GOOD AND FAITHFUL SERVANT

GOOD AND FAITHFUL SERVANT

The unauthorized biography of
Bernard Ingham

ROBERT HARRIS

faber and faber
LONDON · BOSTON

First published in 1990
by Faber and Faber Limited
3 Queen Square London WC1N 3AU

Photoset by Parker Typesetting Service Leicester
Printed in England by Clays Ltd St Ives plc

A CIP record for this book
is available from the British Library.

ISBN 0–571–16108–1

For my mother and father

Contents

Illustrations

PREFACE

'Albion'

'... what greatly concerns me and many other Socialists is that there are thousands of highly moral, upright and indeed religious people who are nevertheless Tory to the bone. They are quite frankly enigmas to simple souls like me.'
   Bernard Ingham, 1965[1]

One day towards the end of February 1964 a small left-wing magazine in the north of England acquired the services of a new columnist. The *Leeds Weekly Citizen* was the journal of that city's Labour Party. The columnist was anonymous. He signed himself simply 'Albion'. As time passed, Albion's outspoken views became famous among local party members. He was at once a familiar and yet mysterious fixture on the Leeds socialist scene. His articles, 800 to 1,000 words long, ran almost every week for more than three years until suddenly, in April 1967, as abruptly as he had surfaced, Albion vanished.

This gentleman (for gentleman he clearly was) begged a number of questions, of which the most obvious was his choice of pseudonym. 'Albion' is the ancient and poetical name for Great Britain: the sort of alias one might expect to see adopted by some mystical, flag-draped, right-wing nationalist. But the Leeds Albion was not that sort of chap at all. In his first column he declared himself proudly to be 'a politically active trade unionist'.[2] In his second, he attacked Britain's possession of nuclear weapons, calling the Conservative Prime Minister, Sir Alec Douglas-Home, a 'political fossil ... dangerous ... bomb-happy'. By column number three, Home ('the incurable waffler') had been rechristened 'Sir Alec Strangelove'.

He suffers, in particular, from the disability of arrogance, which is an hereditary, though not exclusive, disease of those reared in the main forelock-touching belts of Great Britain. (13 March 1964)

I

Home was not the only member of the 'terrible Tory tribe' to feel the thud of Albion's pen between his shoulder blades. When Home's successor as Conservative leader, Edward Heath, made a speech, he apparently 'revealed his party's stagnant mind in all its revolting crudity'. The Chancellor of the Exchequer, Reginald Maudling, was an 'arthritic slug' who 'should hang down his head and cry'. The Minister for Science and Technology, the once and future Lord Hailsham, was usually referred to simply as 'Mr Quintin "Bonkers" Hogg'. As for Enoch Powell, even before his notorious 'rivers of blood' speech, he was 'an anarchist without the sense he was born with ... a menace to civilized society'.[3] Albion, it soon became apparent, did not discriminate much between Tories. He loathed them all:

> As a party they do not give a tinker's cuss for the consequences of Capitalism – the crawling anthill of the South-East and the under-employed, under-privileged muckheap of the North – until they become electorally dangerous. (10 April 1964)

> In the Tory state of the future it is obviously intended that we should all be crawling madly over each other after tax concessions like ants in search of building materials. Our motivating force is not to be anything more than hard cash; not a vision of a better future for society, brighter hope for a largely downtrodden world, a worthier, fuller corporate life. Not on your Nelly. Just a bit more filthy lucre for yourself if you're prepared to flog your guts out for it.

> Well, I can tell you one who won't have any truck with this sort of apology for existence, not to mention life, if he can avoid it. And that's me. I don't mind flogging my guts out. I don't even mind a bit more filthy lucre for myself.

> But Ted Heath and his bandits are not going to have the privilege of treating me like a gormless greyhound. For that is what I would be if I fell for their diabolical plan.

> Under their scheme I – and millions like me – would be like the greyhound given the essentially hopeless task of running against the elite who are also given 10 yards start. (22 October 1965)

> What it amounts to is this: we are to establish in Britain if, God forbid, the Tories ever get the chance, two classes of citizenship – those who help themselves and those, poor dears, who either don't or can't. If

you can't make the first class compartment there will be a place for you in the cattle wagon, providing, of course, you're suitably docketed ... What do they think we are? Serfs? (11 February 1966)

So who was Albion? A regular reader of his column would soon have picked up enough clues to form a rough picture. He was a north countryman. He was irascible. He had been born into a fairly poor background, brought up, he said, in a 'two-up and one-down' terrace house, 'built into a damp hillside'. He had failed his eleven-plus, an exam which he denounced as 'stupidly cruel'. He was an ardent trade unionist ('all companies – public or private – should be made to hand over audited accounts to Trade Unions who are negotiating with them so that they can really have the facts and not some managing director's fiction'). He was passionate in his commitment to full employment, which he called 'the foundation of happiness in the home'.

Sometimes he sounded like a Marxist, talking about the 'economic and social purpose of Socialism'. 'Serf' was one of his favourite words. He began one column 'Dear Fellow Serfs'; three months later, he was addressing his 'fellow slaves'. At other times he sounded more like a lay preacher, his language hinting at a chapel upbringing: for thirteen years, he thundered in July 1964, 'this nation has bowed down before the Golden Calf'. Capitalists, he maintained, 'worship on a much higher altar than Britain, mankind or even God. They have no other gods before Mammon.'[4]

As for Albion's profession, the likeliest bet appeared to be journalism. For one thing, his work seemed to take him to Conservative as well as Labour party meetings; for another, he had a journalist's preoccupation with the media. He denounced 'the Tory Press' as 'part of the Tory election machine': if it 'can convince us that the Tories are going to win,' he wrote in August 1964, 'then it will have done its job'. To correct the imbalance, he urged the creation of a socialist press: 'members of the Labour Party and the Trade Unions had better get interested in the idea of owning their own newspapers pretty quickly'. And if they didn't, Albion had another and, as it turned out, prophetic suggestion: they should employ 'full-time officials who would at least be able to try to make the most of the hostile media'.[5]

Now it is an axiom of politics that as a person gets older, so they tend to move crab-wise across the political spectrum, from left to right. But few, at first glance, can have scuttled quite so far or quite so quickly as Albion of the *Leeds Weekly Citizen*. For in 1979, twelve years after his last appearance in print as a scourge of the capitalist classes, to the astonishment of his old friends, he moved into Downing Street as Chief Press Secretary to Margaret Thatcher, Britain's most ardently pro-capitalist Prime Minister.

That Bernard Ingham and Albion are the same person is beyond doubt. Surprisingly, it has taken a quarter of a century to put the two together. It was in January 1990 that an old colleague of Ingham suggested I try to find back copies of the now defunct *Leeds Weekly Citizen*; another recalled the pseudonym under which his column appeared. One had only to read this to know its author. 'These are facts and interpretations which I defy anyone to dismiss as prejudiced bunkum,' concluded one column on 26 August 1966. 'I may be prejudiced but I try hard not to talk balderdash.' Anyone who has ever had dealings with Ingham knows that 'bunkum and balderdash' is his favourite phrase, regularly employed to knock down some errant reporter's speculative story.

Albion's voice is unmistakably Ingham's: gruff, no-nonsense, didactic, colloquial, colourful, aggressive, humorous, chippy, sometimes surprisingly querulous. I was soon able to match internal evidence from the column with the facts of Ingham's life: for example, that he had failed his eleven-plus. His choice of pseudonym was significant. Albion was the name of the street in which the *Yorkshire Post* and, at that time, the *Guardian* had their Leeds offices; Ingham worked there from 1959 to 1965. More importantly, the 'two-up and one-down' terrace house 'built into a damp hillside', in which the columnist had grown up, turned out to be part of a small row in the Yorkshire weaving town of Hebden Bridge. Ingham's childhood home was in Albion Terrace. So when he picked his alias, he was making a proud nod not to Britain's heritage, but to his own.

How could he do it? That was the question which I encountered again and again in the north of England from people who had known Bernard Ingham when he was, in the words of one, 'the kind of bloke who would stop on the way to his own wedding to argue with someone who was rude about the Labour Party'. How could he work for Margaret Thatcher? Not just work for her, but be part of her inner circle for more than eleven years – indeed, on a twice-daily basis, in meetings with the media, become her very voice? 'I believe what I write,' Albion had asserted in 1966.[6] How, then, did a believer in full employment come to defend

4

policies which produced more than three million unemployed? How did a man who believed in extending trade union rights come to advocate their strict curtailment? And if Albion found Home, Heath, Maudling and Hailsham impossible to stomach, how on earth could he bring himself to make common cause with a Tory Prime Minister far to the right of any of them? One purpose of this book is to trace that ideological journey: a trail, it is worth remembering, followed by millions of working-class voters in the 1970s and 1980s, many of them former Labour supporters with an upbringing similar to Ingham's. In that sense, he is representative of a type.

As to the book's theme, that is summed up in the biblical quotation which provides its title:

> Well done thou good and faithful servant: thou hast been faithful over a few things, I will make thee a ruler over many things: enter thou into the joy of thy lord. (Matthew, xxv, xxi)

Ingham was not the 'rough-spoken Yorkshire Rasputin' to whom John Biffen once jokingly referred. He was not really a Machiavelli or a Svengali or an *éminence grise* or any of the other (as he might put it) bloody foreigners to whom he was regularly compared. His role was much more that of an ultra-loyal servant; a courtier; one might almost say, a willing tool. Like one of those legendary butlers who has been with the same family for years, he would render a service before his employer had even thought of asking for it. 'Bernard is not a Conservative,' claimed one intimate of the Prime Minister. 'He is a fully paid-up member of the Thatcher Party.' He was a True Believer. He was One of Us. 'These last six years,' he told the Media Society in 1985, 'I have been able to operate with the confidence of a Prime Minister constant of purpose and resolve.' Asked what it was about her he most admired, he always answered 'guts'.

Ingham was duly rewarded for his devotion. After his arrival in Downing Street, there were three different Chancellors of the Exchequer, four Home and five Foreign Secretaries. Elections passed. Cabinet and Private Secretaries came and went (or, in the case of Mr Charles Powell, came and stayed). A hundred ministers were bundled out of the back door of Number 10, occasionally speeded on their way by a non-attributable briefing from the Chief Press Secretary. But Ingham, like his mistress and the Mississippi, just kept rolling along. By 1990 four years had elapsed since she last rejected an offer from him to resign, two years since the Civil Service last dared try to remove him. Theirs was the longest partnership between an official and a Prime Minister in British political history.

This fact alone would render Ingham a figure of interest. But in 1989, Margaret Thatcher did indeed make him 'a ruler over many things'. She placed her Chief Press Secretary at the head of the entire Government Information Service (GIS), with responsibility for the careers of all 1,200 of its members. For forty years previously, fearful of charges of politiciz-ation, care had been taken to keep the two posts separate. Moreover, through his chairmanship of the weekly Meeting of Information Officers (MIO), he had oversight of the burgeoning Whitehall advertising budget, which by 1989 was running at £168 million per annum.

Even by the standards of British democracy, a bizarre situation had now been reached. Margaret Thatcher's longest-serving official adviser, a uniquely-placed confidant, who had already held his office almost twice as long as any of his predecessors, was effectively in sole charge of the Government's propaganda machine. Ingham was so devoted to her, and she so trusted him, that he was almost an extra lobe to her brain. Ministers regularly scanned the papers to find out what he was saying about them. Some were careful about what they said in front of their own information officers lest it got back to Ingham and, through him, the Prime Minister. Yet technically he was a neutral civil servant. He was not accountable to Parliament. If he did not wish to speak to MPs, as the Westland affair showed, he did not have to do so. He was not accoun-table to the electorate. In fact, he took care to shield himself from its gaze. His words could not be attributed to him. His media briefings were conducted off the record at meetings which could not be televised because officially they did not exist.

It was at this point that Mr Ingham – his personality, his career, his position and his methods – suggested themselves as a legitimate subject for study. This is the result: the first biography of a British civil servant to be written whilst he was still in office.

It is not an honour which Mr Ingham has taken kindly to having thrust upon him.

The reader has a right to know the relationship between a biographer and his subject. I first met the Prime Minister's Chief Press Secretary in 1982, during research for a book about the media and the Falklands war.

In 1987, I became Lobby correspondent of the *Observer* and, for the next two years, attended his weekly Downing Street briefings for the Sunday press. To me, he was consistently courteous and helpful. To him, I suspect, I must have been a regular pain in the neck – and never more so than in November 1989, when I sent him a letter telling him I intended to write this book and asking for an interview. His reply was a single sentence, polite but succinct: 'I think I would prefer that those who write books about me do so without my assistance.'

I make no complaint. In his place, I might well have said the same. Besides, on a purely practical level, I soon discovered that Mr Ingham's fondness for giving lectures laced with autobiography had already placed a surprising amount of material on the record. In addition, more than eighty friends and colleagues, past and present, were willing to give me an interview. Most asked to remain anonymous; those who did not are named in the text where appropriate. I thank them all for their time and trouble.

I would like also to record my gratitude to the staffs of the Leeds University Library, the Hebden Bridge Library, the British Newspaper Library, the West Yorkshire Archive Service, the *Hebden Bridge Times*, and the libraries of the *Guardian* newspaper, both in London and Manchester.

For helping me with advice, or for lending me various books, documents and photographs, I would like to thank Diverse Productions, Barry Flynn, Andrew Grice, Joe Haines, Ian Hellowell, Lord Houghton of Sowerby, David Hughes, Nicholas Jones, Sir Dick Knowles, Mrs Alice Longstaff, Richard Norton-Taylor, Peter Preston, Laurence Rees, Sally Soames, Neville Taylor and Donald Trelford. Anna Ford kindly gave permission to use the cartoon of Mr Ingham by her husband, the late and much-missed Mark Boxer. Tony Benn generously agreed to let me quote from his diaries.

My editor, Susanne McDadd, had the original idea for a book about Mr Ingham, was unflaggingly enthusiastic, and was ably assisted at Faber and Faber by Julian Loose. My agent, Pat Kavanagh of Peters, Fraser and Dunlop, gave good advice, as always. And my wife, Gill Hornby, read the book chapter by chapter as it was written: her suggestions made it a much better – or at any rate, a less worse – book than it would otherwise have been.

Where, despite the best efforts of those mentioned above, errors have occurred, I am solely responsible.

ONE

Dear Bernard

'The thing about you and me, Bernard, is that neither of us
are *smooth* people.'
Margaret Thatcher[1]

The lights came on in the bungalow in Purley just before 6.00 a.m. By
7.00, he was at the wheel of his car – a vehicle, paid for out of his own
pocket, invariably modest, determinedly British (in 1990 it was a Ford
Escort). As he drove to work through the still-quiet streets south of the
Thames, he listened to the news on Radio Four and to tapes of Elgar. By
7.30, he was at his desk on the ground floor of Downing Street, gutting
the morning's newspapers, as he had done all his life. He began with the
tabloids: 'they get my blood going'. By 9.00 he had finished, and a
secretary was typing up his 1,200-word summary of their contents for his
employer.

Bernard Ingham's daily précis of the press was a staccato compilation
of snappy quotations, facts and figures. He was punctilious about including the bad news as well as the good: it was 'not a sanitised version,' he
once explained, 'you have to reflect the media as it is'.[2]

'There was generally a line from the leaders,' according to one of his
former assistants: '"the *Sun* calls you the Iron Lady, the *Guardian* calls
you a silly old cow" – that sort of thing. The first part consisted of items
just about her; then came a section on the Government; then general
matters; then economics and industrial disputes.' The moment it had
been copied, the press summary was run upstairs to the Private Office.
By 9.30, it was on the Prime Minister's desk. And that – unless someone,
later in the day, drew her attention specifically to an article or editorial –
was as close as Margaret Thatcher came to reading the papers. (Weekends were slightly different: at Chequers over breakfast she was said to
glance through the *Sunday Times* and read the opinion pages of the
Sunday Telegraph.)

According to Michael Alison, her former Parliamentary Private

8

Secretary, she set great store by Ingham's labour-saving digests: 'She's better informed after a ten- or twenty-minute perusal of Bernard's briefings than she would be if she sat down for two hours and read the papers herself.'[3] No other Prime Minister relied on an official to interpret the press for them in this way. It placed Ingham, from the start, in a uniquely influential position – a kind of gatekeeper of information, deciding which facts were worth ushering into the Presence and which should be turned away.

On Tuesdays and Thursdays, when Parliament is in session, the press summary was finished a little earlier and formed the agenda for a morning meeting to prepare for Prime Minister's Questions. At least five people met the Prime Minister in her study. In 1990 they included Sir Brian Griffiths, the head of the Number 10 Policy Unit; Peter Morrison, her current Parliamentary Private Secretary; either Charles Powell or Andrew Turnbull from the Prime Minister's Private Office; John Whittingdale, Mrs Thatcher's young Political Adviser; and Ingham, the only member of this kitchen cabinet whose memory of such meetings went back to 1979. John Wakeham, the minister responsible for co-ordinating Government presentation, would sometimes call to offer advice. By 10.00, the group would have compiled three lists: of subjects likely to be raised by the Opposition, of information required to make an effective counter-attack, and of helpful questions to be 'planted' in advance with the more malleable Tory backbenchers.

Back in his office, Ingham then chaired his own meeting. His bow-fronted room overlooking Downing Street was spacious. There were a couple of armchairs and a sofa upholstered in a rough, mustard-coloured fabric; a large safe for classified documents; a television and a video recorder; and a desk at which he sat with his back to the window. A single line from Hansard, greatly enlarged, hung framed on the wall:

The Prime Minister. Mr Ingham acts in accordance with the duties of his office.

His staff – a deputy, three full-time press officers and a junior on a six-week attachment – were given their orders: Get me *this* from the Ministry of Defence . . . Find out *that* from those buggers at the Foreign Office . . . Environment is making its announcement at *what* time? . . . At 10.45 they trooped back in with the result of their researches. At 11.00, Ingham briefed the Lobby in his office. About twenty reporters turned up. He ran through the Prime Minister's engagements and answered questions, not only about her work but that of the entire Government. What he said here helped shape the coverage of both the lunchtime news and the London *Evening Standard* – and they in turn helped determine the main themes of the day.

The briefing was followed by routine administrative work, correspondence, and possibly lunch with a journalist. At around 3.00, if it was a Tuesday or Thursday, he looked in at the Prime Minister's room in the House of Commons, then took his place in the Press Gallery at 3.15 for Questions. He had become a familiar part of the Westminster furniture over the past eleven years, sitting hunched over his notebook, scribbling his famously accurate shorthand, his bushy eyebrows – now leaping in exasperation, now knitted in a frown – dancing around like a pair of tiny ginger field mice in the mating season. 'He is large and craggy and rather loopy-looking,' wrote Craig Brown, when he was Parliamentary sketch writer for *The Times*, 'like one of the background soldiers who used to be employed on Dad's Army.' (Ingham retaliated in a speech two years later by describing Brown, not altogether inaccurately, as looking 'like Dylan Thomas pulled through a hedge backwards'.)[4]

After a swift cup of tea in the Press Gallery canteen, he climbed the spiral stone staircase to the Lobby room in the eaves of the Palace of Westminster for what is known as 'the four o'clock' – the second of the two daily Lobby briefings – this one attended by thirty or forty reporters. Then it was back to Downing Street and more work until 7.30 or 8.00 p.m. If he was eating in town rather than returning straight to Purley, he would often finish his meal and go back to the office to check all was well. In that case, it might be midnight before he got to bed. And so it went on for more than a decade: twelve hours a day, five days a week, forty-seven weeks a year, not counting the constant telephone calls at home during the night and at weekends, not including the endless foreign trips (two European summits a year, the annual Group of Seven summit, countless 'bilaterals' with foreign heads of government, and always at least two full-scale overseas tours).

Few colleagues, even those who had worked with him for twenty years, knew much about his private life. His wife Nancy, a former policewoman, was always an off-stage figure. 'I've met Nancy, but very rarely,' said Neville Taylor, who was Head of Information at the Department of Health and Social Security when Ingham arrived at Number 10. 'Like many husbands and wives, they're two totally, totally different characters. She's very quiet.' Nancy made the headlines only once, in April 1987, when the IRA sent a letter bomb to the Inghams' home address: it arrived at lunchtime, she took one look at its Ulster postmark and, with admirable coolness, placed it on the front step and dialled 999.

Their son John took a degree in history at Durham in 1980 and won a Fulbright Scholarship to George Washington University. On his return from the US, he decided to follow his father into journalism. 'Bernard asked his friends where might be the best place for him to start,' recalled Geoffrey Goodman, former industrial editor of the *Daily Mirror*. 'I said that in his job he could surely just pick up the phone and someone would help out. But he said no, he'd never do that.' And he never did. John Ingham had to work his own way up through trade magazines and regional newspaper offices before finally landing a job in London in 1990, as defence correspondent on the *Daily Express*.

Many accusations were flung at Ingham, but nobody, not even his bitterest critic, has ever suggested that he put on airs and graces or abused his position for personal gain. His house was as modest and unpretentious in 1990 as it was when he moved into it in the 1960s. You would not find the Inghams – unlike the Powells – at smart dinner parties or on the cocktail circuit. 'Bernard is a workaholic,' said Neville Taylor.

> I don't think there is any time in his life for anything other than work, and I don't think there ever has been ... There is this drive, this total and permanent drive, to do this job better than any other bugger's going to do it. He will go for weeks – and I mean, literally, weeks – before he gets round to reading something that somebody's sent him to read because it was urgent six weeks ago. Bernard will quite honestly say: 'I just haven't had time ...'

Even when his wife was almost killed by a runaway lorry in 1982, and had to spend three months in hospital, Ingham refused to take a day off.

Occasionally, the strain took its toll on his health. Ingham still suffers from the asthma which afflicted him in childhood and which prevented him – to his chagrin – from doing his National Service. A visitor to Number 10 in 1984 noted that Ingham had difficulty mounting the one flight of stairs to the Prime Minister's study: a chest cold had activated his asthma and he was panting heavily.[5] There was also a stage when he suffered blackouts and was ordered by his doctor to stop drinking and lose weight. But, for the most part, he thrived on a diet of adrenalin and mugs of coffee. 'I am still a journalist at heart,' he claimed. His life was one long, rolling deadline.

Only one other person shared such a gruelling workrate for such a long period at the heart of the Government, and that was Margaret Thatcher. A mutual capacity for early starts, long hours and little sleep was one of the planks on which they built their relationship. 'He fell under her spell very quickly,' remembered Goodman. 'He spoke of her with great admiration, first and foremost because of her workrate. I'd say "What does she do in her spare time?" and he'd say "She doesn't watch television or read books because she just works".' Her idea of an annual holiday was a week in Cornwall; his was a fortnight mucking-out on his brother's farm. 'She is not a relaxed person,' Ingham told one reporter. 'I'm not either. We work hard.' To another he confided that he and Thatcher had 'an instinctive rapport . . . My parents regarded hard work as the greatest virtue, and it was impressed on me from the earliest age that education never did anyone any harm . . . She had a fairly hard upbringing, too.'[6]

They treated these similar backgrounds in completely different ways. Ingham nurtured his roots, returning to them whenever possible. He hung watercolours of the Yorkshire countryside (by his friend Donald Crossley) on his walls at home and in Downing Street. He kept up old friendships, proudly inviting acquaintances from his school days and their children to look round Number 10. He made no attempt to disguise his accent; if anything, he hammed it up. To him, the north was a place to which he looked forward to retiring. Margaret Thatcher's approach was in sharp contrast. She loathed Grantham and bent all her immense will to fighting her way out of it. She has virtually no old friends. She married a millionaire from Kent and took elocution lessons to obliterate the last, embarrassing trace of Lincolnshire from her voice.

But all of us, as Ingham once observed, 'are mightily conditioned by our upbringing; few of us escape its consequences or can shake it off like dust from the feet'.[7] The weaver's son and the grocer's daughter, whatever the superficial differences, shared a common inheritance: both were reared in a culture suspicious of metropolitan sophistication, which emphasized the virtues not only of hard work, but of thrift and self-reliance, of discipline and respect for authority. They were practical people; they favoured plain speaking to oratory, facts to theory. Thatcher talked of her father as Ingham did of the people of Hebden Bridge, as a repository of sound, old-fashioned common sense. Here was the basis of what Ingham called the 'instinctive rapport' between them. 'Chemically, it worked right from day one,' claimed a civil servant who was employed in Downing Street in 1979. Donald Grant, Chief Information Officer at the Home Office, also described the 'chemistry' as 'quite amazing'.

It gave Ingham the confidence to be frank in his advice. 'He was not afraid to argue with her if he thought she was wrong,' insisted one insider. 'If he wanted to say something, he said it – you know, wham, bam, he argued back.' Every so often, in the privacy of her study, if one of his briefings had blown back in his face, she would rage against the Lobby system: 'Bernard, just don't do it any more. Just stop talking to them.' To which he always replied: 'You can't do that, Prime Minister. If you did, it would only start up again.' More than once, standing around in a television hospitality suite after an interview, as she reached for another glass of whisky, he was known to tap his watch and loudly tell her it was time to go home.

If his employer resented this occasional bluntness, she did not show it. She knew she was always the boss. Even after eleven years he invariably called her 'Prime Minister'. She referred to him, possessively, as 'my Bernard', or even 'dear Bernard'. 'He's a sort of rock of loyalty,' said her speechwriter, Sir Ronald Millar. 'I think his loyalty to her is something that she absolutely appreciated.' Mrs Thatcher's favourite poet is Kipling; her favourite poem, 'Norman and Saxon', in which an eleventh century Norman baron passes on this advice to his son:

The Saxon is not like us Normans. His manners are not so polite.
But he never means anything serious till he talks about justice and right.
When he stands like an ox in the furrow with his sullen set eyes on your
    own,
And grumbles, 'This isn't fair dealing,' my son, leave the Saxon alone.

She seemed to cast Ingham in the Saxon's role, as a man of old-fashioned, ox-like reliability. He responded in kind. 'The Prime Minister knows her own mind,' he once declared. 'She allows me to get on with my job. She has guts and she supports me.

'I like people with guts.'[8]

TWO

Hebden Bridge

'I want a Government that redistributes wealth. I want a Government that relieves the lowly paid of the magnified miseries of poverty in an affluent society. And I want a Government that produces a society which affords its children an equal opportunity in life. And if the shortest route to securing these, and many other desirable objectives, means pursuing the idea of "consensus", then I'll pursue it.'
Bernard Ingram 1966[1]

Hebden Bridge, a place to which Bernard Ingham constantly alludes and frequently returns, stands on the River Calder in the West Riding of Yorkshire, on the road from Halifax to Burnley. 'Lower the window, lad,' Ingham once commanded a *Guardian* colleague as they passed through it on the train. 'Take a good sniff of that air, because you're nearer to Heaven now than you ever will be on earth.'

They do things differently in Hebden Bridge. The local delicacy is dock pudding, a dish made from the leaves of a common weed, sweet dock (*polygonum bistorta*), chopped up with nettles, boiled with oatmeal, then fried with bacon fat to make a kind of slimy green patty, of which the Prime Minister's Press Secretary is particularly fond. The Yorkshire dialect is thick, studded with words the rest of the country has long forgotten: *carr* (to sit), *gang* (to go), *bahn* (going). There is even a local phrase book. '*Smarrerweeim?*' translates as 'What's the matter with him?' '*Astageniter?*' is 'Have you given it to her?' In a speech in 1990 to mark the fortieth anniversary of the local high school, Ingham spoke with warmth of the 'modesty and unpretentiousness' of his home town:

This was perhaps most beautifully brought out when a *Financial Times* reporter, staying in Hebden Bridge for the General Election, was asked by the waitress if he wanted coffee.

'Yes,' he said, 'Cappuccino.'

14

'Nay lad,' she said, 'you'll have to go to Leeds for that.'

Hebden Bridge is the place he comes from, the place he talks of retiring to. The *Hebden Bridge Times* is still delivered each week to his home in London. One of the yardsticks by which he judges whether a problem is just a passing media squall or a serious storm is whether they are discussing it in the pubs of Hebden Bridge. So it is in Hebden Bridge that we should begin.

Ingham is a Yorkshire name. Members of his family have lived in the Hebden Bridge area for at least three generations. His father, Garnet Ingham, was born at the turn of the century in Charlestown, a small village a couple of miles to the west of the town. He was the eldest of seven children – after him came Maud, Florrie, Arthur, Harold, Clare and Annie – all of them the progeny of the redoubtable Harry Ingham, weaver, who lived to be ninety-four. Garnet was called up to fight in the First World War and joined the Royal Naval Air Service. But he never saw action. The Armistice was signed while he was still in southern England, training. He returned to Yorkshire where, in 1927, he married Alice, then twenty-four years old, the only daughter of the splendidly-named Greenwood Horsfall, of Queen's Terrace, Hebden Bridge.

'In her younger days,' according to her obituary in the *Hebden Bridge Times* in 1967, 'Mrs Ingham was well known in the district as an elocutionist.' She is still remembered by some of the older inhabitants as a 'right good singer' who used to play a leading part in the amateur productions of the Hebden Bridge Light Opera Society. But, like most of the town's 6,000 inhabitants, it was on the weaving sheds that her living depended. When her children were growing up, she worked part-time as an 'odd weaver': someone who was paid by full-time weavers to mind their looms for them while they were off sick or away for a few hours.

Garnet, apart from his brief spell in the armed forces and a period of war-work in a local engineering factory during the early 1940s, was a weaver all his working life. He was employed at the Windsor Shed, in the northern part of Hebden Bridge, owned by the Olympia Manufacturing Company, and also at a grim Victorian fortress in the centre of town called Nutclough Mill. Each weaver operated perhaps four looms. With 250 employees to each shed and up to 1,000 heavy metal looms running at full speed, opening the door to the factory was like walking into a wall of noise. In the words of David Fletcher, a historian who was raised in Hebden Bridge, 'it hit you like a solid substance; you could feel your whole body vibrating in time to the machinery'. Over the roar of the looms, the weavers communicated with one another like deaf-mutes. It is unwise in Hebden Bridge, even today, to make an unflattering remark about someone on the other side of the street. Plenty of sharp-eyed elderly residents remember how to lip-read.

Noise was not the only form of pollution produced by the mills. For the best part of a century, unchecked by law or public protest, they spewed their dirt into the air and their filth into the waters of the River Calder. The effects were worsened by Hebden Bridge's geography. Its mills and grey stone houses jammed the narrow valley floor and clung, sometimes at precarious angles, to the steep hillsides overlooking the river, forming a cauldron of smog. To quote David Fletcher again:

> Hebden Bridge was a very demoralizing place in which to grow up. The streets and houses were dingy, and the air was smokey, especially on still winter mornings. Sometimes you would go for days and the place would stay dark, with a roof of smoke trapped in the valley. You'd go to school on your bike with a handkerchief over your face, and by the time you arrived, the material would be filthy. If you went into the woods and ran your hands down the bark of the trees, they'd be smeared with soot. We didn't have silver birches; we had black birches. Depending on what dye they were using further up the valley, the streams would run blue, black or maroon.

The air which Ingham urged his *Guardian* colleague to sniff thirty years later was the product of the Clean Air Acts of the 1950s: a very different substance to that which he breathed as a child.

He was born, plain Bernard, in the Royal Infirmary, Halifax, on 21 June 1932. A brother, Derek, arrived two years later. As a child he suffered badly from asthma. So did his mother. She was to be a semi-invalid for the last few years of her life, before dying of pneumonia at the age of sixty-four. Derek also contracted pneumonia, in May 1937, when he was three. The Inghams could not afford an ambulance, and he had to be transported to and from hospital by the local greengrocer. The memory of this episode later stirred 'Albion' to a vigorous defence of the National Health Service:

It represents a tremendous advance on the inherently vicious private enterprise system of Dr Finlay's time, and the 1930s. That was when my parents, for example, ran up for them, the colossal bill of £120 when my brother contracted double pneumonia.[2]

Garnet and Alice had to borrow the money, and were still paying it back years later.

A few months after his brother's illness, Bernard began attending the Central Street School, a Victorian establishment bounded on three sides by mills and warehouses. His nickname was 'Bunny' Ingham. He was tall for his age, red haired and raw-boned. As he grew up he became rather fat: years later, in his teens, he and some friends would have to abandon a cycling holiday in Devon after his weight had buckled the spokes of his back wheel. 'He tended to be "Big Daddy" in a group,' recalls one of his schoolmates, Peter Marsland. 'He wasn't brash, but in a quiet way you knew who the leader was.' Cricket and football were his main interests. But he was bright enough at his class work and certainly expected to pass the eleven-plus. Unexpectedly, through sheer panic as much as anything else, he flunked it. He later recalled the shame of how 'after consistently coming out top or second in the class virtually from entering primary school I failed miserably in the eleven-plus and had to go to bed for several days with asthma brought on by the nervous strain imposed by the examination'.[3]

It was a traumatic experience and, again, it was to help shape his political views. In the mid-1960s, when Harold Wilson denounced the 'educational apartheid' of the grammar school system, and his Labour government legislated to end it, he had few more enthusiastic supporters than Ingham. In the *Leeds Weekly Citizen* of 14 January 1966, he attacked 'the anxiety, pain and often downright cruelty' it inflicted.

There are millions being made into second class citizens by an archaic education system, and we are not on this earth to perpetuate a second class system riddled with the strength-sapping pox of class tensions and injustices ... This also implies that I want an end to public schools as such and the fee-paying sector. I do. It is the only way that we shall get a real head of steam behind our educational system.

Fortunately for Ingham, there *was* a fee-paying scheme available in Hebden Bridge in 1943. Parents whose children had failed the eleven-plus were allowed to buy them a place at the local grammar school. Garnet and Alice, in their son's words, 'scraped enough money together' to pay the fees and Bernard went after all. Had he not, he would have stayed another three years at Central Street and then left at the age of fourteen, probably to work in one of the local mills. As it was, he recovered his academic confidence sufficiently to be placed in the A-stream at Hebden Bridge Grammar School, consistently coming a creditable fifth or sixth in a class of about twenty-five.

Outside work and school, the Ingham family's attention was divided between two institutions. One was the Hope Street Baptist Church. Bernard's parents, like most of the town's citizens, were regular worshippers. His aunts helped teach Sunday School and he and Derek were strictly brought up in the Nonconformist tradition. They were expected to devote a large part of their spare time to the church. In 1947, for example, Hope Street's basement was flooded, destroying the electrical system which powered the organ. For six months, the Ingham boys were required to pump it manually. 'The hymns were fine,' recalled Derek, 'but then they decided to do Handel's *Messiah* at Christmas. The Hallelujah Chorus nearly killed us.'

The other institution was the Labour Party. Garnet was of that generation for whom Baptism and socialism were two halves of the same faith. He was the auditor of his local union, the Todmorden Weavers' and Winders' Association; a director of the Hebden Bridge Co-operative Society; and a member of the Executive of the Sowerby Constituency Labour Party. Round-faced, bespectacled, with thick wavy hair and a ready smile, he became one of the town's best-known citizens. 'Garnet were a right good man', is the sort of comment still made about him. 'A right kindly man; had a good word for everybody.' Hilary Varley, whose family knew the Inghams through the church and the local Trades Club, retained a similar impression: 'Garnet was a lovely man. He ran the Labour Party. He *was* the Labour Party.' Bernard's mother, who also did her bit for the socialist cause as secretary of the town's Co-operative Women's Guild, is remembered as 'quiet' and 'supportive'.

His parents' opinions were readily absorbed by their eldest son. Bernard's headmaster, Herbert Howarth, once had to ask the tyro politician to remove a pile of Labour Party pamphlets from the school library. 'I am all in favour of politics,' Ingham recalled Howarth admonishing him, 'but I will not have party politics in this school.'[4] Nevertheless, during the 1945 general election, the voice of the thirteen-year-old Ingham could be heard piping 'Vote Labour' from a loud-speaker van parked outside the school. Perhaps these modest efforts swayed a few minds; at any rate, on 25 July the Labour candidate for Sowerby, John Belcher, defeated the sitting Conservative MP, Malcolm McCorquodale, by 7,000 votes.

From this point onwards, the Ingham household's preoccupation with politics intensified. In March 1946, Garnet became the first candidate to stand for the local council with the official backing of the Labour Party (hitherto, all councillors had stood as independents). He polled 790 votes, only narrowly missing election – 'a good figure for a first contest,' commented the local paper. The following year he tried again. On 29 March 1947, under a dull and rainy sky, the citizens of Hebden Bridge turned out to vote at the polling station in Central Street School. Counting began at 8.00 p.m. 'The space available for the public was packed,' recorded the *Hebden Bridge Times*, 'and a keen interest was taken in proceedings.' Two hours later, with the street lamps doused and in almost pitch darkness, the town clerk posted the results outside the *Times*' office in Market Street. With 906 votes, Garnet Ingham was elected – the first socialist councillor in the history of Hebden Bridge.

That same year, Bernard became a founder member, and sub-sequently Secretary, of the Hebden Bridge League of Labour Youth. In November 1947, he helped organize a meeting for John Belcher in the town's Little Theatre. The MP mounted an outspoken attack on the 'vicious' and 'unscrupulous' attempts of Mr Churchill to divide the nation, and concluded with a little homily on 'the importance of youth in the ranks of the Labour Movement'. According to the *Hebden Bridge Times*, 'a vote of thanks to Mr Belcher was moved by Bernard Ingham'.[5] At the age of fifteen, he had made his first speech – and his first appearance in print.

These were good years for the Inghams. Four decades later, it became fashionable to blame the Attlee Government – with its dreary insistence on 'planning' and 'welfare' – for precipitating Britain's economic decline. But in places like Hebden Bridge it was simply the best thing that had ever happened. 'The valley,' Ingham subsequently recalled, 'was hum-ming. It was a good place to live. The future looked better than the past.'[6]

Garnet and his family were typical beneficiaries of the government they had helped elect. They left the cramped conditions of Albion Terrace and moved to a new housing estate in Mytholmroyd – the local pronunication is 'Marthamroyd' – a mile from Hebden Bridge. Number 1 Birchenlee Close was a post-war prefab, boasting such undreamed-of luxuries as an indoor lavatory, a spacious kitchen and bathroom, and three bedrooms. Round the corner from the Inghams, in Aspinall Street, lived the future Poet Laureate, Ted Hughes. (Hughes was two years older than Bernard, and they did not meet until Ingham was working in Downing Street; since then, however, they have kept in touch.)

When it came to building the socialist New Jerusalem, Garnet was a Stakhanovite. Most of the other councillors were self-employed businessmen who could take time off whenever necessary. Mill workers, on the other hand, were employed in two shifts on a rota basis: 6.00 a.m. till 2.00 p.m., and 2.00 p.m. till 10.00 p.m. Undeterred, Garnet managed to strike a deal with a fellow weaver who preferred to spend his mornings in bed. For the next 13 years he worked the early shift only, leaving his evenings free for council and Labour Party business. This meant getting up at half past four every morning to catch a bus to work at 5.20 a.m. In the evening, after a hurried meal, he would return to Hebden Bridge, to the council's imposing Victorian offices in St George's Street, where he sat on half a dozen committees, including housing, health and highways. It might be nine or ten o'clock at night before he returned home. The council's records show him to have been one of the most assiduous attenders: in 1949, for example, out of eighty meetings held, he was present at seventy-two. Eventually he gave up all outside interests, including his beloved membership of the Hebden Bridge Brass Band, to concentrate on council work.

Garnet Ingham was never a militant, but he was passionate about the aims and achievements of the Labour Party. He regularly berated the council for its 'disgraceful' failure to invest its funds in the Co-operative Society Bank which, he said, offered a higher rate of interest than its competitors. He spoke proudly of the 'pioneers' of the Sowerby Labour Party who, in the early years of the century, 'practically gave their lives in the service of the movement' but who had had the courage to stick to their convictions.[7] He was no theorist: his brand of socialism was very much of the practical, municipal, gas-and-water kind. In 1951, when he stood for re-election, his address to the voters concentrated on health and hygiene: 'it is imperative that no attempt should be made to deter the onward march of the past few years'.[8] He lost on that occasion, swept away when the tide turned against the Labour Government nationally. But he was re-elected the following year and, on 20 May 1957, despite the fact that Labour had only two seats on the council compared with the Conservatives' eleven, was unanimously nominated as Leader. There were affectionate tributes to what one Tory councillor called 'a rabid old socialist'. Some of the phrases used to describe him – that when he had an idea 'he stuck to it with great stubborness' and that he 'had a reputation for calling a spade a spade' – would later be applied equally readily to his son. 'I am proud to be associated with the Labour move-ment,' responded Garnet, the Leader's chain of office glinting on his chest. 'This is not said in a belligerent attitude, but out of respect for the achievements of the Labour Party over the past fifty years.'[9]

'Garnet,' in the words of one elderly resident of Hebden Bridge, 'were red hot Labour.'

If Bernard Ingham had been born ten years later he would almost certainly have gone to university. But in the 1940s such a prospect was far beyond the horizons of the average son of a Yorkshire weaver. 'My parents' attitude,' recalled Derek, 'was that they made sure you got a good education at school. After that it was up to you to get the best job you could.' Ingham's original plan was to become a geography teacher. Then, in the autumn of 1948, the *Hebden Bridge Times* ran an advertise-ment for a trainee journalist. Ingham applied. According to him, they 'made me an offer I could not refuse: the post of junior reporter at thirty bob a week, with use of your own bike to cover Luddenden Valley on Mondays'. He started that October. He was sixteen.

Ingham often refers to these early days of his in journalism. His manner on such occasions is invariably that of a self-made Yorkshire businessman, wi' brass in t'bank, discoursing at a school prize-giving on the homespun virtues of his humble youth. Indeed, this is how Ingham actually expressed it at the local school in 1990:

> Working on the *Hebden Bridge Times*, cheek by jowl with your readers, was the finest preparation for the life I now lead. You either got it right or you got it in the neck, right there in Market Street, Bridge Gate or Hangingroyd Lane.

It was a favourite theme. Covering council meetings, he declared, was 'the finest background for any real life in politics, because you got to know how a country worked from the bottom up.' In 1986, he told an audience in the City of London:

> I share the view Lord Kemsley expressed in his *Manual of Journalism*, a copy of which I acquired when it was first published in 1950 ... Lord Kemsley wrote: 'There is no more important responsibility to the community than that of journalists.' Those words 'responsibility to the community' were the very bedrock of my training. Responsibility to inform. Responsibility to be accurate. Responsibility to be fair. In short, responsibility to the reader.[10]

Asked to lecture on the theme 'The Right to Know' in 1983, he told his audience of newspaper editors that there was no such thing: 'And I am bound to tell you that my training as a journalist put far greater emphasis on responsibilities, duties and obligations than ever it did on rights.'[11]

The *Hebden Bridge Times*, this apparently inexhaustible fount of civic virtue and journalistic excellence, was then housed in a disused eighteenth-century church in the centre of town. It was an odd place to find a newspaper office. Visitors had first to make their way through a small graveyard, filled with sombre reminders of stories past:

> In Memory of
> Henry Riley; whose short existence was marked
> with continued Misfortune, and because he became
> poor, was cruelly murdered on the 2nd of Oct 1818
> in the 37th Year of his Age. He has left a Widow &
> eleven Children to lament his Loss.
> Nor Angel's Blessings, nor the Murder'rs Prayers
> Can wipe away a desolate Widow's Curse;
> And though he shed his Heart's Blood for Atonement,
> It will not weigh against an Orphan's tear.

Beyond the grave stones, fixed to the Ebenezer Chapel's smoke-blackened frontage, was a sundial with the dolorous inscription *Quod petis umbra est* ('What you seek is but a shadow'). If Ingham's first years as a reporter really were marked by such a heavy sense of seriousness and duty, one can begin to see why.

The gloomy atmosphere lingered inside. 'You'd go in,' remembered

Derek Ingham, 'and the reporters were in a dark room on the left, sitting at a long table, with perhaps one telephone between the lot of them.' In 1948, the two senior journalists were veterans of the Hebden Bridge scene, Jack Holroyd and Walter Marsland. Running round the walls, at a height of four feet, was a tidemark, a relic of the same flood which had damaged the organ in Hope Street the previous year. The paper was set in type in a room upstairs. If the compositor had a query, he would fling open a trapdoor above the reporters' heads, swear, and toss down the offending piece of copy, screwed up in a ball. The reporter would flatten it out, make any necessary corrections, screw it up again and throw it back, accompanied by a few choice words of his own.

The *Hebden Bridge Times* then consisted of eight pages, published weekly. Once a month the front page was given over to the council's minutes, which were published almost verbatim. Another staple was the magistrates' court ('Butcher Burnt Cow's Hide/Slaughtered Animal Himself – Fined £50/Horseflesh Dealer to Appeal Against Sentence'). There were the usual births, marriages and deaths. Nature Notes were provided by 'Tawny Owl' ('Don't forget that empty bird table; do it now!'). Advertisements were basic ('Do your false teeth ROCK, SLIDE or SLIP?'). The frequent announcements placed by the Ministry of Food reflected the austerities of post-war rationing. One, a list of recipes for various kinds of dumpling (fish, herb, cheese, curry, sweet and baked), concluded with the bathetic message: 'Good News! There's plenty of Ryvita in the shops now and it's down to only 2 points a packet!'

Bernard's special beat, for which his bicycle was essential, was village news: the whist drives in Luddenden Foot; the old-time dancing nights in Lumb or Heptonstall; bowling club socials ('the Embassy Band played for dancing') in Sowerby Bridge; the talks by the likes of Mr S. Weatherill of Todmorden 'on the signalling system of the railways' or by the Rev. H. Godfrey, who spoke to the Providence Methodist Church on 'Real Romance'. On one celebrated occasion, Ingham found himself interviewing a talking dog in the Spotted Cow at Drighlington. The prosperity of the *Hebden Bridge Times*, like that of most successful local papers, was based on the sound commercial principle of printing as many readers' names as possible. Ingham's job was to lick the end of his pencil and make sure he spelled them correctly. To that end, the paper paid for him to learn shorthand one morning a week at the Todmorden Technical College, where he cut an incongruous figure, the only boy in a class of more than thirty girls.

As it happened, one of the biggest news stories in the history of Hebden Bridge occurred in the very month that Ingham joined the paper. On 7 October 1948, the government set up the Lynskey Tribunal to investigate allegations of corruption against the constituency's MP. John Belcher, for whose election Ingham had campaigned, was by now Parliamentary Secretary at the Board of Trade. He was accused of receiving various gifts in return for dropping an investigation into a firm of football pools promoters. The 'bribes', to a modern eye, seem almost pathetically tawdry: a week's holiday in Margate, a gold cigarette case, a suit. Nevertheless, in January 1949, Belcher was found guilty. In February, in 'the very depths of unhappiness and wretchedness', he was obliged to resign his seat.

The man chosen to replace him was Douglas Houghton, a well-known trade union leader and broadcaster. The executive of the Sowerby Labour Party, of which Garnet Ingham was a member, had no say in the matter: the leadership in London imposed the candidate they thought most likely to win a by-election. More than forty years later, aged ninety-two, Houghton could still recall Garnet: 'a staunch, middle-of-the-road chap; always eloquent on the side of reason; one of the sobersides in the constituency.' He could remember Bernard, too: 'a ginger-headed boy who worked in my campaign; on election day he ran messages between the headquarters and the polling booth'. Among those who came up to speak for Houghton was his former deputy at the Inland Revenue Staff Federation, the youthful MP for South Cardiff, James Callaghan. On 17 March, Houghton duly held the seat with a majority of 2,000. The *Hebden Bridge Times*, normally published on a Friday, kept the printers waiting and managed to get the news on to its front page.

In 1951, Ingham entered what he later called 'my most idyllic and productive years in journalism'. The paper's two senior reporters departed: Jack Holroyd to go to the *Burnley Express* and Walter Marsland to the *Halifax Courier*. That left young Bernard, effectively, to produce the paper on his own.

I wrote at least fifteen columns a week – roughly 15,000 words; sub-edited the lot – that is, cut the stories to fit and wrote the headlines; wrote the editorial column, to my enormous pride and satisfaction; laid out the front page and the sports pages; and then on Thursday mornings put some of the pages to bed, even locking up the forms, the metal frames holding the type together. And the forms had to be locked up properly because they had to be carried down the stairs from the first floor of the old Ebenezer Baptist Chapel and out through the front door, through the graveyard to the waiting taxi in Market Street. The paper was printed in Todmorden ... One bit of bad workmanship and the *Hebden Bridge Times* would have been a page short that week – lying in tiny pieces on the pavement or on the floor of the taxi.[12]

In the interests of accuracy, it should be recorded that Ingham's frequently repeated claim – that 'I had the direct responsibility for producing and editing a local weekly thrust upon me at the age of nineteen'[13] – is contested by Kenneth Lord, son of the paper's owner at that time, who insists *he* was in charge. But if, over the years, Ingham has slightly exaggerated his role, it scarcely matters. Certainly, he had done well enough chronicling the comings and goings in Hebden Bridge to be offered, in 1952, a better job. The *Yorkshire Post*, based in Leeds, needed an extra pair of hands at its Halifax office to help cover news in the West Riding. Ingham applied for the post, and got it.

Superficially, not much changed in his life. Halifax is only seven miles from Hebden Bridge, and he continued to live at home with his parents for the next four years. But in fact this was a decisive moment, for his ambition was beginning to pull him beyond his home town. 'I used to say that Hebden Bridge was like Colditz,' his brother recalled. 'Everyone was planning their escape.' Unlike many of his contemporaries, whom he returns to visit trailing clouds of glory, Bernard made it.

He was ambitious. He was already famous for working extremely hard. He had absorbed, and would continue to revere, the values of a small town in the north of England. Yet he had taken the first opportunity to leave it behind. He had been brought up a Nonconformist. He had a respected father, a councillor, who had sacrificed much of his spare time to civic duties, and from whom he had inherited a passionate

25

interest in politics. In all these respects the young Bernard Ingham already had a surprising amount in common with the woman who, nearly thirty years later, would become his boss.

THREE

Reporter

'I feel for the reporter . . . I have shared with him his perishing funerals, his sodden agricultural shows, his grisly murders, his eerie ghost hunts, his endless doorsteps, his high living at trade union conferences . . .'

Bernard Ingham, lecture to the Worshipful Company of Stationers and Newspaper Makers, 1986

At the age of twenty Bernard Ingham's life settled into a daily routine which was to last for the next four years. He would rise early and leave the house for Halifax. Mostly he went by bus; occasionally, according to his colleagues, he even walked: a two-hour trudge beside the River Calder. Halifax at that time was like Hebden Bridge, only larger: a gritty, smoky Victorian textile town of some 75,000 inhabitants, bounded by steep hills. The local offices of the *Yorkshire Post* and *Yorkshire Evening Post* were above a printer's shop in Horton Street, near the railway station. These Dickensian premises had battleship grey lino on the floor, on to which flowed piles of yellowing cuttings and back-copies. Ingham's first task each morning was to telephone the police and fire stations and the local hospital and check if anything had happened overnight. If it had, he would ring the story through to the *Post*'s news desk in Leeds. Then he would don his raincoat and cloth cap and walk down to the County Court building to check what cases were on that day. The police headquarters were conveniently arranged in the same building, and at 9.00 a.m. an inspector would brief reporters.

After that, breakfast was taken in the Star Cafe in Rawson Street, where a cup of tea and a cigarette could be had for sixpence. Here would gather the cream of the Halifax press corps: Stan Solomon, Alan Cooper and Max Jessup of the West Riding News Service; Jack Knott and David Illingworth of the Bradford *Telegraph and Argus*; Bryan Harwood of the Halifax *Courier*; and Bernard Ingham and his partner on the *Yorkshire Post*, an experienced journalist named Tom Dickinson. The gossip would go on until a few minutes before 10.30. Then they would grab their notebooks and set off at a brisk trot back to the court in time for the start of the first case.

The popular image of a journalist – a solitary creature, endlessly in pursuit of a scoop – is only partially true. Reporters are wolves rather than foxes. Most of the time they hunt in packs. This was especially so in a small town like Halifax in the 1950s where a limited supply of news – crime, sport, the council, the activities of the locally-based Halifax Building Society and British and Foreign Bible Society – had to satisfy the appetites of half a dozen papers. The journalists' main object was to make sure they missed nothing. Accordingly, they filled in for one another. Illingworth of the *Telegraph and Argus* might cover the morning's court case, while Ingham of the *Post* headed up to the Chamber of Commerce. Afterwards, they would exchange notes. Often they would even go on the same stories together. Illingworth had a motorbike and sidecar and he and Ingham would chug up and down the Calder Valley covering the parish councils.

The emphasis was on providing the reader with a good service of news; the reward was never to see your name in print. Everything Ingham and Dickinson wrote for the *Yorkshire Post* was attributed, if at all, to 'our Halifax staff'. Indeed, from the day he walked into the Ebenezer Chapel until the day he received his first by-line, Ingham had to wait more than twelve years. Three headlines from the beginning of 1953, credited to 'our Halifax staff', give the flavour of what would have been considered major stories:

Thieves took cup tie money from shop

Fire in theatre as 1,000 watch show
Audience left without panic

Mill worker dies from smallpox
Two suspect cases at Todmorden

Ingham was renowned among his colleagues for two qualities: dogged thoroughness and first-rate shorthand. The most famous story about him, endlessly retold by Yorkshire journalists, is that he once rang Halifax police station on Christmas Day and, on learning that a man had fallen off his bike and broken his arm, missed Christmas lunch to interview him. That tale, sadly, proves on investigation to be apocryphal.

But the fact that it is still so widely believed shows how well it captures his spirit. 'The man used to turn out twelve stories a day,' recalled Stan Solomon. 'It was phenomenal. He never bloody stopped.' Covering council meetings, where others might take four or five pages of short-hand notes, Ingham would take twenty or thirty. His colleagues would leave in the evenings for a drink and he would still be there, sorting through reams of paper or banging out a story with two fingers on an old Underwood typewriter.

This thoroughness and capacity for hard work shone through in other ways. In 1954 David Illingworth got married and moved to a new house. The 22-year-old Ingham could not afford to buy the couple a present, so he offered to dig their front garden instead. For weeks thereafter, whenever he had a day off, he would turn up, spade in hand. 'He didn't just dig it,' remembered Illingworth. 'He riddled the soil. He carted away bricks and boulders. He'd go on for hours. There were blisters on his hands. It got to the point where we just used to give him the key to the house so he could use the lavatory, and leave him to get on with it. To this day, the front lawn is a yard lower than anywhere else in the garden because of the amount of rubble he took out.'

By this time, Ingham had marriage plans of his own. Nancy Hoyle was a policewoman, Halifax born and bred, more than eight years his senior. She was often to be found behind the desk in the police station when the reporters went for their morning briefing – a pleasant, unpretentious woman, remembered for a capable manner and a quiet sense of humour. One day, Ingham took Bryan Harwood of the *Courier* to one side. 'He said to me: "I do like that police lady, Nancy Hoyle. I'd like to take her to the pictures. Will you introduce me?" So I did. He was quite chuffed.' (Such a liaison was not uncommon. 'Provincial journalists,' says one of Ingham's northern colleagues, 'tend to marry policewomen, nurses or barmaids: they're the only women they meet.')

Nancy came from an Irish family. Her father, Ernest Hoyle, a joiner by profession, was dead. She lived with her mother, Nora, in the terraced house where she had been born. The policewoman and the reporter carried on a discreet courtship for a couple of years – so discreet that when the workaholic Ingham announced he was getting married, some of the Star Cafe regulars were amazed. There was a slight complication in so far as Nancy was a practising Roman Catholic. Her Nonconformist fiancé was thus obliged to take instruction from a local priest, Father

MacMahon, before a wedding could be countenanced. The ceremony eventually took place on 3 November 1956 at St Columcille's Church in Pellon, Halifax. Ingham was twenty-four, his wife a month short of her thirty-third birthday. 'The bride wore a cocktail gown of gold brocade,' reported the *Hebden Bridge Times*, 'and was given away by her brother'. The best man was Derek Ingham. Following a reception in the town's Co-operative Cafe (a concession to Garnet Ingham, perhaps), 'the couple left for their honeymoon in Keswick'.[1]

They returned to a new home. Sixty-two Gleanings Avenue was a small, semi-detached house in Norton Tower, a windy hilltop on the outskirts of Halifax. Nancy gave up work, and a little over a year later she gave birth to the couple's first and only child. An announcement in the *Hebden Bridge Times* in February 1958 recorded the birth of 'a son, John Bernard. *Deo Gratias*.'[2]

Ingham served seven years in Halifax for the *Yorkshire Post*. At length, in 1959, this long apprenticeship was rewarded with a transfer to the paper's headquarters in Leeds. Eighteen months later he was given a further promotion. He was made the paper's northern industrial corres-pondent. From now on he had a by-line. At last he could take full credit for his prodigious output of news stories (when he had finished his day's work in Leeds, he became famous for asking the news editor if there was anything more he could do). Few editions passed without some contribu-tion from him – on the coal or motor industries ('Six ton coal lump sent to Solid Fuels Exhibition at Grimethorpe', 'Skilled workers in short supply'); or on a takeover or a strike ('Merger of liquorice kings', 'Plan for peace in car works'). Only when it came to features was his touch less sure. This, for example, was his idea of a catchy opening to the 'Inside Industry' column on 24 April 1961:

> Life, as the saying goes, is full of temptations as well as surprises. This is particularly true so far as top executives are concerned when they come to deal with the problem of management succession.
>
> It was one of the points made most forcibly at the seminar held this week in Harrogate by Ashley Associates Ltd, the Manchester firm of executive selection consultants . . .

This leaden prose style, only a minor disadvantage in his early years as a journalist, was later to prove a decisive handicap.

That problem, however, lay in the future. In the early 1960s, the northern industrial scene suited him well. His upbringing in Hebden Bridge and his background in the Labour Party gave him a rapport with the local trade unionists, especially the Yorkshire miners. He relished their company. Years later he was still telling the story of a fellow industrial correspondent's attempt to interview a striking miner at Rossington Colliery, near Doncaster.

> The office car he was driving had seen better days – a relic of the '30s. It hissed, puffed, creaked and groaned its way down the pit lane and shuddered to a halt in the yard. As my colleague untied the string to let himself out he heard the crouching miner observe 'Hey up lads, here comes t'capitalist press'.[3]

Ingham got on well with his fellow reporters. Monty Meth, then freelancing for the *Daily Worker*, who became a friend, remembers a colleague who was 'objective and diligent in the extreme', who had brilliant shorthand and 'would do three or four stories where others would be content to do one'. Joe Haines, then with the *Scottish Daily Mail*, who was to become an adversary, remembers 'a very convivial evening' during a TUC conference when 'we were both stuck in a rather shabby hotel on the south side of Blackpool. He was Labour. We had a sympathy of political view.'

Through these contacts, towards the end of 1961, Ingham learned that the *Guardian* was looking for a reporter to work in its Leeds office, a few doors down from the *Yorkshire Post* in Albion Street. There were disadvantages in such a move. He would lose his by-line. His work would appear under the tag 'by our own reporter'. He would be a smaller fish. But then he would be swimming in a much larger pond. He applied for the job.

Ingham was interviewed first by Mike Parkin, the *Guardian*'s Leeds correspondent. Parkin preferred writing about the lighter, more whimsical side of northern life. Ingham these days was concentrating on politics, industry and regional planning: the sort of worthy subjects which needed to be covered, but which few of the *Guardian*'s specialists, based in London, wanted to trail up and write about. Parkin thought him the ideal candidate. Harry Whewell, the paper's northern news editor, came across the Pennines to meet him. Finally, Ingham was dispatched to Manchester to see the *Guardian*'s editor, Alastair

Hetherington. He was approved, hired, and started work at the beginning of 1962.

'Bernard looked like a grafter,' recalled Whewell. 'He *was* a grafter. He just laboured away.' Whewell would speak to him on the telephone from the Manchester news room every morning to assign him his day's work. By chance, several of the ledgers in which the news editor recorded who was doing what have survived. They bear out what every ex-colleague of Ingham remembers: that whereas most reporters undertook to do one or two pieces, he would often submit ideas for five or six. In 1963 alone, Whewell's ledger records 351 stories assigned to Ingham: 133 connected with trade union or industrial matters; 121 with politics and regional policy; the rest mainly devoted to agriculture, tourism or fishing (covering the latter, he fell victim to the *Guardian*'s legendary capacity for typographical errors, and was recorded as interviewing 'a machine biologist').

In the course of that year he attended the conferences of the TUC in Brighton and the Labour Party in Scarborough. He was with the National Union of Public Employees at Bridlington and with the Confederation of Shipbuilding and Engineering Unions at York and Margate. He followed Lord Hailsham across the north-east of England. With John Cole, the *Guardian*'s labour correspondent, he toured Scotland. He was hungry to get his copy into the paper and became a master of the 'Sunday-for-Monday' story: by coming in on his day off and filing an article when fewer journalists were competing for space, he stood more chance of seeing it printed.

Not all his work was quite so serious. In January 1963 he covered the world needle-threading contest. In the same month he reported on the case of a fox and a terrier trapped together in a snow-bound crevice at Hardcastle Crags (the fox escaped, Ingham was able to assure the *Guardian*'s readers, while the dog was rescued and 'went home to a liver and whisky dinner').[4] He described such marvels of science as the development of antibiotics for fish and the strengthening of eggshells. Best of all, in July 1963, was a piece about a peripatetic Yorkshire crab – the first Ingham story, as far as one can tell, ever to make it on to the *Guardian*'s front page:

175-MILE CRAWL BY CRAB?

By our own reporter

A Yorkshire crab now holds the record for the longest known journey by an East Coast crab.

One tagged off Whitby last year by the staff of the Fisheries Laboratory at Burnham-on-Crouch has turned up in a seine net in Aberdeen Bay, about 175 miles away as the crab crawls. Previously the longest known journey was by a Norfolk crab which covered 124 miles from Norfolk to Yorkshire in 21 months ... Mr E. Edwards, of the Fisheries Laboratory, who has just completed tagging another 1,000 crabs off the Yorkshire coast, says a pattern is already emerging. Apparently there is a tendency for the female to wander northwards and for the male to stay where he is.[5]

Parkin found his new colleague to be 'the very embodiment of the Protestant work ethic; a demon worker'. Ingham sat hunched over his desk in their dingy one-room office, smoking so heavily that by the end of the day the air would be thick with stale fumes and the floor littered with cigarette stubs. He smoked cheap Woodbines – not, in Parkin's view, 'because he couldn't afford better cigarettes, but because he thought it was a good working-class smoke: none of your nonsense'. He had turned into a young man of stern values, contemptuous of people he thought had had it soft. He was good-natured rather than witty; dogged, decent, serious. As a journalist he was renowned both for the quantity of facts he would stuff into a story and for their unerring accuracy. But if he was asked to speculate or embroider he was lost, and his sentences, notoriously, 'went on like a club bore's story':

> Yet at least one firm in Sunderland so far speaks only highly of the Board of Trade even if it owes its presence on the Pallion industrial estate there to a combination of circumstances stemming from the Board's policy of refusing industrial development certificates in London for new industrial buildings and extensions of more than 5,000 square feet.[6]

That particular specimen, from January 1964, lurches on bewilderingly through 58 words without the assistance of a single punctuation mark.

*

Ingham by now was notorious for the vehemence of his political views. In Halifax he had made no secret of his socialism. 'He was not just violently anti-Tory,' recalled Stan Solomon, 'he had a vitriolic hatred of them.' Bryan Harwood remembered him as 'steeped in politics; always on about wanting to get into politics'. Like his father, he was a strong union man. He had joined the National Union of Journalists aged sixteen. In Halifax, he had been chairman and treasurer of the local NUJ; in Leeds, vice-chairman. At the 1959 General Election he gathered together a group of Yorkshire journalists to help produce Labour's campaign material.

As the years passed, he became increasingly dogmatic. He could always be provoked into an argument. The man who rented the *Guardian* its office in Albion Street, Ken Ridge, would come in with a gleam in his eye and the sole intention of goading Ingham to fury. No matter how busy he was, his quarry would invariably break off from his work and rise to the bait. 'Gutlessness' was what he claimed to despise most. 'The Tories could kick you in the teeth,' he was fond of remarking, 'and all you would say is: "Sorry, did I hurt your boot?"' His style of debate was demotic, hectoring, often pedantic. 'I gave you an argument,' he would say, 'and all you've given me is an assertion.' One night he was laying down the law to Mike Parkin and Harry Whewell over dinner in Whitelocks, a Leeds hostelry famous for the sawdust on its floor. He became so agitated, his newly-fitted false teeth flew out and skittered across the dining room. Ingham paid no attention. He carried on talking. Eventually Whewell had to tell him to stop and put his dentures back in.

At the beginning of 1964, Ingham's involvement in the Labour Party suddenly intensified. For some reason, he must have let his subscription lapse – at any rate, in February 1964 he simultaneously joined the West Leeds constituency party, and arranged for the Fabian Society, of which he was a member, to nominate him for inclusion on Labour's list of candidates for the City Council. His nomination paper has been preserved. Under 'experience', he wrote of himself: 'Has had a great deal of experience in writing political articles. Has spoken at weekend schools and seminars on "The Press" and also on "Regional Development"'. Under 'adult education' he disclosed that he had taken classes in 'public speaking' at the National Council of Labour Colleges, an organization similar to the Workers' Educational Association, but with a decidedly more Marxist tinge. Clearly, and with typical thoroughness, Ingham had been schooling himself for a political career.

On the evening of 11 February 1964 he was summoned to the Leeds Trades Hall to be interviewed by the Executive Committee of the City Labour Party. According to notes of the meeting made by Dick Knowles, the party's full-time agent, when 'asked why he wanted to go on the Council, Ingham replied: "Planning, Housing, Transport"'. As a known party sympathiser, he must have passed muster, for Knowles noted laconically underneath: 'Moved. Agreed.'[7] Ingham was on the candidates' list – the first step on the road.

The following week, he struck a deal with Solly Pearce, a wealthy Jewish tailor who ran the party's newspaper, the *Leeds Weekly Citizen*. The *Citizen* was unique – professionally produced from a building in Queen Square, well regarded, half a century old, the only official Labour Party weekly of its type. Pearce was always keen to fill his pages. Ingham was always keen to express his views. A columnist was born.

Albion made his debut on 28 February 1964 with an attack on the Prime Minister, Sir Alec Douglas-Home: 'no greater harm could have befallen the country than to have had inflicted upon it by a manifestly undemocratic process, however normal, a Prime Minister who is irrelevent to the problems both at home and abroad.' This, as we have seen, was mild stuff, no more than a polite clearing of the throat, compared with what was to come. In the *Guardian* office, Mike Parkin would occasionally look up from his work to find that his colleague's face, ruddy at the best of times, was turning even redder than usual. That was the sign that Ingham was writing his column.

Five months earlier, Ingham had been with the *Guardian*'s team at Scarborough for the Labour Party conference. It was there that Harold Wilson had made his famous speech about a 'new' Britain being forged by the 'white heat' of technology. The excitement it generated was reflected in the *Guardian*'s own front page report, written by John Cole, which hailed Wilson's performance as 'superb ... the best platform speech of his career', proof that the Labour leader's 'hard political shell covers a sincere and reforming spirit.'[8]

This enthusiasm for Wilson was all the rage in the period 1963–4 and Ingham, in the guise of Albion, was in the vanguard of the cheering crowd. 'Britain under Harold Wilson,' he asserted on 12 June, 'could be sure of thoughtful, professional leadership.' The Conservative Party was perceived, even by many of its supporters, as out of step with the times. Or, as Ingham put it characteristically on 3 July:

> The plain fact is that this raddled lot with their class approach to wages and salaries on the one hand and capital gains and dividends on the other are incapable of securing the co-operation that could produce the conditions necessary for 'controlled development' of the economy.

Or, even more characteristically, on 8 August:

> The trouble with Sir Alec and the whole terrible Tory tribe is that they are stuck with a feudal mentality in a potentially brave new world of social, scientific and technological revolution.

But there was more to Ingham's column than the mere following of intellectual fashion. It did not spring from some temporary infatuation with Harold Wilson and the wonderful world of science. It was founded on the bedrock of an absolute loathing of the Conservatives. 'From now on,' he wrote on 17 April, 'everything must be subordinated to the task of demolishing this battered remnant of an opponent still arrogant in its cowardice.' The Tory Party stood for everything he despised. The words seethed and foamed from his pen with a fluency he could never manage in his everyday journalism. Conservatives were public school southerners who had had it easy – snobs, 'fossils', 'goons', parasites living off unearned income, 'contemptuous of the common man's intelligence', 'diseased' and 'bonkers', forever looking down their long noses at the likes of him, expecting the workers to be grateful for their television sets and similar crumbs from the rich man's table:

> Everywhere the call – nay the demand – is for gratitude. But everywhere, fellow serfs, crude humanity refuses to be grateful for the fruits of this paternal feudalism ... As for my television set, I had that in 1959 when I was last told I'd never had it so good. But I still rebelled at the polling booth, because this is one serf who has not the slightest intention of being grateful for small mercies when others have huge mercies for, in my opinion, less effort, less ability, less application and less work.[9]

These, it is worth bearing in mind, were not the passing protests of some teenage militant. They were the settled opinions of a man of thirty-two.

36

As the opinion polls continued to point to a Labour victory in the coming election, Ingham was jubilant. 'Night is upon the Tories,' he chortled in April 1964. 'And night must fall.' In August he was rubbing his hands in anticipation: 'All the rag bag lot of them are about to meet their Waterloo.'[10]

'Labour will win,' he predicted on the eve of polling. 'My estimate is by a margin of at least thirty-six seats. This would be enough to lift Britain out of the feudal strife into which the country could sink with Sir Alec.'[11] He was over-optimistic. On 16 October 1964, Harold Wilson scraped into Downing Street with a majority of four. It may not have been a victory on the scale he had hoped for, but few can have celebrated the end of the Conservatives' 13–year reign more joyfully than Bernard Ingham.

Privately, he nurtured hopes of becoming a Member of Parliament himself. To several friends he confided his ambition of seeking the nomination in his old home constituency of Sowerby. This was not an unrealistic ambition. Although Garnet Ingham had by now retired from the Hebden Bridge council to nurse his ailing wife, he would still have been a useful ally in any selection battle. Douglas Houghton, the sitting MP, was in his sixty-seventh year. Who better to succeed him than Ingham: a local boy, an ardent trade unionist, a founder member of the local League of Labour Youth, a reporter on a distinguished left-wing newspaper? His acceptance on to Labour's list of candidates was designed to plug the one hole in this promising curriculum vitae: the fact that he had never previously stood for public office.

At the beginning of 1965, he was selected to fight the Conservative seat of Moortown in the forthcoming local elections. It was a daunting prospect. Moortown was one of the Tories' safest wards: street after street of rock solid, respectable Yorkshire bourgeoisie. Nevertheless Ingham set about contesting it with his customary thoroughness. He wrote Labour's campaign pamphlet ('LEEDS/heart of a NEW region/help LABOUR to make it really tick') which, in the opinion of Dick Knowles, was one of the best pieces of propaganda the city party ever produced. After three pages of facts and figures, headlines and pictures, came Ingham's own election address:

Dear Elector,

I have accepted an invitation to stand as Labour candidate for Moortown for three main reasons. I believe that:

1. As a journalist I have served an adequate apprenticeship for membership of a local authority;
2. I have something to offer Moortown, Leeds and Yorkshire through my broad understanding of their problems;
3. The Labour Party should be supported in its effort to bring about radical – and much-needed – changes in our society.

On May 13 YOU have an opportunity to lend your support by voting for ME. And if every Labour voter in Moortown takes the trouble to vote, Labour CAN take this so-called Tory citadel by storm.

Give me five minutes of your time on May 13 and I will give you many hours' service in return. My object is to serve you by securing imaginative, efficient and socially just local government.

Thank you.

Yours faithfully,

BERNARD INGHAM.

This appeal was rounded off with the slogan 'Let's get things done VOTE INGHAM' and was accompanied by a picture of the candidate, fat-cheeked and unsmiling.

He took time off from the *Guardian* to pound the streets, delivering his leaflet. He bussed in colleagues to help with the canvassing, among them Mike Parkin and two reporters from the Manchester office, Victor Keegan and R. W. Shakespeare. They even got up at dawn on polling day to deliver a last-minute appeal: 'if everyone who THINKS Labour VOTES Labour we can WIN'. By the end, Ingham had fallen prey to a syndrome common among first-time candidates in hopeless seats: he had convinced himself victory was within his grasp. It was pure self-delusion. In the local elections in May 1965 Labour performed badly everywhere. Moortown registered an 8.5 per cent swing to the Conservatives, and Ingham ran a very poor second:

Mrs L. E. Henson (Conservative)	5,532
Mr B. Ingham (Labour)	1,485
Mr K. R. Dunn (Liberal)	561
Mr P. Boyles (Communist)	190

For all his hard work, the result was exactly in line with others across the city.

In 1989, Ingham reminisced sweetly that he was 'comprehensively beaten by an extremely nice old lady.'¹² At the time, however, in the *Leeds Weekly Citizen*, his response to his defeat was less magnanimous. He ascribed Labour's poor showing in the local elections to

> stunning apathy on the part of Labour supporters and a relative eagerness on the part of reactionary minds to rush to the defence of their 'brass' ... The Socialistic notion had the same effect on Tory voters – most of whom have plenty to defend – as a bit of sun has on a chrysalis: it hatched them and sent them flitting about their business.¹³

In fact, although Albion's readers did not know it, by the time this article appeared its author had done a little flitting of his own. Defeated in Leeds on the Thursday night, on the following Monday morning he left Yorkshire to begin a new job – at the *Guardian*'s head office in London.

Ingham already had some limited experience of working in the capital. Occasionally in the previous year, if a member of the paper's labour staff had been off sick or on leave, he had been summoned down to spend a few days filling in. At that time the *Guardian*'s labour correspondent was Peter Jenkins. When, in the spring of 1965, Jenkins's deputy, Eric Jacobs, took a job as press adviser to the newly-created Prices and Incomes Board, the Yorkshireman was the obvious replacement.

At first, until he was able to move his family down, Ingham had to stay during the week at a grimy hotel behind the newspaper, only travelling home to Leeds at weekends. In the evenings, with nowhere else to go, he would hang around the Grays Inn Road offices long after his colleagues had gone home. Eventually he bought a bungalow in Purley, on the southern outskirts of London; Nancy and John joined him; they settled into a new life.

In leaving Leeds he had not abandoned his political ambitions. Far from it. He still talked hopefully about the Sowerby nomination. He maintained the Albion column, and thereby kept a toe in the water of Yorkshire politics. But the next couple of years were ones of gradual disillusionment as two of the institutions he respected most – the British trade union movement and the *Guardian* newspaper – badly let him down.

To begin with there were no apparent problems. The fearsome clique of labour correspondents was penetrated without too much difficulty. Monty Meth, his friend from the Leeds industrial scene, had also moved down south; he helped with introductions. The labour lobby tended to divide into two camps, one centred around Keith McDowall of the *Daily Mail*, and the other around John Grant of the *Daily Express*; Ingham gravitated towards the latter. With the Wilson government in office and with the trade unions approaching the peak of their power, these were the days when the labour correspondents were mighty barons in Fleet Street. The 'number ones' – men like Geoffrey Goodman of the *Daily Mirror* and Jenkins of the *Guardian* – supped, if not with princes, then at least with Cabinet ministers and general secretaries. Their deputies, the 'number twos' – men like Ingham and the 26-year-old John Torode of the *Financial Times* – were expected to produce large amounts of copy. Both the *Guardian* and the *FT* prided themselves on a comprehensive service of labour news. Ingham and Torode formed an alliance. One might cover the transport workers while the other would ring round the executive of the seamen's union. They would then exchange information, much as Ingham had done with his colleagues in Halifax a decade earlier.

Yet again the same phrases about Ingham recur: 'brilliant shorthand', 'diligent in the extreme', 'a grindingly hard worker', 'accurate', 'absolutely straight', 'fair'. He was soon churning out news stories at a greater rate than ever. 'After 17 years of straining blood out of millstone grit,' he would later say, 'I found that government, considered in its widest sense, not merely served it up on a plate in London but often washed it down, too.'[14] What were all these pansy southerners complaining about?

Among the trade unions, he had particularly good contacts with the miners, especially those members of the NUM executive from the Yorkshire area. According to Harry Whewell: 'While all the other reporters tended to concentrate on the leaders, Bernard would be off in the pub with some ordinary delegate who was telling him things he wasn't supposed to.' Another valuable source was Vic Feather, then assistant general secretary of the TUC. Ingham and Feather found they had plenty in common: both were north countrymen, both down-to-earth no-nonsense types, both suspicious of Oxbridge intellectuals, yet both deputies to exactly such men – in Ingham's case, Peter Jenkins and in Feather's, George Woodcock.

Given a choice between the worker by hand and the worker by brain, Ingham favoured the former any day. His loyalty to the Labour Party was never in question ('we took it for granted,' said Geoffrey Goodman) but there was a type of socialism which he hated: the theoretical, the airy-fairy, the chic revolutionary, the 'look-at-me-how-radical-I am' tendency of the ultra-left. This was shown most strongly just before Christmas 1965 when Henry Solomons, the Labour MP for Hull North, suddenly died, cutting the government's majority to one and precipitating a by-election. Hull North was highly marginal. Labour's majority was less than 1,200. If ever there was a time for all good men to come to the aid of the party, this was it. Yet what happened? Richard Gott, a Labour Party member – a journalist on the *Guardian*, to boot – decided to stand as a candidate of the Radical Alliance. Gott was protesting at the Wilson government's support for America in the Vietnam War. Albion was outraged.

> He is prepared because of what I accept is a sincere abhorrence of the conflict in Vietnam personally to bring down the Labour Government. As an historian he will no doubt appreciate the niche in history that this would give him.
>
> As an individual he has a perfect right to seek this sort of glory, or infamy, depending on one's point of view. But as a member of the Labour Party he has no right at all. He surrendered his right to act in this way the minute he joined it ... In this situation he classes himself – quite unjustifiably I'm sure – with the Trotskyists who use this party as a respectable cover for their disreputable activities ... He is in these circumstances no better than the meanest Young Socialist who has been corrupted by that miserable bunch of intellectual bullies, whose main deficiency is intelligence, which inhabits the fringes of the Labour Movement.

Ingham's stance on the issue of Vietnam, was equally robust:

> I take exception to those who clamour, often mechanically, for the immediate withdrawal of all foreign troops from Vietnam, meaning, of course, American troops, and the holding of free elections which, in the circumstances of an immediate American withdrawal, would be just about as free as a Great Train Robber in Durham Gaol ... We shall not achieve a thing if the Americans pull out tomorrow. All that we shall do is sanction an even more horrible bloodbath ...
>
> There has to be a negotiated settlement. And those who delay the

return to the negotiating table are the people to whom Mr Gott and the Radical Alliance should direct their challenge. Not the Labour Government. Not Harold Wilson. Not Michael Stewart. This is the Government and they are the statesmen who want a negotiated settlement. And it is they who are trying to get it.[15]

(In the event, Gott's challenge fizzled out. In January 1966 Labour held Hull North with a majority of more than 5,000: a result hailed by Ingham as 'a magnificent Tory-shattering victory . . . a real tonic.')[16]

For students of Bernard Ingham this article is something of a key text. There is, first, the overwhelming personal antipathy to the *Guardian* pointy-head, Gott, which no amount of weasel words ('what I accept is a sincere abhorrence . . . quite unjustifiably I'm sure') can fully disguise. Secondly, with its thuggish denunciation of Trotskyists ('miserable bunch of intellectual bullies') and sympathy for the American presence in Vietnam (essential to prevent 'an even more horrible bloodbath'), it places him firmly on the Healeyite Right of the Labour Party. Thirdly, and most importantly, it shows what might be called Ingham's reverence for authority. It is genuinely incomprehensible to him that people should step out of line and question the wisdom of the 'statesmen' in charge of the nation's affairs: for 'this,' as he puts it in his most revealing phrase, 'is the *Government*'. Here, as early as 1965, inside the shell of a supposedly left-wing journalist, is the future Whitehall press officer struggling to get out.

For Ingham, Harold Wilson could do no wrong. He stood 'head and shoulders above all other political leaders'. He was 'the outstanding national leader in British politics today'. He had 'given the lie to that ridiculous myth about Labour's incapability of governing'. He was 'a Prime Minister with an obvious ability not merely to walk but to command the world's stage'. James Callaghan's Budget was a 'tour de force': 'a springboard from which to launch ourselves on what has already been called the Wilsonian Grand Design'.[17]

At the start of the General Election campaign in March 1966, Ingham proclaimed that 'Labour has exceeded the wildest dreams of those who hoped it would jerk this country out of the inertia into which it had fallen under Conservatism.' Even taking into account the audience at which it was aimed – the Labour faithful – this was laying it on a bit thick. He listed nine factors which made it essential for the Wilson Government to be re-elected, including its 'redistribution of wealth', its 'determination to intervene in industrial trouble spots', its 'substitution of the savage stop-go system with the controlled operation of a flat-out economy' (whatever that might be), and 'its drive for reform of the educational system on comprehensive lines'.[18]

Anyone who attacked the Labour Government was, in Ingham's eyes, an enemy. They were undermining the only party 'likely to act fairly and decently to all groups of people'. If the attackers came from within the Labour movement itself, they were even more reprehensible. They were traitors. When, two months after the election, the seamen went on strike, they received scant sympathy from Albion. Their claim – effectively, for a 17 per cent pay increase – threatened to sail a large hole through the Government's pay 'norm' of 3.5 per cent. The 'saddest part of this whole miserable affair,' wrote Ingham in the *Leeds Weekly Citizen*, 'is that brother has been set against brother.'

> The seamen who have gone on strike – and all the unions fighting the incomes policy – should realise once and for all what they are doing.
>
> If I need to spell it out, they are sabotaging the Government's chances of successfully applying the policies it was elected to carry out. They are conspiring to set back the progressive forces which were unleashed at the General Election.[19]

The strike dragged on for seven weeks and did indeed do immense damage to the Government, reducing exports by 20 per cent, draining £38 million from the gold and currency reserves, and contributing to a run on sterling which eventually turned into the 1966 July Crisis. Ingham spent much of his time covering the strike almost literally camped outside the headquarters of the National Union of Seamen (NUS) in Clapham. In the *Guardian* during the week he was a neutral, strictly factual Dr Jekyll; in the *Leeds Weekly Citizen* at the weekends he became an opinionated, foaming Mr Hyde. At the end of the second week he wrote an article entitled 'The Seamen's Strike: Why we should support the Government'. On 10 June he accused the unions not only of failing 'to show any gratitude towards the Labour Government' but also of lacking any 'intellectual appreciation of the situation'.

At least eight members of the NUS Executive had communist sympathies. They were famously denounced in the House of Commons on

20 June 1966 by Harold Wilson as a 'tightly-knit group of politically motivated men'. Three days before Wilson's attack, Ingham criticized:

> the bulk of moderate Labour MPs who have remained strangely silent about the strike, its consequences and implications.
>
> We were told that the 1964 and 1966 intakes into Parliament were the brightest and best for many a long year. To me, the events of the last few weeks have proved neither their brilliance nor their worth; merely their dumbness ... A lot of things have needed saying over the past four weeks ... It grieves me that I have had to say them in the *Citizen*. I expect MPs to speak out against wrongs, including trade union wrongs ...

For Ingham, the seamen's strike was a kind of Damascene conversion: the point on the road at which he began to be blinded by doubts. Hitherto his vision of the world had been a simple one: the Tories represented a feudal, failed Britain; Labour stood for partnership and progress. Yet suddenly the unions – the institutions he and his family had set so much store by, which he had spent half his working life writing about – were ratting on their side of the bargain. They were behaving as selfishly as any capitalists. Worse, they were jeopardizing the very government they had helped elect. Meanwhile, the Parliamentary Labour Party was in the grip of a new intake of supine intellectuals, unwilling to confront a manifest wrong.

These feelings did not come hurtling out of an entirely clear sky in the summer of 1966. Six months earlier, Ingham had put his finger on what was to prove a central weakness of Labour governments for the best part of two decades:

> Either we trade unionists believe what we say when we talk about the brotherhood of man and social justice or we don't. And if we are not prepared to practice what we preach – often, I suspect, so hypocritically from conference platforms – we should shut up.
>
> We – and that goes for me as well as every other trade unionist – have to show that we have the humanity we so often deny to capitalists. If we don't we shall be branded by history as the biggest hypocrites since the Bible-toting Victorian (and some Elizabethan) mill owners; the Sunday saints who literally overnight became or become Monday devils.[20]

But after the seamen's strike, there feelings coalesced to become almost an obsession. It was as if Ingham felt personally let down by the unions. From now on, week after week in the *Leeds Weekly Citizen*, he berated them with the indignation he had once reserved for the Tory Party. 'I might as well tell you before, instead of after, the event,' he wrote on 3 June, 'that if the busmen come out they will not have much sympathy from me.' In July, Frank Cousins, the left-wing former leader of the Transport and General Workers' Union, resigned from the Cabinet in protest at the Government's incomes policy. Ingham was derisive about this 'prima donna':

> Somehow I'm supposed to get worked up about the resignation of Frank Cousins . . . And yet I can't. This is perhaps because I am one of those who can never make head or tail of what Frank Cousins says when he gets to a rostrum. And, believe you me, I try hard.[21]

He did not have much time for the leader of the white collar workers' union, either: 'I would never bank on Clive Jenkins supporting a Government which secured a drastic transformation of our society. The great strength of Clive's position is that he is insatiable.'[22]

Such blunt home truths did not, predictably, go down well with the more orthodox comrades who subscribed to the *Leeds Weekly Citizen*. The paper began to carry regular letters of complaint. One reader described Albion as the political equivalent of Ken Dodd. Ingham loved it. 'If all this does not provoke a fierce row in the correspondence columns of the *Citizen* then nothing will,' he wrote at the end of one anti-union diatribe. 'Blast away, please!' He delighted in taunting his readers: 'for too long I have felt able to get away with any outrage . . . you are soul-destroying in your apathy.'[23]

The longer he wrote the column, the more self-revelational it became. By the end of 1966, the full Ingham persona, which twenty years later was to earn him from foreign journalists the nickname 'Bernie the Bear', was on vigorous display: earthy, irascible, rude, aggressive – often to the point of self-parody and, occasionally, beyond it. On 14 October he described how he had found himself the previous week with a 'group who were pleased to call themselves rising young executives'.

> And I happened to say some blunt things about our lily-livered national newspaper proprietors collapsing at the first whiff of

grapeshot from the printing unions, breaching the [pay] freeze and then laying all the blame on to the Government for not doing its own dirty work.

'Good Lord,' one of them said, 'we've got a right communist here.'

Had I anything more to do with this particular rising young executive he would neither rise nor continue to execute.

Ingham then described how one of these proto-yuppies, earning four times the national average wage, had denounced as greedy a man on £11 a week who had asked for more. 'I told him,' said Ingham (and it requires little effort of the imagination to hear him doing it), 'that if I were on £11 a week I would not merely want another £1 per week. I'd damn well get it.'

Ingham's column leapt out from the pages of the *Leeds Weekly Citizen* like a firework on a grey day. On 21 April 1967, Solly Pearce forgot to print Albion's by-line and the following week published a wry apology: 'We regret the absence of his "name" from the article, but discerning readers would have known from its individual style who was its writer.' They certainly would. Albion had now been making his inimitable contributions for more than three years. But henceforth the *Citizen*'s readers would have to manage without him. By coincidence, that very week, Ingham had filed his last dispatch from the political battlefield. He had ceased to be a columnist; indeed, he had ceased to be a journalist.

The exact sequence of steps which led to Ingham's resignation from the *Guardian* is difficult to retrace. Those who were involved, when questioned today, tend to be afflicted by flashes of amnesia. Who can blame them? Not many journalists would care to confess that they once helped deprive of a job the man who is now the most powerful press secretary in the country.

The basic cause was the nature of the *Guardian* itself. It was – and is – a progressive, liberal newspaper. But then there is no snob quite like a progressive, liberal snob. Whatever it is like today, a quarter of a century ago there was a definite division on the editorial floor between gentlemen and players. The gentlemen composed elegant leaders and leader-page articles, and provided the front-page stories. The players produced the other nine-tenths of the paper. 'People often spoke of the *Guardian* as a snobby paper,' remembered Harry Whewell. 'For instance, reporters would come into the Manchester office from some local paper to do shift work and no one would speak to them. Bernard, I think, was always a bit over-awed by the *Guardian*, and he felt it more when he got to London.'

The 'number one' labour correspondent was, by tradition, a gentleman; the 'number two' was a player. Peter Jenkins would cover the main story of the day and contribute to the discussions about the leader; Ingham did the rest. 'He found he was a bit of a dogsbody,' recalled one old *Guardian* reporter. 'He was the guy who stood shivering outside the Ministry of Labour waiting for the result of some arbitration.' Years later, in his regular homilies on media standards, there was always something heartfelt about the way Ingham spoke of the Poor Bloody Infantry of the newsroom: he once described ordinary reporters as 'an endangered species': 'One of my ambitions is to elevate the reporter in the hierarchy of newspapers. He is the prospector in the geology of news who digs and pans for the gold of which a service to the public is made.'[24]

'He was very nice to work with: extremely conscientious,' recalled Jenkins, who was two years younger than his deputy. 'He probably thought I was a bit flash and metropolitan.' Keith Harper, who currently has Jenkins's old job on the *Guardian* and who was then a young reporter, remembers Ingham as a red-faced figure, arms akimbo, always in the forefront of office politics, a human dynamo, 'the engine room of the labour coverage'.

> Peter would be turning out the airy features while Bernard hammered out four news stories a day. I remember him in shirt-sleeves in '67 coming in with bits of copy to the news desk complaining about Peter's absence but actually revelling in it because it gave him an opportunity to make a name for himself.

Matters were brought to a head early in 1967 when Harold Evans, editor of the *Sunday Times*, offered Jenkins the chance to write a column. Alastair Hetherington promptly offered him a similar role on the *Guardian*. Jenkins accepted. The post of labour correspondent now fell vacant.

Not surprisingly, Ingham believed the position should be his. He had been Jenkins's deputy for two years. He had worked hard. He had the contacts and the experience. But Jenkins was dubious: 'In those days, the labour correspondent's job was second only to the political correspondent's; it was a stepping stone to greater things.' Jenkins's immediate predecessor, John Cole, was now news editor; Cole's predecessor, John Anderson, was northern editor. Nobody could imagine Ingham in such a senior role on the *Guardian*. He was not, to be frank, regarded as officer material. He was not Oxbridge. He was not even redbrick. He lacked intellectual self-confidence and made up for it by what came across as a belligerent anti-intellectualism. His colleagues would have been amazed by the fluency of his Albion columns: under his own by-line his style was stilted, conventional, dull. In Jenkins's words: 'The view – and it was not just mine – was that Bernard's experience as an industrial reporter just down from the north was not up to being chief labour correspondent.'

Jenkins's refusal to recommend his deputy for promotion was the Black Spot for Ingham. Whatever chance he might have had vanished. There was a painful interview during which Ingham's alleged deficiencies were made brutally clear to him. The *Guardian*, he was told, had decided to bring in an outside candidate and, to Ingham, their final choice must have seemed a calculated slap in the face. John Torode, his colleague on the *Financial Times*, was only 27 years old – seven years his junior. He was also much less experienced. He had been a Fleet Street labour reporter for just eighteen months. What he did have was a university education. Oxford, Cornell and Harvard trumped Hebden Bridge, Halifax and Leeds.

Ingham took it very badly. 'It was pretty rough on him,' remembered Jenkins, 'because he'd moved his family down.' Keith Harper recalled him 'vociferously complaining about his lot . . . [He] felt very aggrieved.' Another *Guardian* reporter describes 'a terrible set-to in public' between Ingham and one of the paper's senior editors. Around the office there was considerable sympathy for him. For he had not been simply passed over; he had been humiliated. It had been made abundantly clear to him that, as things stood, his prospects of promotion were bleak. In his later years, Ingham was to reveal a profound contempt for his old profession and it may well be that it was formed, at least in part, by his experiences at the hands of the *Guardian* in the spring of 1967.

It was at this point, with his career precariously balanced, that a *deus ex machina* appeared. It assumed the form of Eric Jacobs, whose decision to leave the *Guardian* to work for the Prices and Incomes Board (PIB) had brought Ingham down to London in the first place. Jacobs, too, had now been offered a job by Harold Evans. Quite by chance, according to

Jacobs, he rang his old friend Peter Jenkins to tell him he was going to the *Sunday Times*. Ingham, who shared an office with Jenkins, heard the news and spotted the opportunity in a flash. A few minutes later he rang Jacobs back. Would he be willing to recommend him, Ingham, as his successor as press adviser to the PIB? It was the perfect solution for all concerned. Jacobs, who was keen to leave as soon as a replacement could be found, was delighted to have a name – any name – to put forward. The PIB was anxious to fill the post at once. Ingham was keen to get out of the *Guardian*. The *Guardian* was happy to let him go. A couple of days later, he was offered a short-term contract to run from 1 May 1967.

If the Civil Service did not regard this as a permanent arrangement, neither did Ingham. He wanted a break from a newspaper where he felt badly done by. He also, with typically dogged determination, wanted to improve himself: to ensure he would not be treated in such a fashion again. 'I was told it would make me a better journalist,' he subsequently said of his move to the PIB. 'My intention at the end of it was to return to the practice of journalism all the better for the Whitehall experience.'[25] He thought he would be in and out in one year; two at the most. Nobody, least of all him, dreamed he would still be there nearly a quarter of a century later.

On 28 April, the *Leeds Weekly Citizen* published Albion's final column. '"No man is an island,"' he quoted. 'Yet if we rationalize Conservative philosophy, we soon discover that, in their view, man really is an island. And the bigger his island the better they think he is.' With that characteristic observation, he turned his back on the *Citizen*, resigned from the Labour Party (as he was obliged to do under Civil Service rules) – and disappeared into the anonymity of Whitehall.

FOUR

Press Officer

'Bernard Ingham came to see me. He's a very difficult man . . .'

Tony Benn, diary entry, 30 October 1975[1]

It is a prejudice widespread among journalists that all press officers, however grand their rank, are really just failed reporters. In the summer of 1967 this would have been a harsh but not wholly unfair assessment of Bernard Ingham. He was close to his thirty-fifth birthday and had been slogging away at his chosen profession for nearly nineteen years. True, he had risen from a local weekly to a Fleet Street daily. But by the mid-1960s there were ominous signs that he had gone as far as he was likely to get. Already, younger and less experienced men were streaking past him. He was not a fluent writer. He was not a scoop-monger. 'I never felt confident,' he once said of his work as a journalist, 'and never settled for not feeling confident.'[2] This was a revealing admission. The aggressive exterior and the phenomenal work-rate hid a more tentative spirit than might have been suspected.

Once, in a speech in 1986, he quoted Bismarck's maxim, that 'a journalist is a man who has missed his calling'. It was truer of Ingham than most. Having talked to his colleagues, ploughed through his journalism and read his Polonius-like lectures on the profession – with their emphasis on duty, responsibility, service and respect for the integrity of government – it is hard to avoid the conclusion that he was not really cut out for what Francis Williams called the 'Dangerous Estate'. There are all sorts of journalists: the elegant and provocative essayists, the macho foreign correspondents, the show-offs who thrive on being first with the news, the hangers-on of the rich and famous, the gossips, the malcontents, the mischief-makers, the conspiracy theorists (it was a deputy editor of *The Times*, no less, who once advised any young journalist interviewing a politician to keep asking themself 'Why is this bastard lying to me?'). Ingham was none of these. He was a frustrated man of power. Instinctively, he respected rather than suspected authority. He should have been one of those curmudgeonly, northern, right-wing Labour MPs. And who knows? If Douglas Houghton had retired at the 1966 general election he might have become one. Instead, he happened upon the perfect substitute. He became a civil servant.

When Ingham walked into his new office in Kingsgate House, Victoria Street in May 1967, it was like coming home. 'I found, on the inside, how little I had known,' he said later, 'how much there was to learn, and how much enjoyment I could get out of trying to solve problems.'[3] The PIB, set up in 1965, had the power to poke its nose into every wage and price increase in the country. It had the statutory right to summon witnesses and collect information. Its rulings had the force of law. Ingham had long supported it: 'a bold and praiseworthy idea,' he called it.[4] Now his task was to boost its public image.

His predecessor, Eric Jacobs, had had a deputy and four or five clerks who would answer the telephones, write letters to members of the public, and snip out press clippings about the Board and its doings. Jacobs professed himself 'bored stiff'. When the Treasury had suggested that he could manage without a deputy he had readily agreed. He finally left because it seemed to him there was 'nothing much to do'.

Ingham changed all that. A new deputy was hired. He took to coming in himself early in the morning to compile a detailed summary of the day's press. Like so many others, the Board's senior civil servant, Alex Jarratt, was immediately impressed by Ingham's 'immense capacity for work' and by the fact that 'he had strong views on most things'. According to Jarratt, Ingham and his predecessor 'could not have been more unalike. Eric was sophisticated and cultivated. Bernard was much more rugged and from a quite different background. Eric was interested in concepts. Bernard was just very anxious to project the Board and its chairman, Aubrey Jones.'

In fact, rather like the blind man who didn't wish to cross the road, the reserved and donnish Jones didn't always want to be 'projected', Ingham-style. He acidly described his new press adviser as 'very zealous, to the point of excess.' Clive Jenkins recalled a meeting he had with Jones: Ingham attended and 'repeatedly interrupted to protect him.'[5] More than twenty years later, Jones could still recall a vigorous argument at Manchester Airport when he felt his press adviser was trying to browbeat him into doing something he had no wish to. Journalists also claimed to detect a different style at the PIB. Whereas the laid-back and gossipy Jacobs would happily leak stories over lunch, Ingham, in the words of one reporter, was 'a jailer of information'.

This combination of zeal and discretion may not have been to everybody's taste, but it certainly brought its practitioner a growing reputation in Whitehall. This was just as well, for eleven months after Ingham joined the civil service, Harold Wilson embarked on yet another administrative shake-up. In April 1968, the old Ministry of Labour was given cosmetic surgery, and rechristened the Department of Employment and Productivity (DEP). The PIB was tossed in to add to the impression that this was some sort of dynamic new organization. On 5 April Barbara Castle was promoted from the Ministry of Transport to run the DEP as the new Secretary of State. She was now, albeit at several removes, Ingham's boss.

His fate was decided over Sunday afternoon tea two days later at Mrs Castle's country cottage. Denis Barnes, the Permanent Secretary, travelled down to see her to discuss personnel. The conversation turned to the question of who should be head of information at the new department. 'She wanted to import her man from Transport,' recalled Barnes. 'Well, the last thing I wanted to do was say "yes" to that. She already had a reputation for sacking people and bringing in her own team. I would immediately have been seen as being under her thumb.' Barnes's solution was to suggest she appoint the energetic new boy at the PIB, Bernard Ingham. There was one snag. The old Ministry of Labour already had a head of information: a former industrial correspondent in his fifties named Charles Birdsall.

There now occurs such a conflict of evidence and testimony regarding this crucial stage of Ingham's career that the only honest course is to offer both versions. According to Sir Denis Barnes: 'We had to pretend Birdsall was still chief information officer. He was very upset, but he wasn't so far off retirement. Bernard managed it very well and went out of his way to make sure his feelings weren't hurt.' Sir Alex Jarratt, who became Deputy Under Secretary at the new department, has a similar recollection: Birdsall, he has stated, was 'pushed to one side'. These memories are backed up by other sources. On 20 May 1968, the *Financial Times* reported Ingham's appointment as 'Director of Information' at the DEP. Ingham's own *Who's Who* entry reads simply: 'Chief Inf. Officer, DEP, 1968–73'. Barnes says that Ingham 'seemed to suit

Barbara; he got on very well with her'. This impression was shared by other observers: 'He was very close to Barbara' (Geoffrey Goodman); 'He became very attached to Barbara' (Peter Jenkins); 'She had a high regard for him' (Aiex Jarratt).

Barbara Castle's own version is, however, quite different. In her capacious diaries of the period, Ingham first appears on 18 May 1968, when our heroine is suffering from acute toothache and preparing for the Second Reading of the Prices and Incomes Bill:

> I tried to make progress with Bernard Ingham's rough redraft of my speech with very little success. Bernard has tried to liven up the ghastly officialese of the Department but I wouldn't say I have got myself a Kennedy-type speechwriter yet. However, he is still very new, poor man.

A footnote to this entry records flatly: 'When, to my great regret, Charles Birdsall retired, I brought Bernard Ingham over from the PIB where he was Press and Public Relations Adviser, to be my Chief Information Officer.' Yet Birdsall did not in fact retire until September 1969: Castle attended his farewell party and wrote in her diary that she would 'miss [him] terribly'.[6]

At first glance, there is an obvious explanation for this discrepancy: in order to save face, Birdsall was allowed to keep the title for eighteen months while Ingham actually had the power. But that is not Baroness Castle's recollection:

> Charles Birdsall was my main fellow ... From the point of view of press contact and the general feel for how to handle the press, I thought Charles was a wonderful old boy ... I didn't have that rapport with Bernard at all ... I found him a bit dull, a bit stodgy ... He didn't impinge on me at all ... I can't say I was massively impressed by him.

Nor is it the picture drawn in her diaries. These show Birdsall ('a pocket dynamo of a man,' according to one former colleague, 'restless and unremittingly energetic')[7] to have been at her side throughout the first, turbulent eighteen months of her rule at the Department. On 24 April 1968, for example, 'poor devoted Charles' is still hanging around the office at 2.30 a.m.; on 18 October 'Charles was doing his usual magnificent stuff, seeing that the press got the picture right'; on 18 June 1969, after the collapse of *In Place of Strife* (see below), 'Charles could not have been more loyal and comforting'. Ingham, by contrast, merits half a dozen perfunctory entries, conspicuous for their lack of flattery. Therefore, unless memory and diary have both been severely edited, it would seem that Ingham was not nearly as important to Barbara Castle as his contemporaries suggest: not least because he can only have been her 'main fellow' from September 1969 (when Birdsall went) to June 1970 (when the Labour Government fell), a period of a mere nine months.

There is a slight but poignant element of unrequited love about all this, for if she scarcely noticed him, he obviously adored her. Jarratt detected in him an element of protectiveness, almost of chivalry. 'He was devoted to her,' recalled Geoffrey Goodman. 'He thought she was an outstanding person in every respect. I think it was partly the Yorkshire connection. One got the impression that here was red-haired Yorkshire Bernard devoted to red-haired Yorkshire Barbara.' A former *Guardian* colleague watched him in action with her during an official visit. 'She'd say: "Right, come along Bernard!" and you could see that he loved it. She was to him what a duchess was to Ramsay MacDonald.' He shared her accent, her background, her political beliefs. Above all, he admired her for trying to tackle the trade unions.

Castle's White Paper on the future of the unions, *In Place of Strife*, was published in January 1969. It contained three particularly controversial proposals: a twenty-eight day 'cooling-off' period for unofficial disputes, during which strikers would be obliged to return to work; compulsory pre-strike ballots in industries where the government believed a dispute would damage the economy; and the establishment of a Commission on Industrial Relations with the power to impose fines on trade unionists who breached its rulings. All this, of course, met with Ingham's warm approval. 'The Government,' he had written three years earlier, 'was not elected by trade unions to serve trade union ends. It was elected by the nation to serve the nation and – at least in the minds of many who voted for it – the wider cause of humanity.'[8]

He thus required no prodding from Barbara Castle to defend her policy: on this issue, both in 1969 and, ten years later, under Margaret Thatcher, he was more royalist than his Queen. 'When Bernard got on that side of the fence he became even more disillusioned with the unions,' remembered Peter Jenkins. 'People who wanted the Labour Government to succeed were increasingly frustrated with the bovine selfishness of the union bosses, and Bernard became very indignant.'

But from the start *In Place of Strife* was a doomed venture, an idea a decade ahead of its time. James Callaghan, then Home Secretary, opposed it. Labour's National Executive rejected it. A special conference of the TUC came out against it by a majority of 8 million votes. In desperation, the Government decided to produce a 'pop' version, written in the style of a tabloid newspaper, designed to appeal over the heads of the union leaders to the ordinary members. This was entrusted first to an official in Ingham's department, but Number 10 was unhappy with the result and passed it on to Joe Haines who had recently joined Harold Wilson's staff from the *Daily Mirror*. Haines rewrote it in a way which Ingham felt breached civil service rules on impartiality. 'I can remember,' Haines recalled, 'Ingham fuming at me: "The trouble with you is you're too political!" Which I think, given today's circumstances, is amusing.'

It hardly mattered. The pamphlet was never published. On 17 June ('the most traumatic day of my political life,' as Castle called it) the Cabinet rebelled and she and Wilson were obliged to capitulate to the TUC. 'You're soft, you're cowardly, you're lily-livered,' the Prime Minister railed at his colleagues, but he decided not to resign. This was one of the great turning points in British politics, clearing the way for the union militancy of the 1970s and the consequent rise of Margaret Thatcher. It was a turning point, too, in Ingham's life. According to Geoffrey Goodman: 'He was deeply disillusioned by the whole experience of *In Place of Strife*. It conditioned his attitude to the trade unions, without any question. The way the unions rounded on Barbara persuaded him that something had to be done to destroy their power and influence. That whole department, Bernard included, was in a state of shock.'

One year later, almost to the day, the Conservatives won the general election. The 'terrible Tory tribe,' as Ingham had once called it, was back – and this time he, as a civil servant, was obliged to work for it.

Ingham's political ambitions, at least in a party sense, had now been abandoned. He had resigned from the Labour Party on the day he entered Whitehall. Eighteen months later, at his request, his short-term contract had been converted into full, professional membership of the civil service. But he was obviously no ordinary mandarin. He had never tried to pretend that he was neutral. 'He made no secret of his political views,' recalled Neville Taylor, then a public relations adviser at the

Ministry of Defence. 'There was a general awareness that this chap was different, because the rest of us didn't make a political comment, even among friends ... He was very open about his support for the Labour Government.'

The advent of a Conservative administration in June 1970 therefore left him in a peculiarly exposed position. Moreover, Edward Heath was pledged to introduce statutory controls on the unions. The Department of Employment was bound to be at the centre of a political storm and Ingham would have the crucial task of explaining its plans to the media. Could he do it? More importantly, would the new Secretary of State, Robert Carr, trust him to do it? According to Carr:

> Practically on my first day, Sir Denis Barnes came to see me and said Bernard Ingham wanted to have a word with me. What Bernard wanted to tell me was that he was still a committed supporter of the Labour Party and that he had stood as a local candidate. He said he wanted to tell me before anybody else did, especially as we were bound to be heading towards controversy over the Industrial Relations Bill. However he also said that, contrary to the views of most of the Labour Party, he was a passionate believer in creating a new framework of industrial law for the unions. He had been a very strong supporter of *In Place of Strife* – it wasn't just a matter of professional support. I made a few enquiries and everyone said he was very good: forceful, able, absolutely first class. So I kept him on.

Here was the clearest measure yet of how far Ingham had travelled politically, and how bitter was his disillusion with the unions. Five years earlier he had written in the *Leeds Weekly Citizen* that Tory plans to legislate on industrial disputes would be 'the kiss of death ... It is not in the Conservative nature, whatever they may say to the contrary, to wish to see a stronger and healthier trade union movement.'[9] In 1966, he had denounced the ideas which Heath now proposed to put into effect as 'dangerous drivel ... designed to appeal to the simple-minded':

> If you make procedures legally enforceable you have to have a means of enforcing them. This means fines and ultimately imprisonment if you don't pay the penalty ... But how do you enforce fines on, say 1000 miners? ... If they refuse [to pay], do you send them to prison? And if you send them to prison, do you have enough cells to go round?

Of course you don't. The whole miserable business would collapse the very day those 1000 miners marched to the doors of Armley Gaol and demanded instant incarceration.[10]

As it happened, this was one of Albion's more prescient pieces. By 1974, even the major employers' organization, the CBI, wanted the repeal of Heath's Industrial Relations Act, which they saw as inflammatory and unworkable. But at the time Ingham threw himself into the battle with a full heart, confident that Carr was only doing what Castle had tried and failed to do. He produced a series of five information films extolling the virtues of the Act ('for which, believe it or not,' he later claimed, 'there was a very brisk demand indeed').[11] He developed a considerable respect for his new boss, and the feeling was reciprocated. 'He knew his stuff,' said Carr.

Rather more unexpectedly, Ingham also got on well with Carr's successor, the charming, reformed alcoholic Etonian, Maurice Macmillan – a Treasury minister who was as startled as anyone else to find himself transferred to the Department of Employment. 'Bernard was frightfully good at covering for Maurice,' recalled Denis Barnes. Geoffrey Goodman also remembered Ingham saying how much he admired and respected Macmillan: 'What impressed Bernard was the way he handled the unions during this difficult period.' On one memorable occasion, in April 1972, Macmillan, Barnes and Ingham found themselves confronted outside the Department by a group of striking railwaymen, protesting at the Government's decision to order a ballot. Ingham was unimpressed. 'If you don't hold a ballot yourselves,' he growled at them, 'we'll hold the bloody ballot for you.'

Ingham's yeoman service during the industrial battles of the Heath years established his reputation in Whitehall. No longer was he seen as a creature of the Labour Party. Sir Donald Maitland, the former diplomat who had been brought back from the British embassy in Tripoli to serve as Heath's Press Secretary, was aware that Ingham supposedly had left-wing sympathies. 'But I would not have guessed that from his behaviour, from the way he carried out his job . . . He was utterly reliable, a safe pair of hands, and gave me great support.' Maitland did not, at that time, rate him as the best information officer in the government, but certainly placed him 'in the top rank'.

These were the years of Edward Heath's grand, Gaullist press conferences in Lancaster House, as the Government struggled to put together a 'tripartite pact' with the CBI and the TUC to tackle the country's economic problems. Ingham was trusted enough to be part of a small, four-man team, chaired by Maitland, including Peter Middleton from the Treasury and Patrick Shovelton from the Department of Trade and Industry, which met weekly at Number 10 to co-ordinate press coverage. According to Maitland:

> Bernard's role was to mark the trade union side. He was not only on very good terms – terms of mutual respect – with the TUC, but also with the industrial correspondents. I had total confidence in his handling of that sector of these negotiations. His contributions at our own co-ordination debates were characteristic of Bernard: very much to the point, no mincing of words, short, concise . . . He did have what people call 'northern directness'. He didn't go in for diplomatic niceties. He may have been a bit impatient: I wouldn't deny that. But I wasn't at the receiving end . . .

For all the efforts of Ingham and his colleagues, the tripartite talks failed. Heath, like Wilson before him, had to impose a statutory prices and incomes policy. In November 1973, the miners began an overtime ban. A state of emergency was declared. With the country facing power cuts and on the brink of a three-day week, the Prime Minister played one of his few remaining cards. He brought back William Whitelaw from the Northern Ireland Office (where he had established a formidable reputation as a conciliator) and put him into the Department of Employment, replacing Macmillan. Whitelaw's brief, effectively, was to save the Government.

This, in turn, had alarming consequences for Ingham, for it quickly transpired that part of the price Whitelaw had demanded for his services was the right to bring across his own public relations officer from Belfast: Keith McDowall, former industrial editor of the *Daily Mail* and an old rival of Ingham from his labour corps days. Ingham fought desperately to retain a job he loved and at which he was held to be good. He enlisted the support of the Cabinet Office and of his superiors at the Department of Employment – to no avail. As Whitelaw subsequently explained: 'I was in a fairly powerful position because I didn't want to come back anyway . . . So they had to take it.'

At the beginning of December, Ingham had a series of painful interviews with Barnes and Whitelaw. 'I had to tell him that I was sorry,' said Whitelaw, 'that I had nothing against him personally, but that Keith McDowall had worked for me in Northern Ireland and I wished to bring him back. He obviously was disappointed because he enjoyed the job. He thought it was unreasonable.' At lunchtime on Wednesday 5 December, Barnes told him he would have to be sent home on what the Civil Service euphemistically called 'gardening leave' – suspended on full pay, whilst they tried to find him another job. It leaked to the press. It was deeply embarrassing. 'He was very upset,' according to Barnes. 'He took it badly.'

For a workaholic like Ingham, having to sit at home in Purley as the country was gripped by the biggest industrial crisis since 1926 must have been torture. Five weeks dragged by. Eventually, in January 1974, he was given a new job. At an annual salary of £8,000, Ingham was made Chief Information Officer at a new ministry: the Department of Energy.

The formation of the Energy Department, in the words of its first Secretary of State, Lord Carrington, was an exercise in 'crisis management'. Electricity was being rationed, coal stocks were dwindling, the price of oil had quadrupled. 'I was plucked from the Ministry of Defence to go and head it,' wrote Carrington. 'I went without enthusiasm ... For the weeks that this lasted I retain no affection.'[12] Less than two months later the Heath Government had fallen and Labour was back in power.

Ingham might reasonably have hoped that with Whitelaw gone, he could have returned to his old post at the Department of Employment. The new Labour Employment Secretary, Michael Foot, certainly toyed with the idea of reinstating him. A few days after the formation of the government, he sat near Peter Jenkins at a dinner party and asked his opinion of Bernard Ingham. Jenkins gave a non-committal reply. The idea was dropped.

Instead, Ingham passed the next fifteen months at Energy in the congenial service of Eric Varley. Varley was exactly Ingham's type of minister: a north countryman, a former miner, moderate in his views, efficient in the dispatch of business. His Chief Information Officer was soon making his presence felt in the new department in his accustomed manner: part-gruff, part-cheerful; part-helpful, part-bully. Ronald

Custis, Varley's Private Secretary, had a 'friendly' but sometimes 'uneasy' relationship with him. They had a series of running battles over access to classified information:

> At the time [recalled Custis] there was a little bit of sensitivity about how much heads of information saw which wasn't relevant to their own departments. And I was applying the rules, saying 'No, you can't see this' or 'Yes, you may see that'. And he found this a bit upsetting and once or twice we had 'I'm-not-talking-to-you' sessions for a few days.

Another civil servant with whom Ingham had frequent rows was the deputy secretary responsible for energy conservation, Philip Jones. 'I often used to say to him,' Jones remembered, '"It's your job to present policy, not make it." He was always wanting to write great papers and there used to be stormy minutes flying between us as a result.' At heart, Ingham was what he always had been: a frustrated man of power. And although, in Jones's view, he 'ran the best public relations department in Whitehall', this propensity to argue and to involve himself in everyone else's business hampered his effectiveness:

> If Bernard has a fault, it is that he gets over-assertive and over-aggressive and promotes policies more strongly even than their authors. The danger is that you get Bernard's policy rather than government policy.

Under an easy-going character like Eric Varley, this was less of a problem. But in June 1975, Ingham's world was turned upside down by the arrival of yet another Secretary of State. Tony Benn was a public school-educated, far-left intellectual, determined to go his own way, deeply suspicious of the entire civil service, at war with the media, semi-detached (to coin a phrase) from the Labour Government, the most controversial figure in British politics. He was, in short, Bernard Ingham's idea of a nightmare.

During his eight years as Prime Minister, Harold Wilson appointed forty-two different Cabinet ministers. Of these forty-two, three published diaries. Of these three, Ingham worked for two: Barbara Castle and Tony Benn. This statistical freak may have been Ingham's misfortune; it is certainly of the greatest assistance to a biographer. 'I had a call from Bernard Ingham, my new press officer at the Department of Energy,' recorded Benn on 11 June 1975, the day of his appointment. For the next two and a half years, theirs was to be one of the most fascinating and well-documented relationships in Whitehall.

Benn had been demoted to Energy from the Department of Industry, and viewed his new job as the equivalent of a posting to run a Siberian power station: it was 'an absolutely major political reverse ... From the point of view of the party and the country, it was a position of disgrace, or intended to be.'[13] This attitude was not calculated to endear him to his new department. Nor was the reputation he brought with him. At Industry he had become famous for treating his civil servants, especially his Permanent Secretary, Sir Antony Part, as if they were Fifth Columnists. Part has left a telling description of what even their most routine tête-à-têtes about the ministry entailed:

Usually for such informal talks the Secretary of State and his Permanent Secretary would sit in armchairs in a corner of the office. Mr Benn wished us to face each other across the long narrow conference table next to his desk. As he did at meetings with deputations, he put a block of paper in front of him and drew a line down the middle. As the conversation proceeded, he noted my remarks to the left of the line and any comment or counter-argument of his to the right of the line. This did not make for a relaxed atmosphere and occasionally it was as though he were pointing a pistol at my head. Metaphorically, I would watch his finger tightening on the trigger and when I judged that he was about to fire I moved my head to one side. With any luck, I heard the bullet smack harmlessly into the woodwork behind me.[14]

As if to underline his contempt for the regular civil service, Benn trailed around with him two ideologically-sound 'special advisers': Frances Morrell and Francis Cripps. The trio was portrayed in the press as a nest of revolutionaries at the heart of the Government. Benn's house in Holland Park was routinely staked-out by the media. 'I'm sorry to see you lot going,' the Chief Information Officer at the Industry Department, Ray Tuite, told Frances Morrell as they packed their bags. 'There's been nothing like it since the Berlin airlift.' He had cause to be cheerful. Benn's relations with the press were now Ingham's responsibility.

For the first few weeks, all was quiet. 'Benn was sulking in his tent,' according to Ronald Custis, who had stayed on to serve as his Private Secretary. 'We saw very little of him. Then he appeared and the weight started flying around.'

What brought Benn dashing out of his tent was an economic crisis. On 30 June 1975, the pound lost more than five cents against the dollar. The next day the Cabinet went into emergency session. To strengthen sterling, the Treasury was demanding cuts in public expenditure and an incomes policy – both of them anathemas to the Labour left. Ingham saw Benn first thing in the morning on 2 July and asked him about his personal position. 'I told him I was strongly opposed to the proposed economic package,' recorded Benn, 'and that there were four options: to put up with it, to oppose it from the inside, to come out and oppose it constructively, or to come out and oppose it destructively. I thought opposing it from the inside was perhaps the best thing to do.'[15]

In theory, Benn's personal political position should have had nothing to do with Ingham: as a press officer, he was employed by the taxpayer solely to explain the policies of the Energy Department. In practice, of course, he was immediately sucked into the political controversy. Ingham suggested they brief his old friend, Ian Aitken, political correspondent of the *Guardian*, on Benn's thinking. Benn agreed. In the following morning's paper, Aitken reported that the Energy Secretary was 'known to have serious reservations' about the Government's direction.[16]

The real crunch came the following week, when the Cabinet had to vote on the Treasury's demands. On 10 July, minutes before he was due in Downing Street, Benn had a discussion about tactics with his media adviser. 'Bernard Ingham said the press would be interested today in whether or not I would resign,' wrote Benn. 'I told him I wasn't sure what to do but the movement wanted us to stay in. He thought I might have to explain to my constituents the agonizing choice I'd had to make.'[17] In the event, it was not Benn who explained his 'agonizing choice' to the country; it was Ingham, using the medium of an off-the-record briefing to John Bourne of the *Financial Times*.

Bourne's account ('"Grave doubts" by Left after marathon talks') based in part on his conversation with Ingham, was the lead story in the following morning's *Financial Times*. It provided a good illustration of some of the baroque euphemisms of British political journalism, and of the grey area in which supposedly neutral civil servants operate. First came an account of the Cabinet's deliberations (a clear breach of the then Official Secrets Act, incidentally); then this explanation of Benn's position:

> Some left-wing ministers, led by Mr Anthony Wedgwood Benn, the Energy Secretary, expressed grave doubts about the policy. But Mr Wedgwood Benn has for the moment let it be known that he has no intention of resigning from the Government.
>
> However, he is worried about the policies in the Government's White Paper, to be published at 11.30 today, because he believes they are bound to fail.
>
> Some political friends of Mr Wedgwood Benn maintain that Mr Michael Foot, the Employment Secretary, would destroy himself by supporting the Chancellor's package. But they also claimed that Mr Wedgood Benn's refusal to resign at the moment was because he regarded the economic situation as extremely serious and although very unhappy about today's measures, he thought he ought to do his best not to break Cabinet solidarity at this stage.
>
> According to the same sources, Mr Wedgwood Benn believes that now for the first time a Labour Government is imposing pay cuts by law, that public expenditure reductions and higher unemployment are also in the wind – all points that ran counter to Labour's election manifesto . . .

'*Mr Benn has let it be known . . . political friends of Mr Benn . . .*' – it did not require Sherlock Holmes to detect Ingham's fingerprints all over this piece. It was too ham-fisted an operation even for Benn (whose more subtle ploy to distance himself from his Cabinet colleagues had been to walk into Number 10 with a copy of Labour's election manifesto tucked prominently beneath his arm). 'When I went into the office, Bernard Ingham told me he had been talking to John Bourne of the *FT* about how I thought the policy was bound to fail, and how I was anxious about wage cuts and public expenditure cuts and rising unemployment and so on. I was slightly nervous, as I think was Bernard, that they had printed it so fully.'[18]

Ingham was now experiencing at first hand the dilemma which had confronted Sir Antony Part. What was an official to do when his political boss, although opposed to Government policy, nevertheless refused to resign? In Part's words: 'To whom does his loyalty lie – his Secretary of State or the Prime Minister?' The dilemma was a particularly acute one for Ingham, who had built his career on his reputation for loyalty. Suddenly he was finding himself having to brief against the interests of the Government he served. More than that, he was briefing against his own deepest beliefs, for everything in his personal history suggests he would have been an instinctive supporter of the policy his minister opposed. The 'Social Contract' between Government and unions which Wilson, Foot, Denis Healey and Jack Jones were struggling to devise was exactly the sort of partnership for which Ingham had argued in the *Leeds Weekly Citizen* a decade earlier. Not surprisingly, his relationship with Benn began deteriorating fast.

The week after the Bourne briefing, Benn, accompanied by Ingham and Custis, travelled up to Aberdeen to inspect a North Sea oil rig. They spent the evening in Glasgow. 'We were due to come down on the night sleeper,' recalled Custis, 'and we found ourselves with a couple of hours and Benn said: "Let's go and see the chaps in the *Scottish Daily News*."' This was a pet project of Benn: a workers' co-operative, born three months earlier out of the ashes of the *Scottish Daily Express*, into which the sacked printers and journalists had been encouraged to invest their redundancy money in return for a Government loan of £1.2 million. According to Custis:

> We walked through this huge old printing shed, and there in one corner was a group of men working a machine and getting it ready to go to press and it was obviously doomed to failure. The whole atmosphere of the place was black. And here were all these chaps who had, in a sense, been duped into putting their redundancy money into this venture. They were obviously going to lose it all. But nevertheless in walked Benn and there was a bit of hero worship going on ... That was quite a night.

Ingham knew enough about journalism to recognise a sinking ship when he saw one (the paper closed in November) and the whole incident left him, in Custis's view, not merely 'saddened and depressed' but 'sickened'.

Benn's starry-eyed view of the working-classes, his mugs of tea, his regular quotations from the 17th-century Diggers and Levellers, his well-aired obsession that the secret service was out to get him – all these idiosyncrasies grated on Ingham. 'At times one could find him very, very depressed,' Custis remembered. 'He was glum and humourless. You could sometimes go into his room late in the day and find him slouched over his desk looking very fed up with things.' It was around this time that Ingham swore one journalist to secrecy and then confided his firm belief that his minister was 'stark raving mad'. Word of his disenchantment filtered back to Benn's ever-vigilant inner circle. 'I can't believe I'm doing this,' one sympathetic left-wing journalist told Frances Morrell in September 1975, 'but I heard the head of your PR department vilifying Tony Benn so much I felt I had to come and tell you.'

Ingham, in turn, suspected Morrell of leaking confidential information behind his back. 'PLAN TO MAKE BRITAIN WORLD'S NUCLEAR DUSTBIN' was the *Daily Mirror*'s front-page headline on 21 October. The *Mirror* reported that Britain might soon be sent '4,000 tons of lethal waste' by Japan, in a reprocessing deal worth up to £400 million. According to 'sources close to the secret talks . . . the contract could be signed before Christmas'. The story spilled over on to page two. 'Would you fill your house with bottles of poison just because someone paid you to do it?' demanded the paper's editorial. 'What a lethal legacy to leave to our children and our children's children.'

The 'source' was undoubtedly inside the Energy Department. Ingham went immediately to see Benn and accused Morrell of being responsible for the story. Such was his agitation ('hot, flushed and angry,' according to one eyewitness) that Benn himself went off to find his special adviser. He was away for what seemed a suspiciously long time. When finally he returned with Morrell, she loudly denied any involvement. Ingham did not believe her, and the next day's *Mirror* seemed only to confirm his suspicion that Benn was now running his own private press operation within the department. Under the headline 'Well done the *Mirror* – Praise by Benn for Doomwatch Report' was a comment from the Energy Secretary actually praising the leak: 'The *Mirror* has performed a very valuable function and now there will be a lot of public pressure put on the Government and my department. This breakthrough by a big popular newspaper gives us the opportunity to discuss these problems.'

Ingham's reaction to this extraordinary statement, in which a damaging leak suddenly became a 'breakthrough', can be easily imagined. Certainly, he was not the sort to bottle his feelings and he appears to have confronted his Secretary of State. 'Bernard Ingham came to see me,' recorded Benn the following week. 'He's a very difficult man ... I think when Eric Varley was at Energy, he and Ronnie Custis did exactly what they liked. Eric is entirely guided by his civil servants. I think part of my problem has been trying to get control of those two.'[19] Benn suspected that Ingham would have taken over the running of the entire department if he had been given half a chance. Many years later, asked if he believed the rumours that Ingham was virtually Deputy Prime Minister under Margaret Thatcher, he replied: 'I wouldn't put it past him.'[20]

This battle of wills between Secretary of State and civil servant reached a farcical, indeed almost physical, climax a fortnight later, with the passing of the act which opened the North Sea oil pipeline. Benn wanted to make a ministerial broadcast to mark this historic step. Ingham advised against it 'on the grounds that it would not be interesting enough'.[21] Benn insisted and was eventually given permission by Number 10. But he was granted leave to give a radio talk only: the BBC had ruled that a television broadcast would be too party political and the Opposition would be entitled to a right of reply. Ingham and Custis duly accompanied Benn to Broadcasting House where he made his radio recording. 'Then,' recalled Custis, 'he said: "Well, let's go and do this television piece." We said: "No, you're not allowed to." And he went right to the door of the television studio and we were almost literally standing in his way and saying "No, you mustn't." He eventually said: "Well, have it your way. I'll get the Party on to this." We just came back and Bernard and I reported what had happened to Number 10.'

This seems to have been the final straw as far as Benn was concerned. He had already demanded the removal of Custis from his Private Office on the grounds that he was 'unsympathetic'. Now he set about securing the dismissal of Ingham. On his way out of Cabinet on 18 November he had a word about Ingham with Joe Haines, the Prime Minister's Press Secretary. According to Haines: 'He said he couldn't stand him and he wanted to know how he could get rid of him. He just thought that Ingham was obstructive to what he was trying to do.' Benn announced that he wanted to bring over his old press adviser from the Industry Department, Ray Tuite. Haines suggested they might arrange a straight swop, but he warned him (or so Benn noted in his diary) that 'Ingham was capable of creating trouble if I got rid of him.'[22]

Nevertheless, Benn was not prepared to let the matter drop. The next day he raised it with Jack Rampton, the department's Permanent Under Secretary.

I said, 'While we're on staff matters, I'm a bit worried about Bernard Ingham.' He told me Bernard had gone to see him, saying he feared he'd lost the confidence of Ministers. I said, 'I think that's true but it's a much deeper problem. He doesn't seem to take an interest and he's not very helpful.'

'He's an energetic chap,' Jack said. 'He has an idea of what a Minister should do and he bullies him until he does it.'

I said, 'On the principle that everybody does best what they most enjoy doing, wouldn't it be a good idea to give him a full-time job on energy conservation?'

'That might be one way of doing it or else I could have a word with Douglas Allen of the Civil Service Department and see what can be done.'[23]

In terms of personal relations between a minister and a press adviser, where trust is of the essence, this is about as bad as things could get. Each man was convinced the other was trying to undermine him. Yet ridding himself of Ingham was not as easy as Benn had hoped. Shunting him off to look after energy conservation was the best hope. But that could not be done immediately: no such division existed within the ministry, and it would take time to persuade the Treasury to put up the extra money. For a time, Geoffrey Goodman – an old friend of Ingham and one of the few journalists Benn respected – seemed to offer a solution. He had been seconded from the *Daily Mirror* to work for Harold Wilson at Number 10 as head of the Counter-Inflation Unit. When James Callaghan replaced Wilson in March 1976, Goodman decided to return to journalism. He nominated Ingham as his successor. 'Callaghan said to me: "Why him?" I said: "Because he's absolutely straight, he's worked for Labour and Conservative governments, and of all the Whitehall press people, he's the best."' Ingham was enthusiastic, but nothing came of it. Callaghan eventually appointed Hugh Cudlipp.

The weeks turned into months, and a curious thing happened. Ingham and Benn started to get on better. The air had been cleared. In addition, Ronald Custis had been replaced by Bryan Emmett, a civil servant more to Benn's taste, and who seems to have helped smooth relations. At the beginning of April, Ingham and Emmett took Benn out to lunch at a restaurant near the ministry. At the end of the month, they travelled back on the train with him from the NUM Conference. 'Every time I talk to them they tell me something interesting about the last Government,' recorded Benn. Among the matters discussed on this occasion was how the Energy Department's 'Switch Off Something' campaign during the three-day week had been 'purely political, designed to prolong the community's capacity to beat the miners; and how many Tories had thought the 1974 Election was a revolution.' Benn responded by describing the way he had been treated by Sir Antony Part at the Department of Industry. 'Gradually they are beginning to understand what it is all about,' Benn dictated into his diary that night. 'I like them both.'[24] On Ingham's side, too, a certain wary respect began to replace his earlier hostility. 'Stark raving mad' Benn might well appear on occasions; but on others he could be stimulating, inspiring and (a quality for which few were prepared) immensely charming.

In February 1977, Benn made a delightful speech at the Energy Department's annual party for journalists, during which he claimed that the ministry was run not by him but by the Press Office. As proof, he read out Ingham's characteristically thorough briefing paper on the evening's festivities: 'Tonight's party for the Press Office will give journalists the full opportunity to explore through casual conversations with Ministers and officials progress on two oil-related items . . . Since all who will be representing the Department tonight will no doubt wish to maintain a consistent line if asked about these issues, it might be useful if I describe the line that the Press Office has been authorized to take.' The reporters laughed. Benn paused and looked up. 'I have to stop there because the last two paragraphs – which tell you the Press Office line – have been classified top secret by Sir Jack Rampton.'

'There was,' noted Benn, 'a lot of giggling and amusement.'[25]

In the meantime, after much clanking and groaning, the Whitehall machine was finally on the point of coughing up enough money to establish a proper Energy Conservation Division. Ingham's final months as Benn's Chief Information Officer were peripatetic – together they visited Brussels, Washington, Saudi Arabia, Norway and Luxembourg – until at length, on 12 December, Benn recorded their last press conference: 'he is leaving to take over as head of the Energy Conservation Department, something I suggested to Jack Rampton when I was getting on badly with Bernard, but I'm sorry to see him go now.'[26] Three months later, he was still grieving over the loss. One of the last entries under 'Ingham' in Benn's diary is for 22 March 1978. It reads simply: 'I miss Bernard.'[27]

The details of Ingham's three months in charge of energy conservation need not, mercifully, detain us long. Ingham himself subsequently referred to it as 'this rather agreeable life ... during which I rediscovered the luxury of reading books and listening to music uninterrupted by calls from newspapermen'.[28] He had reached the rank of Under Secretary. He was entitled to an entry in *Who's Who*, where he listed his recreations as walking, gardening and reading. He presided over a department of some thirty or forty. He helped launch the Government's 'Save It' campaign, an initiative which was later held to have had mixed results, concentrating as it did on domestic users rather than on the real profligates of power, industrial consumers. He launched a newspaper with the uninspiring title, *Energy Management*.

As an administrator he was a natural empire-builder, a tendency he had displayed ever since his days at the PIB. 'I felt he would be expanding his department at times more than it deserved,' recalled Philip Jones, one of his superiors. 'You would find, say, that if there was a need for regular discussions with the building societies, Bernard would create a building society section. Then he'd want more people and more space.' He was not a high-flier. He was an ordinary, competent, middle-aged civil servant. If he had stayed at the Department of Energy, according to Jones, he would, in due course, have been 'moved across to another Under Secretary's job. I doubt whether he had the ability to go up the policy-making ladder. He wasn't a deep enough thinker. I don't think he could have formulated, say, North Sea policy, or gas policy.'

By the summer of 1979 he was forty-seven years old and a pleasant, routine life beckoned: his son was away at Durham University; he and Nancy had time on their hands; he had a secure job and a pension; there would be weekends in Hebden Bridge, summers spent on his brother's farm on the dales overlooking Halifax; early retirement, perhaps, and a return to the north of England; whatever happened, the next fifteen years promised to be easier than the last fifteen ... Then, quite without warning, these modest expectations were utterly transformed by a summons to see Sir Jack Rampton.

FIVE

Prime Minister's Press Secretary

'The Press Secretary is employed by the Prime Minister and for the Prime Minister, not by or for Fleet Street. He has no function in helping Fleet Street. Everything he says and everything he does is designed to help the Prime Minister first, and after that the Government as a whole. If, in the end, it means ditching another minister ... then you ditch that minister.'

Joe Haines, former Press Secretary to Harold Wilson, 1989[1]

It was August 1979. The Labour Government had fallen three months earlier. Benn had gone from the Energy Department, taking his pint mugs of tea and his miners' lamps and his union banners with him. In his place was a Thatcherite Conservative, David Howell. The atmosphere in the complex of offices overlooking the Thames was noticeably less tense.

When Ingham arrived in the Permanent Under Secretary's office, Rampton took him by surprise. Was he, he inquired, happy in his work as an administrator? Were there any circumstances under which he would consider returning to the Government Information Service? Ingham replied that he preferred to stay where he was: 'Unless, I suppose, I am being asked to go to Number 10 as Chief Press Secretary. But that's not going to happen, so . . .' Rampton said nothing. The conversation ended. But his smile, Ingham recalled, 'was more inscrutable than that of the Sphynx'.[2]

One of Margaret Thatcher's first actions on entering 10 Downing Street in May 1979, had been to appoint as her Press Secretary a man named Henry James. James was an experienced Whitehall hand who had started his career as a government press officer at the old Ministry of Pensions in 1951. Since then he had swung from branch to branch – from the Admiralty to Education to Downing Street to Housing back to Downing Street and on to Environment – before finishing at the top of his professional tree as Director-General of the Central Office of

Information (COI) in 1974. He had since retired from the civil service and was working as public relations adviser to the main board of Vickers when Mrs Thatcher asked him to come back and work for her.

Why she did so is not entirely clear. True, James had done a couple of stints as a junior press officer at Downing Street; true, also, that the Parliamentary Lobby had let Mrs Thatcher know, whilst she was still Leader of the Opposition, that his would be a welcome appointment (she had sent her Parliamentary Private Secretary, Ian Gow, to make discreet enquiries). But he was nearing sixty and it quickly became apparent that he and the Prime Minister had no real rapport. He once sent her a memorandum about media arrangements for a forthcoming trip in which he claimed to have visited the location 'to case the joint'. Thatcher, a stickler for correctness, announced to one of her advisers that she had no idea what the man was talking about. In the words of one doyen of the Lobby: 'Our recommendation turned out to be a complete disaster. They just didn't hit it off. It became clear to us that he hadn't got her confidence and he had nothing to tell us. It was conveyed to her by the Lobby that this just couldn't go on.'

James had only been in place three months when Downing Street began putting out feelers for a replacement. The Head of the Home Civil Service, Sir Ian Bancroft, in strict confidence, asked for suggestions from the Permanent Secretaries. There were three potential candidates considered to have sufficient seniority: Donald Grant, Director of Information at the Home Office for the past five years; Keith McDowall, Ingham's old rival, who had just left the Department of Employment to become Managing Director of Public Affairs at British Shipbuilders; and Bernard Ingham. What helped swing it Ingham's way was the enthusiastic lobbying of Jack Rampton who insisted from the start that he had the ideal man.

There followed an intricate courtship, more like an oriental marriage negotiation than the appointment of a senior government official. After Rampton had established that Ingham, at least in principle, was interested in the match, he arranged for the bride and groom to be brought, discreetly, face to face. Mrs Thatcher was then engaged in her infamous tour of all the Whitehall ministries – a regal progress which, legend has it, had left several of her shattered hosts bobbing like driftwood in her wake. The Energy Department was next on her list. At the last minute, Ingham was invited 'to take tea and cucumber

sandwiches with the Prime Minister' in the company of thirty-five colleagues. Rampton engineered a meeting. 'I talked to her,' said Ingham,
'for all of two minutes.'[3]

A few days later he was telephoned by Thatcher's new Principal
Private Secretary, Clive Whitmore. Even at this late stage Whitmore was
unwilling to come out openly and admit what was going on. He began by
recalling that they had met on an open government seminar six months
earlier. Then he asked if the Head of the Civil Service had been in touch
with him. Ingham replied that he rarely spoke to Sir Ian, and 'had not
recently had the pleasure.'

'Oh dear,' Whitmore groaned, 'not another cock-up.' He asked
Ingham if he had got the 'drift' of what was happening. Of course,
Ingham had. He asked for time to think the matter over.

He sought the advice of his colleagues. Most urged him to go. 'It's the
best place to give rein to your talents,' Philip Jones told him. Ingham was
understandably excited by the prospect, but had two major reservations:
he wondered whether he was up to it, and he doubted whether he could
work with Margaret Thatcher. He was ambitious enough to take a
gamble on the first; the second was more troubling. 'I'd put my bottom
dollar,' one friend of his insisted, 'on Bernard having voted Labour in
1979.' Whatever else he was, he was not a Tory. But then – and this is
what finally convinced him he should take the job – neither was she.
Thatcher, like Ingham, had been born without privileges. She had never
quite lost the aura of an outsider. She did not want to conserve Britain's
institutions: she wanted to abolish a lot of them, or shake them up, or
dismantle them. She was not a member of the Establishment. She was
suspicious of it. She thought it had gone soft and let the country down.
With all of this, and especially with her conviction that an economic
recovery depended on a reduction in trade union power, Ingham was in
full agreement. 'I think I'll do it,' he confided to one colleague. 'The
thing is: we're both radicals.'

Alex Jarratt, his former boss at the PIB had agreed to address a
seminar on energy conservation Ingham was organizing in Birmingham.
At the last minute, Ingham failed to appear. He had been summoned,
Jarratt later discovered, to see Mrs Thatcher in her study at Number 10.
Ingham thought this was his final interview. It was not. The decision had
already been made. She merely outlined his duties and welcomed him
aboard. He was in and out in twenty minutes.

So it was that on 9 September 1979 the Downing Street Press Office announced that its next head would be Bernard Ingham. He was to begin work on 1 November at an annual salary of £16,714. In Fleet Street and Westminster and, indeed, in Conservative Central Office, the news was greeted with astonishment. In the words of Peter Jenkins: 'We all said: "She's appointed a Labour man!"'

It has been presented as if it were a baffling question: why did an ideologue like Thatcher choose a man like Ingham? In fact, there is a simple answer: she didn't. The civil service chose him. After her experience with Henry James she was happy to leave the appointment of her Press Secretary to her officials. This was not because she was in thrall to Whitehall – on the contrary, few Prime Ministers have more frequently spurned its advice – but because she gave the matter a generally low priority. 'Prime Ministers,' in William Whitelaw's words, 'have different approaches to the press. Some, like Wilson, never stopped reading the newspapers and were obsessed with what was written about them. Attlee never read any papers at all. Margaret Thatcher is much closer to Attlee than she is to Wilson.' That was why, where other leaders might have agonized over such a sensitive appointment, she was prepared to approve it on two minutes' acquaintance. She had been told, by people who were paid to know, that Ingham was the best. She accepted that judgement. Over the next decade, it was to be her relative indifference to what appeared in the press, as much as his ambition, which made Ingham so powerful.

Mrs Thatcher's surprise appointment moved Ingham from the periphery of the Government to its very heart. He was only the fifteenth man in history to serve as Press Secretary to the Prime Minister.

The post – or, at least, its forerunner – had been created exactly fifty years earlier, in 1929, by Ramsay MacDonald, Britain's first Labour Prime Minister. MacDonald wanted professional advice on how to handle what was then, as now, an overwhelmingly Conservative press. To provide it, he brought in an official from the Foreign Office News Department named George Steward.

No picture of Steward decorates any government office. Little is known of him. Yet, serving MacDonald, Stanley Baldwin and Neville Chamberlain in turn, he did as much as anyone to shape the way politics is reported in Britain. He took the Parliamentary Lobby system – which had been created in 1884 and which permitted certain journalists to wander the corridors and lobbies of the Palace of Westminster, talking freely to MPs and ministers, on condition they did not directly attribute what were told – and imposed upon it a formal structure. Henceforth, he announced, he would brief the Lobby at daily meetings. Naturally, no journalist could afford to miss these events and they quickly assumed a pivotal importance. The system gradually became more rigid. In 1930, according to the Lobby's annual report for that year, 'definite times were arranged for conferences and rooms were provided at Number 10 for meetings'.[4] Three years later, Steward told the journalists that 'although he was formally appointed to act for the Prime Minister and the Treasury, he was also required to act for the Government as a whole in all matters of a general character' – a sweeping job description which, as the Lobby presciently recorded, carried 'certain dangers' as 'it may become too much a personal service of Prime Ministers'.[5]

It was indeed to prove a significant blow to the independence of the Cabinet, centralizing power in Downing Street by enabling Number 10 to impose its interpretation of events on the press. Chamberlain used Steward repeatedly to bypass the Cabinet and promote his policy of appeasing Hitler. In the autumn of 1937, for example, Lord Halifax, the Foreign Secretary, had received a private invitation to visit Germany. The Foreign Office was anxious to play down the importance of the trip. Chamberlain's purpose was precisely the opposite. Steward briefed the Lobby with the Number 10 version. The next day *The Times* and the *Daily Telegraph* appeared with almost identical stories about the visit's vital significance in the eyes of 'the Government' – an interpretation which horrified the anti-appeasers and caused delight in Berlin. By exploiting his press secretary's contacts with the Lobby in this way, Chamberlain was able to raise 'news management,' in the words of the historian, Richard Cockett, 'almost to the level of an exact science.'[6]

Thereafter, every Prime Minister had a motive for keeping a Press Office. When Labour returned to power in 1945, Clement Attlee soon appointed Francis Williams, a former editor of the pro-Labour paper, the *Daily Herald*, to be the first official 'Adviser on Public Relations to the Prime Minister'. (Attlee had a famously other-worldly approach to the press: when Williams arrived at Number 10 he found there was not even so much as a news agency tape machine installed, and he only persuaded a suspicious Attlee to have one put in on the grounds that it would enable the Prime Minister to keep up with the cricket scores; one afternoon, or so the story goes, Attlee, ignorant of Williams's morning press briefings, came rushing in demanding to know why his 'cricket machine' was carrying details of what had been discussed in Cabinet that morning.) In 1951, Winston Churchill, who had an old-fashioned view of these matters, did try to dispense with the Press Office. But he soon found that its abolition was having such an adverse effect on the Government's standing that he was forced to relent. In May 1952, Fife Clark, Press Officer at the Ministry of Health, was appointed 'Adviser on Public Relations to the Prime Minister and the Government'. As Churchill refused even to have Clark under the roof of Number 10, he was obliged to work out of an office in the old Treasury building next door.

Contacts between Government and the media now settled into a pattern which has persisted, virtually uninterrupted, until the present. Clark would see the Lobby twice daily, at 11 a.m. in his office and at 4 p.m. in the Commons. He was kept fully informed of Government policy throughout occasional monologues from Churchill and regular meetings with Rab Butler, the Chancellor of the Exchequer, and Viscount Swinton, the Commonwealth Secretary. Prime Ministerial press secretaries invariably rose and fell with their masters. In June 1955, after succeeding Churchill, Anthony Eden moved the Press Office back inside Number 10 and offered the job to William Clark, diplomatic correspondent of the *Observer*. This was hailed as an imaginative appointment – a phrase which generally preludes disaster, and so it proved. 'The PM is tired and fretful,' Clark noted in his diary at the end of his first six months.[7] When the Suez crisis erupted, there was a complete breakdown in confidence between the two men. Eden gave orders that his Press Secretary was to be kept away from all sensitive papers: 'you must stay down at your end of the building.'[8] Clark was driven to record in his diary what must be the most damning assessment any press officer has ever made of his Prime Minister.

It seems to me that the PM is mad, literally mad . . . My mood towards him is extraordinary. I never see him, worn, dignified and friendly, but a surge of deep and almost tearful compassion surges up in me: I leave him and my violent bitter contempt and hatred for a man who has destroyed my world and so much of my faith burns up again. Then I long to be free as a journalist to drive this government from power and keep the cowards and crooks out of power for all time. God, how power corrupts.[9]

Following this fiasco, Harold Macmillan, Eden's successor, was understandably reluctant to bring in another outsider, and appointed Harold Evans, Head of Information at the Colonial Office. Evans, by common consent, was the most successful of Ingham's predecessors. He stayed for almost seven years – a record until Ingham overtook it in 1986. 'He understood better than most what power at the top is all about,' wrote James Margach, Lobby correspondent of the *Sunday Times*, 'he never attempted hard or soft sells and always avoided becoming involved even remotely with party politics.'[10] He had what has always proved the most essential prerequisite for the job: an easy relationship with the Prime Minister. Most mornings, he would climb the stairs to Macmillan's private flat for a 'gossip'. Macmillan would usually 'still be in bed, wearing a brown cardigan over his pyjamas and surrounded by dispatch boxes, having begun work on his official papers several hours earlier'.[11] Evans was allowed access to most papers in the Prime Minister's Private Office. There was also a standing instruction to the Private Secretaries to 'let Evans know' everything that was going on. Such was the effectiveness of Evans's emollient manner that, in his words, he had 'no serious disagreement' with the Lobby in the whole of his seven years, despite the fraught atmosphere of Macmillan's final months in office. When he left in 1963 they gave him a valedictory silver dish inscribed 'to Harold Evans, for seven years the flawless voice of 10 Downing Street'.

In 1964, Harold Wilson, like Eden, brought in a journalist. Once again, but for different reasons, it proved a less than satisfactory arrangement. Trevor Lloyd-Hughes had been the Lobby correspondent of Wilson's constituency paper, the *Liverpool Daily Post*, for the past thirteen years and the new Prime Minister thought that appointing an insider would smooth relations with the Parliamentary press corps. His plan backfired. Far from flattering the Lobby, this elevation of a provincial newspaperman offended the *amour-propre* of many in the national press. Suddenly they were obliged to go cap in hand for briefings to a man who only yesterday had been a junior member of the club. Aware of this, Lloyd-Hughes became anxious and uncommunicative. He took his new status as a civil servant so literally, according to Marcia Williams, Wilson's Political Secretary, that he shrank 'from any connection with any part of the work of the Government which could in any way be regarded as political'. He became 'more of a civil servant than the civil servants, and so impartial as to make his news statements sometimes sound devoid of content'.[12] Lloyd-Hughes, in his own words, resisted 'fiercely' any suggestion that he should play a political role: 'It is quite wrong for a civil servant . . . to peddle a party line.'[13]

Another reason for his relative ineffectiveness was that Wilson was obsessed by the press and wanted to deal with reporters personally. Against Lloyd-Hughes's advice, he instituted what became known as the 'White Commonwealth', regularly summoning selected political journalists to drinks in Downing Street. Editors and owners were invited down to Chequers for the night, often to hear their political correspondents trashed by the First Lord of the Treasury: David Wood of *The Times* should be given 'a golden handshake', Nora Beloff of the *Observer* was incapable of taking down 'a monumental scoop at dictation speed', and so on. Eventually, so preoccupied was Wilson, a second, 'political' press secretary was appointed, in the person of Gerald Kaufman. Finally, as if this were not enough, at the beginning of 1969, Wilson brought in yet another Lobby correspondent, Joe Haines, to serve first as Lloyd-Hughes's deputy and then, six months later, as his replacement when Lloyd-Hughes was made 'Chief Information Adviser to the Government' (a grand title which, according to Haines, 'didn't mean anything'). Haines never pretended to be neutral. He was always a Labour partisan.

Edward Heath had noted carefully how his predecessor had behaved and was determined not to do likewise. Having thought hard in Opposition, when he came to power in 1970, he appointed Donald Maitland, a career diplomat. 'You know what this job's about,' was Heath's only instruction. 'Get the facts out.'

Maitland was the first Number 10 Press Secretary since George Steward never to have had any journalistic experience. He had met and 'got on well' with Heath in the mid-1960s, when he was Head of the Foreign Office News Department. He was forty-seven: a short, tough-minded Scot, famous in Whitehall for having stood up to George Brown when he was Brown's Private Secretary ('You do not imagine, Foreign Secretary,' he is said to have remarked during one row, 'that a person of my stature has got where he is today by kow-towing to bullies?')[14] For him, the Downing Street Press Office was not the summit of his career; it was not an end in itself; it was just another job. 'I regarded this as a posting, like any other Foreign Office posting.' He thus looked on the Parliamentary press with a cooler and more impartial eye than most of his predecessors. There were by the 1970s, more than one hundred reporters in the Lobby and, to Maitland, 'the idea that this was a conversation which was not taking place seemed to me to have a slightly ludicrous character.'

Maitland soon became tired of seeing simple statements of fact refracted through the distorting lens of the Lobby. He would read (to quote his phraseology) that 'the Government were at pains to do so-and-so' or 'Government plans to do so-and-so suffered a setback,' when the reality was that they had taken no pains, suffered no setback. The reader was often unable to assess the relative weight of such judgements because the stories in which they appeared were seamless robes, with no indication as to where their material had been gathered. 'Everyone is entitled to comment and criticize,' Maitland insisted. 'They should do so. But I don't think they should do so in presenting the actual statement of policy.'

Criticism of the Lobby system was familiar enough, even in the 1960s ('all this grey anonymity has really become a farcical charade,' wrote Anthony Howard, himself a former Lobby correspondent, in 1965).[15] But this was different. A Prime Minister's Press Secretary was in a position to do something about it. Accordingly, in 1972, Maitland suggested to the Lobby that 'as far as possible we should have briefings on the record but by mutual agreement we could go on to a non-attributable basis'. The journalists were at once suspicious, seeing in this a plot to make the Government's image more attractive: good news would be attributable; bad news would be off the record. They rejected Maitland's proposal. Maitland promptly came up with a new idea:

> Instead of coming to the Lobby with a piece of paper from which I read, and then have that 'processed' through the Lobby system, we would issue a press release. They would be given it on arrival so they could read it. Then they could ask me questions on that, on a Lobby basis.

This was tried a couple of times. It seemed to work. The sky did not fall in. As Maitland had shrewdly judged, once the news agencies and the broadcasters began carrying the Government's actual words, Fleet Street news editors wanted 'to have something which was in quotes' to put in their pages as well. This innovation was still being tried in April 1973, when Maitland's posting came to an end.

Joe Haines returned in March 1974 even more determined to forge the Downing Street Press Office into a political instrument. Out of the staff of eleven which he inherited, he promptly sacked five. 'For Joe,' wrote Marcia Williams, 'the building up of an efficient and loyal Press Office meant, quite rightly, having a staff who were loyal to him personally, and who thought and felt the way he did. In sum, he wanted a Labour-orientated organization.'[16]

Haines was one of the more colourful figures to occupy the Press Secretary's chair. A Labour councillor, born in Rotherhithe in 1928, brought up in what he called 'one of the worst slums in south-east London', he had the look of a Mafia hit-man and a wit to match. (Shown a film of the Ronan Point tower block disaster, his response was to murmer the slogan from President Nixon's 1968 campaign: 'The risks are too great for you to stay home.') He operated in Number 10 as if under siege – which, in a sense, he was. He surveyed the British press and concluded there were only two news organizations – the *Guardian* and the Mirror Group, – which he could trust. 'I have long remembered,' he wrote a decade later, 'the occasion when three members of the Lobby, separately, went to the Conservative Chief Whip and told him what had been said at the four o'clock meeting.'[17]

After five bruising years as Wilson's press adviser, in power and out of it, Haines felt he owed the Lobby no favours and soon began tightening the screw. He stopped journalists travelling on the Prime Minister's plane during visits overseas. He abandoned the practice of answering questions across the whole range of Government activities, believing it was 'crazy' that he should have to speak for every Whitehall department. ('This greatly upset the Lobby,' he recalled. 'They were really put out that they actually had to make their own enquiries.') He adopted Donald Maitland's technique of issuing a regular press statement: it 'took up an enormous amount of bloody time [but] at least nobody could misreport it.' Finally, on 19 June 1975, he took the biggest step of all, writing to the chairman of the Lobby, John Egan, announcing his decision to end Downing Street's off-the-record briefings entirely:

From now on, it will be my general rule that if a statement needs to be made on behalf of the Prime Minister, that statement will be made on the record.

This will not lead to any loss of information to the general public. Indeed, they will then know its source. And it will eliminate the kind of extreme absurdity where, under the rules governing the present meetings, even the name of the annual Poppy Day seller who calls on the Prime Minister is given unattributably.

By the time Wilson's final premiership came to an end in March 1976, Haines had ceased to function as a Press Secretary in any traditional sense. He had stopped the Lobby briefings. He had palmed off the administrative work on to his deputy. He rarely talked to groups of journalists, except the Americans based in London ('they were a higher class of correspondent, frankly, and I could trust them and talk freely to them on political matters'). Instead, Haines became a sort of general Prime Ministerial factotum. He wrote almost all Wilson's speeches. He helped draw up the frequent (and extensive) Honours Lists. He acted as an informal adviser to the Number 10 Policy Unit. On one occasion, he even appointed a minister, suggesting her name to the Prime Minister and then interviewing her ('Harold didn't know who to give the job to, so he left it up to me').

Stormy though his relations with the Lobby were, Haines did not exceed his authority. He 'handled them in exactly the way Harold Wilson wanted,' wrote Bernard Donoughue, 'which was quite roughly at times'. Wilson's successor, James Callaghan, could be equally testy with the Fourth Estate but, perhaps wisely, chose as his Press Secretary a man quite different to Haines.

Tom McCaffrey, a professional civil servant, had been Callaghan's Chief Information Officer at the Home Office from 1967 to 1970. He was known to be a Labour sympathizer but, like Maitland, he was nobody's poodle. A few weeks after the new Home Secretary's arrival, McCaffrey had told him bluntly that he was not living up to expectations. Callaghan rather admired him for his candour, or so he claimed. At any rate, when Labour returned to power and he was made Foreign Secretary he readily fell in with Haines's suggestion that the 'politically sensitive' McCaffrey should join him at the FO. Two years later nobody was surprised when Callaghan took McCaffrey with him to Number 10. On their first night in the building, McCaffrey rang the secretary of the

Lobby and told him briefings would resume at 11.00 a.m. the next day – a deliberately flamboyant demonstration that the war was over; it was business as usual.

Callaghan trusted McCaffrey. 'It was thanks to him,' he conceded, 'that I enjoyed a less barbed relationship with the press than I might have done, for his patience and modesty were greater than mine.'[18] McCaffrey, in turn, trusted the Lobby system, of which he was a staunch defender. 'I believe that as a result of Lobby meetings over the years the public know more today than ever before of what the Government is doing in their name,' he said in 1986.[19] Nevertheless, he soon had direct and painful experience of what a combustible device it had become.

In the spring of 1977, Callaghan was prevailed upon to appoint his son-in-law, Peter Jay, as the British Ambassador in Washington. On the morning of 12 May McCaffrey had the delicate task of announcing this to the Lobby. Afterwards, in the corridor, he fell into conversation with two old friends, Robert Carvel of the London *Evening Standard* and John Dickinson of the London *Evening News*. They asked him what was wrong with the present incumbent, Sir Peter Ramsbotham. McCaffrey, caught off guard, replied to the effect that he was stuffy and a bit of a snob. This accurately reflected Callaghan's view, and that of the Foreign Secretary, David Owen, who had talked to McCaffrey about it a few weeks previously. A few hours later, the two London evening papers, the *News* and the *Standard* – one quoting 'the Callaghan camp', the other 'Government circles' – carried similar stories with an identical headline: 'SNOB ENVOY HAD TO GO'. Several Lobby correspondents on Conservative newspapers told Tory MPs that McCaffrey was source.

The controversy which followed was immensely embarrassing, not only to McCaffrey (who offered to resign) but to the entire Lobby. There had, after all, been a time when such confidences were as sacred as secrets whispered in the confessional box. The swiftness with which McCaffrey's role was exposed was a warning that times were changing. The days of the old Lobby stalwart – of Jimmy Margach of the *Sunday Times*, who knew every Prime Minister from Ramsay MacDonald to James Callaghan; of Harry Boyne of the *Daily Telegraph*, who once appeared in the Commons in a morning coat; of Francis Boyd of the *Guardian*, who retired with a knighthood – the days when such men might spend thirty years with the same paper in the same place were passing, and with them went part of that deference to tradition, the shared assumptions, which had underpinned the Lobby system.

This, then, was the situation as Ingham inherited it at the end of 1979. As with so much else in Britain, the job he was about to undertake had never been properly defined. It had grown up, like the fabled unwritten constitution, according to custom and usage: mysterious, crenellated, sham-antique. By the late 1970s, most countries had a straightforward government spokesman – a political appointee who would brief the press, appear on radio and television, and promote the official line. But in Britain, the spokesman was not only anonymous: he acted in accordance with quasi-masonic rules drawn up in Queen Victoria's time. A system which had been designed to preserve the quintessentially English atmosphere of a gentleman's club had been imported into the television age. Not surprisingly, it had begun to look rather shaky.

On the other hand, the very vagueness and secretiveness of the office – the fact that it had always meant different things to different administrations, that its anonymous holder spoke for both government and premier – rendered it a source of potentially enormous influence. The powers were there, waiting to be picked up. Given a sufficiently ruthless, determined Prime Minister and an appropriately ambitious, domineering Press Secretary, it was a superb instrument for imposing the views of Number 10 on the media, for pre-empting debate, and for undermining dissident ministers within the Government. Between them, Margaret Thatcher and Bernard Ingham were to use the Downing Street Press Office in a way which her predecessors – even men as astute and manipulative as Neville Chamberlain and Harold Wilson – would never have dared attempt.

1 Bernard Ingham, Chief Press Secretary to the Prime Minister, photographed
in his Downing Street office in the summer of 1990.

2 The Yorkshire weaving town of Hebden Bridge, Ingham's birthplace, as it looked in the 1930s when he was growing up.

3 Garnet Ingham, Bernard's father, the first socialist councillor in the history of Hebden Bridge, photographed in 1957 when he became council leader.

4 Bernard Ingham (second row, centre) at Hebden Bridge Grammar School in 1948, aged fifteen.

5 & 6 Ingham was a keen sportsman: (above) as a member of the Hebden Bridge Grammar School football team (front row, extreme right); and (below) of the Salem Methodists cricket team, winners of the Halifax Amateur League (back row, fourth from left).

7 Ingham's first office: the *Hebden Bridge Times*, housed in a disused Baptist Chapel, where he started work as a junior reporter, aged sixteen.

8 Ingham (fourth from right, top of steps) with members of a local history society, preparing to fly over Hebden Bridge in August 1951.

BERNARD INGHAM for MOORTOWN

Dear Elector,

I have accepted an invitation to stand as Labour candidate for Moortown for three main reasons. I believe that:

1. As a journalist I have served an adequate apprenticeship for membership of a local authority;

2. I have something to offer Moortown, Leeds and Yorkshire through my broad understanding of their problems;

3. The Labour Party should be supported in its effort to bring about radical—and much-needed—changes in our society.

On May 13th YOU have an opportunity to lend your support by voting for ME. And if every Labour voter in Moortown takes the trouble to vote, Labour CAN take this so-called Tory citadel by storm.

Give me five minutes of your time on May 13th and I will give you many hours' service in return. My object is to serve you by securing imaginative, efficient and socially just local government.

Thank you.

Yours faithfully,

BERNARD INGHAM.

19 Green Hill Mount
Leeds 13
Tel. Pudsey 76900

BERNARD INGHAM. Married, one son. Journalist covering general Trade Union/political and Yorkshire affairs for The Guardian. Reported local government, ranging from Parish to County Councils, for 17 years. Studied recent moves towards regional government in Yorkshire and North-East England. Member, Leeds West Constituency Labour Party, Leeds Fabian Society.

POLLING DAY
THURSDAY
MAY 13th
1965
8 a.m. to 9 p.m.

Let's get things done VOTE INGHAM

Printed and published by Leeds Labour Publishing Society Ltd. (T.U.), 9 Queen Square, Leeds 2.

9 Ingham was an outspoken supporter of the Labour Party. In 1965, he stood as Labour candidate for the Leeds City Council.

10 Ingham's wife, Nancy, was a policewoman in Halifax in the 1950s. She was photographed at their home in Purley, in 1987, after receiving an IRA letter bomb addressed to her husband.

11 Ingham in February 1986 at the height of the Westland crisis, delivering a lecture on media standards at the Stationers' Hall. He was suspected of leaking a confidential letter, and spent the rest of the evening dodging reporters' questions.

12 Outside Number 10, Downing Street. Since 1979 Ingham had been consistently at Margaret Thatcher's elbow. 'Bernard's marvellous,' she once declared. 'Isn't he marvellous? He's great. He's the *greatest*.'

3 Whenever Mrs Thatcher met a journalist, Ingham insisted on being present.
'It was evident that he was very much part of the inner Cabinet,' wrote the editor
of the *Sunday Express*, Sir John Junor, after one such meeting. 'It was obvious
from the way the Prime Minister listened to what he had to say that she
respected his judgement.'

14 Bernard Ingham and friend.

SIX

The Yorkshire Rasputin

'One would begin to imagine that we have in Mr Bernard
Ingham some sort of rough-spoken Yorkshire Rasputin who is
manipulating Government and corroding the standards of
public morality.'

Rt Hon. John Biffen MP, speech in the House of Commons,
February 1983[1]

For a man who relished being at the centre of events as much as Ingham,
entering the office of Chief Press Secretary at Number 10 Downing
Street was like wandering into Aladdin's Cave. He had only been in place
three weeks when the Prime Minister overruled the advice of the Cabinet Secretary, Sir Robert Armstrong, and decided to make public the
treachery of the so-called 'fourth man', Sir Anthony Blunt. Her Chief
Press Secretary, naturally, was closely involved and he later described it
as 'the best story I have ever worked on'.[2] On the day Mrs Thatcher
made her announcement, interest rates were raised to 17 per cent,
inevitably inviting charges of news management. Ingham was alert to the
danger. 'If only you knew,' he recalled, 'how hard I worked to stop those
two things happening, because I thought it was Wilsonian to a fault . . .'[3]

Naming traitors, raising bank rates . . . This was high politics. There
were no more minor officials fussing around, stopping him from seeing
Government documents. Now, Armstrong had instructions to send
Ingham some Cabinet papers direct. If he wanted to read the others, he
had merely to climb the stairs to the Prime Minister's Private Office and
browse through them. After Cabinet meetings on Thursday mornings,
either Armstrong or the Prime Minister herself would brief him on what
had been said. The lad from the *Hebden Bridge Times* who had left school
at sixteen – the man whom the *Guardian* had turned down because he
wasn't clever enough – had finally made it. He could hardly believe his
luck.

From his earliest years, Ingham had shown a capacity to identify completely with whatever task he was given. He was always ferociously loyal, whether it was to the Labour Party or to the *Guardian* or to Barbara Castle. Now he transferred his formidable powers of devotion to Margaret Thatcher. Partly this was due to sheer professionalism; partly to a streak of old-fashioned chivalry – a protectiveness towards a woman he saw as courageous and embattled. But mostly it was down to a passionate belief that what she was doing – knocking Establishment heads together, making the unions face up to the consequences of their actions, putting the emphasis back on traditional values – was long overdue. After twelve years in Whitehall during which, as a press officer, he had often been made to feel like a second-class citizen, he shared her instinctive hostility towards Oxbridge mandarins – he once spoke heatedly of 'the administrator's natural elitist arrogance and the intensely hierarchical and generally secretive nature of our Civil Service'.[4] When Mrs Thatcher made her famous remark, after a particularly rough press conference – that neither of them was a 'smooth' person – she was putting her finger on what made theirs such a strong working relationship. They were two of a kind.

The Lobby journalists soon picked up the Whitehall gossip and concluded that Ingham, unlike his predecessor, was on the inside track. Indeed, the Prime Minister and her Press Secretary were held to be so close that he was credited with almost supernatural powers. What Bernard said today, ran the Lobby cliché, Thatcher would be thinking tomorrow. 'Ingham has learned to read her mind,' claimed Andrew Thomson, her former constituency agent. 'He does not need detailed briefings from her or other Downing Street officials. Hand him a pile of Government papers outlining the problem and setting down a series of choices of action and Ingham will know almost as quickly as the Prime Minister what decision to take.'[5]

When, soon after Ingham arrived, the Government began to run into severe political turbulence, he seemed almost to embody the Thatcherite spirit: embattled, aggressive, often brutally frank. The official guidelines for Government Information Officers, issued in 1980, state that an official 'should not get himself involved in the political battle by fierce advocacy of a controversial policy in his discussion with journalists.' But that was not Ingham's style. 'I got a bit worried at one stage that he seemed to have fallen out with virtually every political correspondent,' recalled one Whitehall Head of Information. 'The first twelve, eighteen months – the Lobby meetings were almost a shouting match.'

For a Government whose message was 'there is no alternative', there could have been no better-equipped delivery boy, either physically or temperamentally, than Ingham. At last he could give free rein to his natural obduracy and penchant for hectoring. 'I have been able to operate with a Prime Minister constant of purpose and resolve,' he subsequently boasted. 'That is why I spent the first two years playing spot the U-turn with the media – and why they never found one.'[6]

In this endeavour, Ingham's previous, well-known attachment to socialism and corporatism was not a handicap but an asset: he personally had travelled down that road in the 1960s, he frequently declared, and had found it led only to a dead end; it was time to try a different route. Like so many Thatcherites, he had the zeal of the recently-converted. To Jim Prior, the 'wet' Employment Secretary in the first Thatcher Cabinet, 'he was another of the left like Paul Johnson who, having decided to change sides, has moved right across the political spectrum,' the only difference being that Ingham 'did not qualify as an intellectual: he was more in the mould of a political bruiser.'[7] When, during an industrial dispute, one Lobby correspondent suggested Government mediation, Ingham was contemptuous: 'That's beer and sandwiches at Number 10. We tried that and look where it got us.' Another reporter with whom he had regular rows on industrial issues was John Cole – part of the *Guardian* team who had refused to promote him in 1967, and who had now resurfaced in his professional life as the BBC's political editor.

It was Ingham's passionate conviction that the trade unions had to be tamed and, like Thatcher, he chafed at Prior's cautious approach to union reform. During the steelworkers' strike of 1979–80, the Employment Secretary came under orchestrated attack from the Tory Right over the slow progress of his department's legislation. He resolved to defend himself and accepted an invitation from Radio Four's *The World at One*. 'Then my private office received a call from Number 10,' recalled Prior. 'Bernard Ingham was saying that I should not go on. That convinced me that I should appear.'[8]

The following year, in October 1981, Ingham briefed the Lobby on a threatened strike at British Leyland. 'It took the steelworkers thirteen weeks,' he said grimly, 'and the civil servants twenty-one weeks to realise that we meant business.'[9] Coming from a once-ardent trade unionist, industrial correspondent and Labour candidate, this tough-talking carried more conviction than it would had it come from some plummy ex-diplomat. In Peter Jenkins's words: 'He used to speak as if he was still of the Labour movement but could justify her policies.' In this sense, he represented a valuable propaganda weapon in his own right: that a man with his background could argue the Government's case so robustly was itself an indication that There Was No Alternative.

Indeed, there is an argument that the Thatcher persona of those crucial early years was, at least in part, an Ingham creation. Prior describes how important a part the right-wing press played in setting the tone of Cabinet debates. 'Battling Maggie Under Attack from Wets' would be the morning headline in the *Sun* or the *Daily Mail*. The issue would be thus reduced to a simple question: were you pro– or anti-Maggie? In October 1980, at the time when the Cabinet was agonising over cuts in public spending, the *Sun* proclaimed that 'Premier Margaret Thatcher routed the "wets" in her Cabinet yesterday in a major show-down over public spending. She waded into attack . . .' But, recalled Prior, 'this was not what had happened . . . When the *Sun* finally reported a month later that the Prime Minister and her Treasury team had not secured the cuts they sought, its headline typified the view that Margaret was somehow separate from her own Government: "Maggie at Bay: Tories baffled as the battle for £2 billion extra cuts is lost." '[10]

Ingham created a (literally) vicious circle: he would brief the Lobby emphasizing her toughness and determination; the following morning, he would relay the resulting headlines to the Prime Minister in his press summary; this would fire her up to be still more tough and determined, giving him yet more ammunition for his next Lobby briefing. This was certainly the opinion of Andrew Thomson, who observed her at first hand for six years:

> In private she was at times cautious, hesitant and uncertain. So instead of waiting to see whether other ministers would be able to capitalize on her weaknesses, Ingham took the essence of Margaret Thatcher out to the media. He scoffed at the idea of U-turns. He disparaged faint-hearts in the Cabinet. A crisis over proposals to cut planned rises in Government spending? Ministers would just have to find the cuts or she would sort them out. Listening to Ingham gave the media the certain impression that there was a ferocious tigress on the loose in Whitehall.[11]

'It was Bernard Ingham who made Margaret Thatcher what she is,' claimed one of Ingham's colleagues. 'He went out and sold the Prime Minister to the Lobby correspondents. But the Prime Minister he sold was not quite the woman she was, at least not at the time he was selling her.'[12]

One should be careful not to overstate the case. After all, Margaret Thatcher was not invented by her Press Secretary: there *was* a 'tigress on the loose in Whitehall', one which had prowled around for several months before he arrived in Downing Street. But it is equally true that Ingham – growling and red-faced, with his frequent snorts of 'Dammit!' and his eyeballs swivelling upwards in exasperation – took care to give no hint of the doubts which sometimes crowded in upon her in the precarious days of 1980–82. He was more furious, more impatient, more intolerant of the 'wets' even than she.

Lobby journalists are quick to spot such hints. Twenty years earlier, Harold Evans, Macmillan's Press Secretary, used to adopt for briefings what Macmillan called his 'Lobby face'. According to Evans: 'an outwardly relaxed and unhurried manner is a necessary part of the equipment of a spokesman, whose demeanour, no less than his words (sometimes more than his words) comes under close scrutiny. A poker face is part of the business . . .'[13] Evans's phlegmatic style helped reinforce Macmillan's reputation for unflappability. Ingham's approach was exactly the opposite. He did not merely speak for Thatcher, he out-Thatchered Thatcher – to an extent she may not fully have realized. On the rare occasions, usually before Prime Minister's Questions, when she studied the press at first hand, she often declared herself baffled at her own reflection. 'Why do they always make me out to be so angry?' she would inquire, with an air of apparently genuine innocence. In time, this, too, became part of Ingham's repertoire of complaints against the media. 'Mrs Thatcher it seems can never be happy, sad, sorry, ecstatic or bored,' he told the International Press Institute in 1985. 'The only emotion permitted is fury.' If that was the case, he was himself in large measure to blame.

Only very rarely, even in private, did he so much as hint at any doubts about Government policies. In 1980, unemployment rose by 830,000, the largest annual increase since 1930. Confronted by images of the Depression, with three million out of work, it would have been strange if Ingham had not felt his father's ghost at his back. 'I suppose you think I've sold out?' was his plaintive remark to one former *Guardian* colleague during this period. On another occasion, he and the Prime Minister went to lunch at the *Daily Mirror*. An argument broke out over unemployment. Ingham, uncharacteristically, sat silently, looking down at his plate. 'He never rebuked me for what I wrote,' recalled Geoffrey Goodman, who had remained a Labour supporter and who was present on that occasion. 'I would tease him about Government policy and he'd just shrug. It was a sign that it was the sort of thing he didn't want to get involved talking about.'

But such reticence, even despondency, was rare. 'The word that he most often uses,' according to his former colleague in the Government Information Service, Neville Taylor, 'is "screw": "Got to screw the Foreign Office" . . . "Can't understand the Lobby – just got to screw the buggers" . . .'

On 2 February 1982, when Margaret Thatcher's unpopularity was at its peak and the 'wets' were in open rebellion, Ingham screwed, stuffed and mounted his first Cabinet Minister.

What Ingham was to do to Francis Pym was not without precedent. On at least two occasions, Harold Wilson, like Margaret Thatcher, used the Downing Street Press Office to undermine ministerial colleagues. On 3 April 1969, he instructed Joe Haines to tell the Lobby that James Callaghan had been reprimanded at that morning's Cabinet for openly opposing *In Place of Strife*. In fact, as Barbara Castle noted in her diary, Wilson was 'unnerved' by Callaghan's coolness and, despite his tough promises, 'the thunderbolt never materialized'.[14] Nevertheless, the papers the next morning were full of Callaghan's supposed 'dressing down' at Wilson's hands. It was a fiction. Haines, taking individual correspondents to one side ('I wouldn't have dared do it to the Lobby generally') and whispering in their ears, had done his bit; but the Prime Minister had failed to do his. Six years later, in 1975, according to Haines:

> Harold told me that Hugh Jenkins [Minister for the Arts] was stupid and he was going to get rid of him. And as the *Evening Standard* had been running a big thing about the arts, he told me to have a word with Bob Carvel. So I went to Bob and told him that Hugh Jenkins was going to be sacked. I told him without equivocation because there was no equivocation. Except that after Harold saw the story and one or two

people went to him and said 'You're not going to do this to old Hugh, are you?' he chickened out. And so Bob had a perfectly genuine splash and he kept coming to me and saying 'When's it going to come true?' And Harold kept saying 'Tell him to wait, tell him to wait.' And in the end it never happened.

Ingham had disapproved of Joe Haines precisely because of antics of this sort. Yet once he was in Haines's old job, he was soon up to similar tricks. On 6 January 1981, the Leader of the House of Commons, Norman St John Stevas, had the dubious distinction of becoming the first Cabinet Minister to be sacked by Mrs Thatcher. Naturally, Ingham was asked by the Lobby why the Prime Minister had dismissed him. He had gone chiefly because he was the most vulnerable of the 'wets', and sacking him would serve as a useful warning to the others.

But that was not what Ingham said. In the words of the *Daily Telegraph* the following day: 'sources close to her [a coded phrase for Ingham] were suggesting that he had borne the brunt of concern about open and at times inaccurate portrayals in the press of what had been going on in Government.' The *Daily Express* claimed Stevas had been sacked because he 'blabbed out of school'. A leader in *The Times* declared: 'One of the reasons for dismissing Mr St John Stevas was to provide a warning to other members of the Cabinet that leaks would not be tolerated.'

This 'guidance' from Ingham, coupled with remarks made by the Prime Minister in a television interview that afternoon ('Leaks there have been . . . I hope it will happen less and less') were too much for Stevas to bear. The next morning, having read the papers at breakfast, he was so upset he sat down at his typewriter in his home in Montpelier Square and tapped out a letter, full of errors and mis-spellings, saying he was 'greatly distressed and indeed angered' and demanding an apology. Mrs Thatcher had little option but to give him one, but it came dripping with disingenuousness: 'I believe it unreasonable that my remarks should have been interpreted in the way they apparently have been.'

The beauty of using the Lobby in this fashion was precisely this: that the stories which resulted were deniable; indeed, that they could be blamed on the 'unreasonable' behaviour of the reporters themselves.

The Stevas briefing, however, was only a curtain-raiser. He had, after all, been sacked: the briefing was merely salt in the wound. It was the treatment meted out the following year to Francis Pym which provided

the first textbook example of the way Thatcher and Ingham were prepared to use the Lobby to undermine a senior colleague still in the
Cabinet. Pym, formerly the Defence Secretary, who had replaced the
hapless Stevas as Leader of the House, had always been a particular
bête noire of the Prime Minister. She openly regarded him as a gloomy,
disloyal, vacillating snob. On 1 February 1982, he made a speech to the
Allied Brewery Trades Association which was unusual for its pess-
imism, even by his standards. 'This Government is completely committed to a long-term economic recovery,' he announced. 'But this cannot
lead to an early return to full or nearly full employment, or an early
improvement in living standards generally.' He spoke of a 'formidable
challenge', of 'a very painful period of transition', of living standards
which 'generally can only fall': 'We have to find ways of coping with
higher levels of unemployment than we have been used to ... Let
nobody think it is going to be easy.'

Pym was saying nothing in public which the Treasury had not already
warned ministers about in private. His words were literally correct.
Newspapers as loyal to Mrs Thatcher as the *Daily Express* and the *Daily
Telegraph* praised him for his courage and honesty. The Prime Minister,
however, was incensed. Only four days previously, the Chancellor of
the Exchequer had made a speech emphasizing the signs of recovery in
the British economy. Now Pym had destroyed the Government's
attempts to accentuate the positive, and done it, moreover, without even
consulting Number 10. She could not disown him without sacking him,
and he was too powerful for that. She therefore did the next best thing.

On the day following his speech, at 3.15 p.m., she rose in the Commons to take Prime Minister's Questions. The Opposition's blood was
up and Michael Foot, the Labour leader, was quickly on his feet
demanding to know whether she agreed with Pym. Thatcher's reply
floored him: 'My Right Honourable Friend made an excellent speech
last night, so good that I wish to quote from it.' This she proceeded to
do, at length. In that case, inquired Foot, why had the *Daily Telegraph*
given it such prominence (under the headline 'Bleak view of the economy by Pym')? 'Because,' said Thatcher, sweetly, 'it was a very good
speech.'[15]

Down on the floor of the House, all might be smiles; but up in the
Lobby room, the knife was flashing. Half an hour after the Prime
Minister had sat down, Ingham was telling the journalists, non-

attributably, a very different tale. According to the *Daily Telegraph* the following day:

> The Prime Minister was dismayed by some of Mr Pym's phraseology . . . She was also angry that Conservative Central Office, which distributed the speech to correspondents early on Monday evening, did not give her office a copy at the same time . . . Discount was being made for a general tendency towards pessimism by Mr Pym. There was an off-stage comparison of him with the wartime radio character whose lugubrious catch phrase was 'It's being so cheerful as keeps me going'.

The *Guardian* had almost exactly the same words:

> In spite of Mrs Thatcher's defence of Mr Pym, it was clear that the Leader of the House was by no means popular among his Treasury colleagues. He was compared to 'Mrs Mopp' whose wartime catch phrase on the *Itma* radio programme had been 'It's being so cheerful as keeps me going'.

(In fact, the phrase belonged to a character called Mona Lott; Mrs Mopp's slogan – which, under the circumstances, would have been rather an appropriate one for Ingham – was 'Shall I do you now, sir?')

The story was everywhere, and everywhere it took precedence over the Prime Minister's soft words. 'Maggie sends grim Pym to the doghouse,' chortled the *Sun*. 'If Mr Misery Pym does not believe the good news,' ran the paper's editorial, 'then he is not merely in the wrong job. He is in the wrong Government.' The *Daily Mirror* reported that 'the word being put around by Mrs Thatcher's friends yesterday was that Mr Pym was known to be a pessimist.' 'Maggie cross at Pym's gloomy view,' was the headline in the *Daily Express*. In the *Daily Mail*, which quoted 'senior Whitehall sources', it was 'Fury over Pym's bleak warning of gloom'. According to *The Times*: 'It was admitted openly in Government quarters that Mr Pym's speech on Monday night . . . had upset Mrs Margaret Thatcher . . . Mr Pym's main sin, in the eyes of Mrs Thatcher, was that he approved the release by Conservative Central Office of extracts of his speech which made little of the good news and much of the bad.'

The Lobby had witnessed some skulduggery over the years, but never anything quite like this. In 1969, Joe Haines had reported what he believed to be a fact – that Wilson had given Callaghan a dressing-down

– and he had done it to correspondents individually. Similarly, in 1977, Tom McCaffrey had made his disparaging remarks about Sir Peter Ramsbotham off the cuff to two old friends. But never before had the Government's official spokesman, a civil servant, deliberately disparaged a minister for speaking what he saw as the truth – and done it, moreover, to the entire Lobby only moments after the Prime Minister had given an entirely different version of events. To Anthony Bevins, political correspondent of *The Times*, it was 'despicable for a servant of the Crown to be backstabbing colleagues of the Prime Minister. He wasn't selling the policies of the Government. He was acting as her personal advocate. I had never seen that before.' John Nott, who had replaced Pym as Defence Secretary the previous year, later called Ingham's use of the Lobby 'sickening ... deplorable and malicious'.[16]

Was Ingham's action really any different to, or worse than, what had happened before – than, for example, Wilson's treatment of Hugh Jenkins in 1975? With hindsight, it is clear that it was significantly different and, in some respects, worse. Different because the disparaging of Pym was not some private tip-off, which would have been reprehensible, no doubt, but a recognized stroke in the dark art of politics; it was not inadvertent; it was a premeditated abuse of the main channel of communication between Government and media. And it was worse, because at least Haines had openly admitted that his role was a partisan one; Ingham had always insisted he was the neutral spokesman of the Government as a whole.

In the end, Ingham's style, like the style of his predecessors, was conditioned by the nature of his boss. What was also striking about this episode was that Pym never heard a word of complaint from the Prime Minister herself. He had to read it in the press. For a leader with a reputation for straight-speaking, it was an oddly devious means of issuing a reprimand. Donald Maitland was shocked by this sort of behaviour because, under Edward Heath, whatever that difficult and autocratic man's other faults, the situation 'could not have arisen':

> There was never any occasion when I commented on the performance of any member of the Cabinet, for the very good reason that the Prime Minister never discussed his Cabinet colleagues with me ... My relationship with Ted Heath was obviously a very close one, but on no occasion did that arise in any conversation he had with me, and I didn't expect it to.

Margaret Thatcher, on the other hand, was notorious for keeping up a private running commentary on the failings of her ministers and their policies, as if the Government was in some way nothing to do with her. Stevas has described how she once stood on a chair during a party in Downing Street and announced herself to be 'the rebel head of an establishment government'.[17] Diatribes against her 'spineless' male colleagues occurred all the time when Ingham was with her: at the 9.30 a.m. meetings in her study, during her preparations for Prime Minister's Questions, on her long plane journeys abroad, in the evenings, after a reception, when she would kick off her shoes and hand round the whiskies to her Downing Street advisers. Knowing her as he did put Ingham in a quandary. When he was asked about her opinions at a Lobby meeting, how much should he disclose? A civil service smoothie would have answered 'Nothing'. But then, a civil service smoothie would not have been privy to such confidences in the first place, let alone have lasted eleven years as Margaret Thatcher's Chief Press Secretary.

Nevertheless, certain of her advisers were worried that, to adapt Attlee's phrase about Aneurin Bevan, where she needed a sedative she got an irritant. 'There's always a danger that Bernard exaggerates her reactions,' said one. 'She's going to react in the privacy of her own room with her close associates one way – like an actor in a hotel who's just read some bad reviews. But what can happen is that he sees her reaction in the morning, shares it, and then recycles it to the press. They wind one another up in private.'

How much of the 'fury', the intransigence, the distancing of the Prime Minister from colleagues, was Thatcher and how much Ingham? That was the question which increasingly preoccupied nervous ministers over the next decade. And, of course, there was never any way of telling. That was the point.

The invasion of the Falkland Islands, exactly three months after the Pym briefing, provided another graphic illustration of how much Ingham's views had changed. In his 'Albion' years, when he was opposed to nuclear weapons, he had been violently pacifist – an aggressive dove. Labour's failure to slash the defence budget in the mid-1960s he called 'an abject failure'. 'Whom are we defending ourselves against?' he asked in 1967. 'It hardly seems likely these days that Russia wants to chuck her weight about.' On this issue, he was an extremist, to the extent of advocating that half the defence budget – £1 billion – should be switched to 'agricultural, irrigational and medical development schemes which Mr Wilson, before he lost his idealism, so movingly pressed upon a receptive Labour Party Conference. Such a policy would soon sort out the men from the boys in the Labour Movement. We would soon discover then what socialism meant to many who now have the honour to call themselves socialists.'[18]

But on this, as on so much else, the wheel had turned. In the first week of the Falklands crisis, as the task force sailed, he gave a briefing to the Lobby correspondents of the Sunday papers, looking, in the words of one, 'like an old sea dog, with the salt spray lashing his face'. He was asked about reports that some Conservative MPs – most notably the Member for Clwyd, Sir Anthony Meyer – were opposed to the Prime Minister's stated willingness to use force. 'Is that what they're saying?' he demanded. He was assured that this was indeed the case. 'So it's true then,' he growled, glaring at the reporters, 'she is the only man among 'em!'

In the course of that extraordinary ten-week conflict, Ingham certainly did his share of hand-to-hand fighting: not in the South Atlantic, but rather in the treacherous terrain of Whitehall. His enemy – implacable, cunning and numerically superior – was located a few hundred yards east of Downing Street in the Ministry of Defence, commanded by the MoD's Permanent Under Secretary, Sir Frank Cooper.

Cooper, sixty years old and due to retire in a few months' time, had travelled with Thatcher to Bonn and Paris in 1979 and 1980, as well as to Washington on her first visits to see Presidents Carter and Reagan. He had observed her relationship with Ingham often enough and closely enough to have become distinctly wary. He had worked for Francis Pym for two years and had just seen what had happened to him at Ingham's hands. The Falklands operation was a purely military affair as far as Cooper was concerned. He wanted Number 10's influence kept to a minimum, and his first objective was to neutralize Ingham.

Ingham's primary aim was equally clear. In 1981, he had secured the appointment of a friend, Neville Taylor, the Chief Information Officer at the Department of Health and Social Security, to the equivalent position at the MoD. But Taylor had been ill. He was not due to take up his new duties for another two months. In the meantime, public relations at the MoD were being run by Ian McDonald, an assistant secretary previously responsible for pay and recruitment. Even in normal times it was a preoccupation of Ingham, amounting almost to an obsession, that all Whitehall heads of PR should be fully-trained information officers and not ordinary career civil servants. Now, with war imminent, he was especially keen to get one of his own kind in place at the MoD: first, because he thought they would do the job better; secondly because McDonald reported to Frank Cooper and was not under his direct control; thirdly because Margaret Thatcher's position as Prime Minister was in the balance and the presentation of news naturally had to take account of this political dimension. Thus, in the shadow of the greater conflict, were the battle-lines drawn for the lesser.

All Ingham's fears appeared to be borne out by the events of the first weekend. The Navy at first refused to allow any journalists to sail with the task force. Ian McDonald persuaded them to take ten: five places were to go to television, one to the Press Association (PA) and four to reporters from national newspapers; the winners were literally picked out of a hat. Naturally, this produced a howl of resentment from all those – the four other Fleet Street dailies and the eight Sunday papers, the regional press, Reuters, independent radio, the foreign correspondents based in London – who felt they had been unfairly excluded. The telephone began ringing in Purley on Friday night with calls from newspaper editors and executives, and it barely stopped all weekend. Ingham later recalled how, 'having spent the first four nights . . . literally on the phone all the time, I said "This has got to stop".'[19] On Monday morning, using the authority of the Prime Minister's name but without actually consulting her, he instructed the MoD to increase the allocation of media berths on the task force. Eventually, some twenty-eight journalists sailed with the fleet: 'more people,' in Frank Cooper's view, 'than we could properly cope with'.[20]

More disturbing to Ingham even than the chaos surrounding press accreditation was McDonald's decision to end all off-the-record briefings. Defence correspondents, like most specialist journalists, operated their own mini Lobby system, as part of which they were given regular 'guidance' by Cooper. On the day of the Argentine invasion, McDonald severed these contacts on the grounds of security. Ingham was incredulous. 'I certainly took the view that when you are in a crisis of this kind, the last thing you do is withdraw the service to the media,' he said later. 'I think that is not the time to withdraw your service to your clientele.'[21]

Ingham acted quickly. He arranged with the DHSS for Neville Taylor to be relieved of his post and sent to the MoD nine weeks earlier than planned. Cooper made his counter-move equally smartly. When Taylor walked through the door on the morning of 13 April he was handed a letter welcoming him to the ministry and informing him that he was now in charge of all areas of public relations – except the Falklands. It was a bureaucratic master-stroke, justified by Cooper on the grounds that Taylor (who had not worked at the MoD for twelve years) needed time to reacquaint himself with military matters. The real reason, as Taylor swiftly discovered, was Cooper's deep-rooted suspicion of Ingham. 'I was known to have a rapport with Bernard,' recalled Taylor, 'which made Frank Cooper incredibly suspicious of me. He didn't trust me. This was a recurring theme throughout the Falklands – actual instructions from Cooper: "Don't tell that bugger anything about it." '

Ingham, who learned of Taylor's treatment with 'ill-concealed fury', now found himself in danger of becoming sidelined. On 8 April he had set up a 'co-ordinating committee', with himself in the chair, which met at 10.00 a.m. each day in his office in Downing Street. The MoD, the COI, the Cabinet Office and the Foreign Office were all obliged to send representatives. The purpose, in Ingham's words, was 'to take stock of developments and their implications for the public; to bring the departments and offices up to date with events; to anticipate, in so far as this was possible, events over the next 24 hours; and to agree on or make recommendations about the action required.' Cooper saw through this ploy at once. Ingham was trying to run the entire information effort from Number 10. Once again, Cooper's response showed what a master he was at Whitehall in-fighting. He simply instructed McDonald not to attend. Instead, the MoD made it a point of principle to send the lowliest official in its news department. As McDonald was the only information officer empowered to be present at the morning meeting of the Chiefs of Staff, Ingham's 'co-ordinating committee' was left with little to co-ordinate.

After a few days of this, Ingham complained to the Prime Minister. She was sympathetic and instructed Cecil Parkinson, Chairman of the Conservative Party and a member of the War Cabinet, to help him out. Parkinson summoned Cooper and the other Permanent Under Secretaries over for drinks on a couple of occasions in order (in his words) to let them know 'that they would have to explain to a member of the

Cabinet why a junior representative had been sent to the key co-ordinating meetings'.[22] Cooper took the hint and McDonald duly started attending the Downing Street committee. Ingham also told Mrs Thatcher of his anger at the MoD's decision to abandon all off-the-record briefings; these were re-started in May. Both victories were a telling demonstration of Ingham's power. He might be outwitted some-times by nimbler minds, but in any dispute he always had at his disposal the ultimate deterrent: the Prime Minister.

Cooper was not antagonistic towards Ingham because he regarded him as incompetent; on the contrary, he thought him a first-class political information officer. His concern was that Ingham would inevitably be tempted to let political imperatives override military ones. On 6 May, for example, two Harriers crashed in fog in the South Atlantic. As the task force had only twenty of these aircraft in the first place, and as no Argentine forces had been involved, the MoD wanted to delay the announcement of their loss. 'In no way do you tell the Argentines that you have lost 10 per cent of your capability,' argued Admiral Woodward, the task force commander. 'It's obvious.'[23] But 6 May was also the day of the local elections. In the House of Commons Press Gallery after Prime Minister's Questions, Ingham was asked if the official release of the bad news was being held up until the polls had closed. Such a cynical tactic would certainly have rebounded on the Government. As Ingham later explained: 'It is very often disadvantageous not to release information which is disadvantageous.'[24] He therefore urged an immediate announcement. The news was promptly released and the Navy, under-standably, was dismayed.

As the fighting intensified, the tension in London between Downing Street and the MoD increased. It was soon an open secret among the journalists covering the war in Whitehall. 'We got the distinct impres-sion,' said Bob Hutchinson, defence correspondent of the PA, 'that Number 10 was more than unhappy at the way the MoD were handling the war – *more* than unhappy – and there were times when Number 10 were briefing on subjects which the MoD refused to talk about.'[25]

It was obviously in the Government's interests to convey an impression of irresistible momentum. 'We're not going to fiddle around,' Ingham told the Lobby on 23 May, two days after the British forces landed on the Falklands. Later that week, on 27 May, Cooper was incensed to hear reports that Ingham had given a briefing hinting that Goose Green had already fallen. At that moment Cooper knew that the 2nd Parachute Regiment was only just beginning its assault. He telephoned Ingham and told him that if he ever did it again, he'd have his bloody head off. He hung up before Ingham could reply. He subsequently criticized the Downing Street Press Office in a radio interview:

> On one particular occasion they let out that something had happened that hadn't happened . . . because, I think, they wanted to influence the political scene. Happily, it was captured quite soon afterwards. They may say that's a very fine distinction. I happen to think it's quite an important distinction in a wartime situation when lives are very much at risk.[26]

Eighteen paratroopers, including their commander, Colonel 'H' Jones, were killed in the assault on Goose Green, and there were bitter complaints from the survivors that the plan had been leaked behind their backs in London. Indeed, there were allegations from some military commanders that the entire operation was strategically unnecessary and had only been mounted due to political pressure at home. 'Goose Green,' said one anonymous 'very senior MoD civil servant' after the war, 'was a push from Number 10.'[27]

Two weeks later there was a further skirmish between Ingham and the MoD. On 8 June, Argentine aircraft attacked the landing ships *Sir Galahad* and *Sir Tristram*. Fifty men were killed. The MoD decided not to release the casualty figures. 'We knew from intelligence,' claimed the Chief of the Defence Staff, Sir Terence Lewin, 'that the Argentines thought they were very much higher.'[28] For the next three days, rumours were allowed, even encouraged, to swirl around Fleet Street and Whitehall that up to 800 men had been killed or wounded. Eventually, on 11 June, Ingham decided that the speculation had gone on long enough. It was proving politically damaging. He made it clear to the Lobby that fewer than seventy had died. The MoD was furious: the Downing Street briefing, said Neville Taylor, 'became the subject of pretty heated discussion between Bernard Ingham and myself.'[29]

Even after white flags had been hoisted over the Falklands and the war had been won, Ingham and Sir Frank Cooper continued to bicker about the part played in the conflict by the Number 10 Press Office. In July, Cooper told the House of Commons Defence Committee that Ingham had definitely not played a 'co-ordinating' role. Ingham read that, and in

October sent the committee a paper claiming that his morning meetings had been throughout 'the main instrument of co-ordination' for media relations. The following month, he appeared before the MPs and blamed the discrepancy between their two versions on the fact that Cooper was not properly briefed. Finally, Cooper took his revenge at a major lecture, attacking Ingham's general role in Government in outspoken terms:

> the aim now is the management of the media with a very much higher degree of central control from Number 10 Downing Street and with the connivance of a part of the media. There is now public relations – which I would define as biased information. I suggest that the post of Chief Information Officer at Number 10 Downing Street is in fact a political job in a party sense and is not a job which it is proper for a civil servant to fill unless he or she resigns from the Civil Service on appointment.[30]

How much truth was there in Sir Frank's assertion? Undoubtedly, the Falklands War served further to cement the relationship between the Prime Minister and her Press Secretary. Ingham, although few in the media realised it at the time, had been operating under a considerable personal strain. On Tuesday 11 May – the day Margaret Thatcher attacked the BBC in the House of Commons for failing to support 'our boys' – Ingham was called away and told that his wife had been gravely injured in an accident. That lunchtime, Nancy Ingham had been shopping in the local market in Surrey Street when a runaway lorry had careered through the stalls and up on to the pavement, injuring nine pedestrians. She was trapped under the wreckage for several hours. Once in hospital she was found to have, among other injuries, a broken pelvis. The Prime Minister told Ingham to take leave. He refused.

This was devotion to duty of an order which surprised even those who knew him of old. Nancy, according to her brother-in-law, 'was on her back for three months'. She eventually had to leave hospital on crutches. 'Most of us,' in Neville Taylor's words, 'given the nature of our marriages and the nature of the injuries suffered by his wife, would have said: "Terribly sorry, even if there's a war on I've got to take half a day off". Bernard didn't. He snatched odd hours. He had a car, visited his wife, then came back again. It was hardly noticeable that there was anything else going on in his life.'

The Falklands War had transformed the Government's fortunes. From third place in the opinion polls it had moved to first. There was talk of a quick General Election to exploit the after-glow of victory. On 10 September, in the Cabinet Room, the Prime Minister convened the first meeting of the pre-election Liaison Committee, designed to co-ordinate the efforts of Tory Party and Government. Five ministers attended (Sir Keith Joseph, Norman Tebbit, John Biffen, Norman Fowler and John Wakeham), together with three senior party officials (the Chairman, Cecil Parkinson, the marketing director, Christopher Lawson, and the research director, Peter Cropper). Somewhat surprisingly, Bernard Ingham was also present.

The Liaison Committee's confidential minutes show how close Ingham now was to playing a party political role. The group, which met many times in the run-up to the election, was essentially concerned with propaganda. The gentlemen from Conservative Central Office undertook to revise a Government paper on the National Health Service and to publish a brochure to accompany it; to 'advise on a more appealing presentational approach of [sic] the Government's privatisation policies'; and to help combat the Campaign for Nuclear Disarmament. Ingham himself addressed the problem of deflecting the Labour Party's attacks on the high level of unemployment: 'the Government,' he said, 'must emphasize the importance of wealth creation'.[31] The Committee's work had nothing to do with the objective publication of facts and everything to do with securing an election victory for the Conservative Party.

Before any election could be contemplated it was necessary to deal with one last piece of unfinished business from the Falklands War. Early in the conflict the Government had been obliged to set up an inquiry under Lord Franks to investigate ministers' conduct prior to the invasion. The inquiry, which included two former Labour Cabinet Ministers, had been given access to all classified documents. There was a risk that its findings might puncture the post-Falklands euphoria, and with it the Government's new-found popularity. Publication was set for 18 January 1983.

Number 10's response was to mount two pre-emptive strikes. On 8 January, the week before the report appeared, the Prime Minister, accompanied by her Press Secretary, paid a dramatic secret visit to the Falklands. What could more graphically remind the nation, in the run-up not only to Franks but to polling, of the victory she had won? Ingham

organised an RAF flight to ferry a couple of Lobby friends, Chris
Moncrieff of the Press Association and John Warden of the *Daily Express*,
down to the islands.

Words were easy to arrange; television pictures were more difficult.
For reasons of security, the visit could not be announced in advance,
Ingham did not even tell his wife where he was going. Despite strong
hints dropped to ITN that it would be worth its while to send a team to
the South Atlantic, they did nothing. When the Prime Minister landed,
the BBC had the only crew on the Falklands. Ingham nonetheless was
determined to have Mrs Thatcher's triumphal entry into Port Stanley
shown on all news bulletins.

His first words to the BBC's reporter, Nick Witchell, waiting by the
runway, were a demand that the material he and his crew were shooting
should be given free of charge to ITN. Witchell replied that that was a
matter for the BBC in London. Ingham responded in a menacing tone
that he would have him thrown off the island unless he did as he was
told. He then rang the BBC's Assistant Director General, Alan Protheroe, and ordered him to 'pool' the material with ITN. Protheroe,
understandably, was reluctant. 'I really find it very difficult to accept that
Number 10 can actually just declare a pool when necessary, Bernard.'
Ingham began to splutter with indignation. A radio ham was recording
the call, and the tape is a treasure. His Yorkshire vowels pierced the howl
of interference across a distance of 8,000 miles like some latter-day
Heathcliffe bellowing into a moorland storm.

INGHAM: It is this childish behaviour that when indeed we have done
you a signal service – a signal service – by keeping your people in the
islands, as I say and to repeat, at considerable risks to ourselves –
and I, I, I, I frankly don't believe that the British public, when it is
explained to them, will understand this childishness. I do expect more
actually from the BBC and I am deeply hurt.
PROTHEROE: It would have been a lot easier if somebody in your office
had asked us or told us twenty-four hours beforehand –
INGHAM: I am sorry there is absolutely no question of us doing that, and
you have got to get it into your mind, and the media has got to get it
into its mind, that we don't operate for your convenience, we operate
for the security of the Prime Minister! I'm fed up with this! I had it in
Northern Ireland.

At considerable cost, the BBC had booked a satellite and flown engineers out to Ascension Island. The plan was for the film to be flown there from the Falklands on an RAF Hercules due to take off at 4.00 p.m. This provided Ingham with his trump card. 'No film is coming out tonight,' he threatened, 'unless I have your absolute assurance that it will be freely available to ITN and Independent Radio News.' He went on: 'I'm sure the Prime Minister, if I had to tell her what is going on, she would scarcely credit it.' Protheroe had no answer to that. He capitulated. 'When I get home,' shouted Ingham, 'we have got to have a meeting. We can't go on like this.' He hung up on the BBC and called Number 10 in triumph:

INGHAM: I've won!
DOWNING STREET: You've won?
INGHAM : Yep!
DOWNING STREET: What happened?
INGHAM: I rang Protheroe and I told him in no uncertain terms that he
    wouldn't get it back tonight unless it was freely available . . .

For the next five days, images of the Prime Minister – graciously accepting the cheers of the islanders, manfully firing an artillery piece, tearfully laying a wreath – dominated all networks. The visit was a great success, although Ingham privately confessed to finding the Falklands a gloomy and charmless place.

He had spent the first leg of the flight down, from RAF Brize Norton to Ascension, reading the Franks Report.' ('In thirteen hours,' he said later, 'you can shift an enormous amount of work, even if you come up for air every five minutes.'[32]) Personally, he had never been in any doubt about where the blame lay for failing to anticipate the Argentine invasion. 'Typical bloody Foreign Office,' Neville Taylor recalled him grumbling. 'They didn't see this coming. Even when some of their own people were telling them something was going on they didn't take any bloody notice because they're all Arabists and Arabists don't know anything about the South Atlantic . . .'

However, the Franks Report did not bear out this trenchant analysis. It was an odd document. Its first 338 paragraphs gave a devastatingly detailed account of Government incompetence, from which the Foreign Office actually emerged better than either Number 10 or the MoD. Lord Carrington, the Foreign Secretary, was revealed to have sent three separate minutes to the Defence Secretary urging him not to withdraw HMS *Endurance* from the South Atlantic lest it send the wrong signal to Buenos Aires. Carrington, clearly, was alert to the danger. The Cabinet's Defence Committee, on the other hand, chaired by the Prime Minister, which had approved *Endurance*'s removal, did not even discuss the Falklands between January 1981 and 1 April 1982, the day before the Argentine attack.

But then came the final paragraph – 339 – at which point, in Lord Callaghan's memorable phrase, Franks 'got fed up with the canvas he was painting and he chucked a bucket of whitewash over it'. The Committee announced it did not feel 'justified in attaching any criticism or blame to the present Government' for the invasion of 2 April 1982.

For Ingham, with all the instruments of news management at his disposal, this was a gift: the opportunity for the second pre-emptive strike against Mrs Thatcher's opponents in as many weeks. The Franks Report was due to be presented to Parliament four days after her return from the Falklands. It was rumoured to be long (it actually ran to 109 pages) and the media, anxious to prepare comment and detailed analysis, were pleading for the chance to see embargoed copies a few hours prior to publication. This had been standard practice for years with Government White Papers. But in October, in retaliation for what he claimed was a 'disgraceful' breach of the embargo on the Falklands Honours List, Ingham had withdrawn this 'privilege', making good his threat to leave 'Lobby correspondents waiting outside Number 10 in the snow'[33] for official documents.

Now, confronted with requests for advance copies of the Franks Report, Ingham turned them down flat. He told the BBC that if they could cover Budget speeches without knowing their contents, they could do the same with Franks (another disingenuous reply, given that the report was seven times the length of the average Budget, took at least a day to read, and was much more detailed). Instead, the report was to be distributed at 3.30 p.m., at the moment the Prime Minister presented it to Parliament. Ingham planned to offer only one piece of assistance: he would meet the Lobby at 2.45 p.m., 'to point out the important paragraphs'.

This was too much, even for some Lobby journalists. Fourteen hours before the proposed briefing, in the early hours of 18 January, the Labour MP Tam Dalyell rose in an almost deserted House of Commons to reveal Ingham's plan. He had been forewarned of it by a Lobby correspondent: 'not a member of the left-wing press,' claimed Dalyell, but a reporter who was 'professionally and personally outraged' by Ingham's manipulative behaviour. To head off a Parliamentary row, the Prime Minister had to tell Ingham to postpone his briefing until after her statement. He was outraged by this fresh evidence of treachery in the Lobby. Never before had the mechanics of its operation been revealed in advance. He was still sore about it several days later when Roy Hattersley, author of a weekly column on press matters, asked him about the purpose of the reconvened briefing. Ingham snapped that he had merely been helping the Lobby 'find their way around Franks'. If people did not believe him, 'that is their problem'. According to an amused Mr Hattersley: 'He gave me that assurance in such bellicose language that failure to report his disclaimer would put my person at risk when next I meet the burly Mr Ingham.'[34]

Politically, despite the last-minute embarrassment, Ingham's handling of the Franks inquiry paid rich dividends. With only a couple of hours available to study the report, almost every paper and news bulletin portrayed it as a document essentially uncritical of the Government. It took some days for its implications to be properly digested. By the weekend, the coverage had become distinctly hostile ('Why the Falklands invasion could have been foreseen,' was the headline in the conservative *Sunday Telegraph*) but by then the Franks Report was the stuff of history. The Government had scored a short-term, knock-out victory – and, in politics, those are the only victories that count.

But in the longer term, and personally, Ingham had done himself considerable damage. A narrow line divides the anonymous civil servant from the official who is too powerful and controversial to ignore. Ingham crossed it in that third week of January 1983. On the Monday he was named on the floor of the House of Commons and accused of trying to manage the news. On the Tuesday, the allegation was reported in the press. On the Friday, the Channel Four programme, *The Friday Alternative*, broadcast the tape of his browbeating of Alan Protheroe. On the following Monday, the 24th, it was revealed that Ingham was considering taking legal action over the unauthorized transmission of a private conversation.

Then on Tuesday, the 25th, there was a fresh controversy. The *Daily Mirror* disclosed that 'a number of Irish journalists' had written to the

Prime Minister complaining that Ingham had 'knocked microphones aside and made liberal use of his elbows, buttocks and shoulders' during her recent visit to Belfast: 'I admit I did bang into them with my backside,' the paper reported Ingham as saying, but he insisted that the reporters were 'behaving like sensitive plants and they should grow up'.

Harold Evans or Donald Maitland would never have spoken in such terms. Fife Clark would have shrivelled into a corner at the mere thought of being quoted by *name*. Even Joe Haines made it a rule that any member of the Downing Street Press Office who was identified in the media had to pay a forfeit of a bottle of wine. But it was not in Ingham's nature to let such slights pass. He fought back – in public. On 6 February, he took the unprecedented step of granting an on-the-record interview to the *Sunday Telegraph*. 'I do not bear grudges,' said the man who, for five months, had persistently refused to let the Lobby see Government papers in advance. 'I play no part in politics,' maintained the official who sat on a Liaison Committee with employees of Conservative Central Office. Most risibly of all, the Press Secretary who regularly turned Lobby briefings into what one colleague called 'shouting matches' was recorded as insisting: 'I keep my views to myself'.

Until this point, the discreet conventions of the Lobby had protected Ingham, more or less. When he had compared Francis Pym to Mona Lott, for example, not a single newspaper had named him as the source. But henceforth, such niceties would not be observed. Anonymity, like virginity, once lost, is gone for good: even prolonged periods of self-denial will not rest%re the *status quo ante*. In any case, Ingham was too colourful, too combative, too ready to give offence and too swift to take it, for him now to relapse back into the shadows as just another 'senior Government source'. From the episode of the Franks Report onwards, he no longer simply released the news; the manner in which he released it often *was* the news.

Proof of that came within twenty-four hours of the *Sunday Telegraph* interview, when Ingham became the first Prime Minister's Press Secretary to be the subject of a Parliamentary debate. True, the debate took place at breakfast time, lasted just fifty-six minutes and involved only two speakers. But such attention had never before been focused upon any civil servant, let alone one in Ingham's position. 'The Prime Minister's press relations,' stated Tam Dalyell, 'are being handled at senior level by someone whom I can only call a thug.' Protected by Parliamentary privilege, unfettered by the risk of a libel action, the MP let fly.

> Why do we have to tolerate a Lobby system in which able, gifted journalists are forced to become beholden to men in the position of Mr Ingham who threaten assistant directors-general of the BBC with 'incalculable consequences'? Why should men and women of calibre, chosen by editors to represent newspapers at Westminster, be put in the position of prostituting their profession by keeping in with truculent, arrogant bullies of the species that the Prime Minister's Press Secretary has clearly become?

The 'heady air of Downing Street has warped his judgement,' concluded Dalyell. He 'should be redeployed to other duties'.[35]

The minister required to respond to this diatribe was the new Leader of the House of Commons, John Biffen, who had patiently sat up all night awaiting the start of Dalyell's debate. He ridiculed the suggestion that Ingham was a sinister, all-powerful Machiavelli lurking at the heart of Number 10. 'One would begin to imagine,' he mocked, in a phrase which became justly famous, 'that we have in Mr Bernard Ingham some sort of rough-spoken Yorkshire Rasputin who is manipulating Government and corroding the standards of public morality.'

Biffen would not have been so sanguine had he known what lay in store for him at Ingham's hands.

SEVEN

Conducting the Orchestra

'I have waxed eloquently indignant about the Tory plan for bringing the Welfare State up to date. For "up to date" you should read "to an end".'

Bernard Ingham, article in the *Leeds Weekly Citizen*, 25 March 1966

'... news stories about deaths due to the shortage of resources for kidney dialysis machines and transplants would certainly arise ... the emotive nature of the subject created present-ational problems.'

Bernard Ingham, quoted in the minutes of the Meeting of Information Officers, October 1983

On 1 May 1983, Ingham travelled to Cardiff to address a conference of British newspaper editors. These large-scale lectures were to become quite a hobby of his over the next few years, and he devoted considerable care to their preparation. After their delivery, he would have the text immaculately reproduced, placed between printed covers, and circulated to selected colleagues in Government and the Lobby. The contents invariably fell into three sections: first, a panegyric to journalism as he practised it in his early years; second, a contrasting of those high princi-ples with the low standards now prevalent in Fleet Street and broad-casting; third, a vigorous defence of the Government's integrity, with himself cast in the role of weary and misunderstood servant of the public good. The routine is so unchanging, the language so trenchant, it is difficult not to believe that he is – ever so slightly – sending himself up.

His speech in Cardiff on 'The Right to Know' set the pattern. He quoted approvingly the words of Sir Angus Maude, the minister responsible for co-ordinating Government presentation in the first Thatcher cabinet:

When people talk about a right of access to information, I am not clear from what that right derives. The right is not written into the constitution. It does not arise from law ... I do not even accept that there is a moral right to know everything that goes on.

This was certainly, said Ingham, his own experience on the *Hebden Bridge Times*:

I was taught that the newspaper I represented had no rights in the community beyond those of the ordinary citizen ... As for responsibilities, they were legion. But in essence the dominating obligation was to inform the reader accurately, objectively and comprehensively of matters affecting the public interest; to keep him abreast of developments; and responsibly to cultivate an informed public opinion. And don't miss anything, lad.

I am not aware that this concentration on responsibilities to the virtual exclusion of rights was inimical to the public interest – or detrimental to our performance in the service of the community.

How different, how *very* different, from the media of the present day:

This is in part due, I suppose, to the changed attitude to authority. But it may also be that a second Watergate is pursued these days much as the Knights of the Round Table sought the Holy Grail. Too often these days the assumption seems to be that Government is either automatically wrong, naturally perverse, chronically up to no good, or just plain inept.

Nowadays, the stock in trade of most newspapers was speculation (as in 'The Government may be on the verge of ...' or 'The Government could soon ...') and breach of confidence (witness the widespread desire 'to lay hands on any document but preferably those marked secret'). Truth was defended by a thin blue line of '1,200 information officers engaged on a whole variety of communications tasks'. They were a much-maligned group. Ingham quoted Shylock: 'Sufferance is the badge of all our tribe.' The suggestion that they spent their time conspiring to 'manage' the news was nonsense.

With respect, the Government does not manage the news. You do, you and the rest of the media are the real news managers. My colleagues and I present the news on behalf of the Government and offer an interpretation of its importance and significance. You either accept that interpretation or reject it ...

If by news management you mean I seek to present the case for the policies and measures of the Government I serve as effectively as possible, I plead guilty a thousand – nay 10,000 times ... If by news management you mean I try to avoid the Government's coming out with five major announcements on the same day – or worse still on Budget Day, or even worse than that on Bank Holiday Monday, I again plead guilty ...

I only wish I was as sophisticated, as devilishly clever, as Machiavellian, as some make out. Not even a combination of Einstein backed up by the world's most advanced computer could achieve the presentational coups with which we – indeed I – have been credited.

This was to be the standard Ingham line for the next seven years, albeit with ever more lurid metaphors and increasingly apocalyptic diagnoses of the 'raddled, disease-wracked body' of the British media. None of the charges he levelled against the press – that it was over-mighty, irresponsible, speculative and unhelpful – was new; they are the traditional complaints of those in authority, as old as the press itself. ('The degree of information possessed by *The Times* with regard to the most secret affairs of State,' grumbled Lord John Russell to Queen Victoria 140 years ago, 'is mortifying, humiliating and incomprehensible.') But it was the first time he had made plain in public what many were aware of in private: that he had developed a deeply antagonistic view of his old profession.

Tony Benn had encountered this five years earlier, in 1978, when the science correspondent of the *Guardian*, Anthony Tucker, had complained to him that he was being victimized by Ingham. Tucker at that time supplemented his income by writing harmless articles for the Central Office of Information magazine, *Spectrum*, about astronomy and medicine. The magazine was distributed overseas to publicize Britain's scientific achievements. Tucker alleged that Ingham disliked him because of his outspoken anti-nuclear views and, in retaliation, had arranged for his COI work to be stopped. Benn investigated and found that this was indeed the case. Ingham had written a minute to the Director-General of the COI stating that Tucker was 'completely unreliable, that he had joined the anti-nuclear lobby and that his opinions "weren't worth paying for in washers"'. Benn tried to persuade Ingham to retract it, but found him 'rigid and dictatorial in his attitude'. He told Benn: 'I don't see why we should pay people to write articles for the

Central Office of Information who are critical of the Government, who don't come for a departmental briefing and who are not balanced and objective.'[1] Tucker never worked for the COI again.

For Ingham, the media, essentially, were the enemy. He later likened Government press officers to 'riflemen on the Somme' shooting down an advancing army of hostile stories. Although he reserved the right to be sceptical about the information *he* was given to pass on ('I am never satisfied that anybody is ever telling me the whole truth and nothing but the truth, and I look them in the eye when I am in real difficulty and put them up against the wall and say, "Are you going to let me down?"'),[2] he appeared to regard similar suspiciousness on the part of reporters as a personal insult.

Yet they surely had good reason to be sceptical. Just as Margaret Thatcher had come to dominate the machinery of Government, so Ingham had established an unusual degree of personal control over its Information Service. He did this, like her, not by taking more powers, but by bending the existing structure to suit his ambitions, overcoming any opposition by sheer hard work and force of character.

Every Monday afternoon at five o'clock, in Conference Room 'D' of the Cabinet Office, Ingham would assemble some twenty-two heads of information from all over Whitehall. This weekly Meeting of Information Officers (MIO) had been established more than twenty years earlier to keep departments in touch with one another and was, by tradition, chaired by the Prime Minister's Press Secretary. In the past it was of limited importance. Indeed, several of Ingham's predecessors virtually ignored it. Donald Maitland, for one, never attended its meetings ('I didn't find that my presence was all that useful') nor did Joe Haines ('They were dreadfully boring ... I put all that kind of thing on to my deputy').

Ingham, by contrast, was soon treating it as a sort of below-stairs Cabinet, even to the extent of encouraging sub-committees on the economy and other policy areas, in imitation of the real thing. By all accounts, the MIO under Ingham resembled nothing so much as a butler's pantry during an Edwardian house party, where the butlers of the various guests would gather after hours and disport themselves according to the stations of their masters. Thus those information officers whose ministers were out of favour with Mrs Thatcher found themselves out of favour with Ingham. According to one participant: 'If someone said, "Look, is it a good idea to say this?" Bernard got very short: "You're the same as your bloody Secretary of State – always arguing!"'

You didn't criticize Government policy because Bernard took that as a personal attack. People who tried got their fingers burnt, so they didn't do it the next week. I've heard colleagues say, 'Well, I've got to go to this bloody meeting but I'm not going to say anything.' It was similar to the Cabinet: there was no proper discussion, and if you criticized you had to be disloyal.

On one occasion, Ingham made an announcement and invited his colleagues to give their opinions. Nobody spoke. Whereupon, in the words of another member, 'Bernard got very red-faced and shouted, "Dammit, what point is there in having this meeting if nobody makes any comments?" So Janet Hewlett-Davies [Chief Information Officer at the DHSS] said, "The main reason, Bernard, is that if anyone seems to disagree they'll be regarded as hostile". Ingham grunted "Rubbish!" Everyone else was silent.'

For twenty years, ever since the days when his passion in argument had been sufficient to send his dentures flying, Ingham had loved to lay down the law. Even then, as a member of the Labour Party, he had been notably intolerant of dissenters. Now these twin characteristics of vehemence and authoritarianism were harnessed to the cause of Government presentation. His all-embracing approach was first adumbrated in 1980, a few months after his arrival at Number 10, when he was asked to prepare a report on what the Government should do to encourage public support for the European Community. The point should be made, he wrote, in a phrase reminiscent of Albion, that a community of 250 million could achieve more than a 'debilitated nation of 55 million, however much the latter may trade on its past imperial glory'. Government publicity should stress this, 'with all the instruments of the orchestra, not only central Government, reading the same score, playing the same tune and coming in on cue'.[3] This potentially discordant ensemble was to be conducted by him through the MIO.

Departments were required to notify the Number 10 Press Office by close of business on Wednesday of all announcements and media engagements planned for the following week. This then became the central item on the agenda for the Monday afternoon meeting. The

MIO's minutes are marked 'Restricted', the lowest of Whitehall's four security classifications: their release is defined officially as 'undesirable in the interests of the nation'. Nevertheless, in the autumn of 1983, three sets of minutes were leaked to Richard Norton-Taylor of the *Guardian*, revealing both the dominating role Ingham had assumed and the level of detail he insisted on discussing.

On 12 September, for example, he began by announcing that he had written to the Manpower Services Commission 'to express his concern' at its 'failure to observe its own embargo arrangements in the handling of its Annual Report'. He gave a *'tour d'horizon* of current news issues following the summer break'. On the economy, he looked ahead 'to the New Year and beyond' and warned that 'Economic Departments should expect a rough ride'. He raised no objection to Cecil Parkinson, Secretary of State for Trade and Industry, appearing on *Panorama* to discuss the economy, but instructed the DTI Press Office to consult with the Treasury 'to ensure a comprehensive presentation of the economic policy and the state of the economy'. He circulated figures on the impact of breakfast television on early morning radio audiences.

Five weeks later, on 17 October, he was to be found bemoaning the circumstances of Parkinson's resignation over the Sara Keays affair ('the behaviour of the news media in creating news stories out of nothing caused great concern'). He thanked those present for their help in compiling a list of departmental achievements since the General Election: 'Ministers might find it a useful aid to presenting the Government's case'. He welcomed the visit of President Mitterrand of France as providing, in the week of a huge CND demonstration, 'a useful opportunity' to stress the 'continued need for an independent nuclear deterrent' (no more talk now of Albion's 'bomb-happy' Tory Party). He warned of the 'presentational problems' caused by the shortage of kidney dialysis machines. He called for departments 'to make a practice of preparing and circulating speaking notes for Ministers on topical issues': all such notes 'should be copied to the Prime Minister's Office'.

At the instigation of the Chairman [Ingham], it was agreed that the Ministry of Defence should liaise with the Foreign and Commonwealth Office and the Home Office and Scottish Office to prepare a Ministerial speaking note on the Government's defence policies. It was further agreed that *Ministers should be encouraged* [author's emphasis] to use the platform provided by weekend newspapers to present these policies to the full. This would provide a 'trailer' to the NATO Nuclear Planning Group meeting which was to take place in Ottawa on 27–28 October.

At the MIO on 31 October, in the wake of the United States' invasion of Grenada, Ingham blamed the media's criticism of the Prime Minister on her 'failure to live up to their caricature of her, either as a Reagan "poodle" or as a warmonger'. At the same meeting, he welcomed the decision of the Conservative Party Chairman, John Selwyn Gummer, to keep ministers off the Radio Four *Any Questions* programme, leaving it instead as 'the preserve of Government backbenchers'. On the economic front, he regarded it as 'essential that the importance of continuing wage and cost restraint was put over in Ministerial speeches' . . .

All this may seem at first glance the small change of Ingham's work as Chief Press Secretary. But it is in its very smallness that its fascination lies. For at the MIO, information officers were required not only to list every forthcoming announcement – hospital closures, retail sales figures, crime statistics and the rest – but to indicate whether these were expected to be good or bad, and what dealings their departments were having with the media: would Minister A be on *Newsnight?* should Minister B take part in a phone-in? In the case of longer-term documentary programmes such as *Panorama* or *This Week*, the MIO might well go so far as to discuss the names of individual reporters and producers: was C to be trusted; did D not once give Minister E a rough ride? In all these decisions, through the MIO, Ingham was consulted and became, effectively, the final arbiter. He made no secret of this process. In October 1981, he spoke at a private seminar organised by the Independent Broadcasting Authority:

> Since ministers are not primarily in the entertainment business, they do not see why they should be the objective of blood sport, and we shall do our level best to deny you it. If you remain incorrigibly preoccupied with staining the sand with ministerial blood, please find a more sophisticated way of doing it than with the invited audience, replete with statutory Trot, bra-burner and barrack room brawler. Finally, do not expect me or my colleagues to move heaven and earth to help you if you have a reputation for seldom, if ever, examining anything constructively as distinct from destructively . . .

Television, he warned his audience darkly, was 'corrupting no less of those who work for it than those who appear on it'.

Of course, Ingham was not in a position actually to forbid a minister's appearance on a particular programme. But he could make his feelings plain to that minister's Chief Information Officer (whose advice would usually be decisive) and he could even lay down the 'line' Number 10 would like pushed. Hence his directives, quoted above, that Government speeches should stress 'the importance of continuing wage and cost restraint' or that ministers should be 'encouraged' to promote the deployment of Trident and Cruise missiles in the Sunday papers.

As Ingham's reputation spread, the question which was asked increasingly was whether this was not an abuse of the system. In 1952, when Lord Swinton urged Winston Churchill to re-establish a Number 10 Press Office, he conceded that 'a centralized information agency of this character might, in the hands of an unscrupulous extremist Government, prove both a powerful and dangerous weapon of propaganda'.[4] Three decades later, there was a growing number – including some Whitehall information officers – who believed that Swinton's warning was fast coming true.

Ingham was seeking to do something which none of his predecessors had attempted. He was trying to reconcile two hitherto unreconcilable functions. He wanted to be both the civil service spokesman for the Government as a whole, along the objective lines of a Trevor Lloyd-Hughes, and to act as the Prime Minister's ultra-loyal lieutenant, after the partisan style of a Joe Haines. And in his urge to meddle in detail, to centralize, to take personal control, to brook no opposition, one is struck, once again, by the parallels between servant and mistress. 'L'état, c'est moi,' Louis XIV's famous motto, was often applied to Margaret Thatcher. What could be more natural than that her spokesman should seek, in his gruff tones, to embody the voice of the entire Government?

Behind his back there was considerable grumbling about Ingham's domineering manner, particularly his habit of answering for every department when he met the Lobby. 'I've never known anyone so keen to have all the minutiae and deliver it all himself,' claimed one independent-minded Chief Information Officer. 'I said to him: "What am I bloody well here for, if not to give out news?" He thought I was just trying to protect my territory. But if we'd got the news, why shouldn't we give it out?' These concerns erupted in public in the summer of 1983 when it became known that Ingham wanted to link all Whitehall information departments to Number 10 via a new computer system. He commissioned a plan, 'The Potential for Information Technology in the Information Service'. A mole in the MIO promptly leaked it to Fleet Street. 'Every morning,' complained an anonymous 'colleague' to *The Times*, 'departments would have to put up what was happening that day. If Number 10 did not approve of Minister X appearing on *News at Ten*, the appearance would be cancelled.'[5] It also emerged that Ingham was floating the idea of downgrading the post of Head of the COI and putting himself in charge of the Government Information Service.

Five days later, under the impassive gaze of the Director-General of the COI, Donald Grant, Ingham told the MIO that two quite separate ideas – the acquisition of information technology and changes in his own role and status – had been brought together to somehow suggest he aimed at becoming 'a so-called "Information Overlord"'. He dismissed the reports as 'inaccurate, ill-informed and possibly malicious'. But he did not, it was noted, deny that he had ambitions to aggrandize his role in some fashion. Ingham's denunciation of the leak was itself immediately leaked. That Thursday, the leader of the Social Democrats, David Owen, wrote to the Prime Minister asking her to explain what was happening and reminding her of the 'classical definition' of the role of the Government Information Service given by Lord Swinton in 1953: that it should

> give prompt and accurate information and give it objectively about Government action and Government policy. It is quite definitely not the job of the Government Information Service to try to boost the Government or try to persuade the press to.

It took Mrs Thatcher almost two weeks to reply, but when she did her answer was emphatic. Ingham, she said, was

> in an especially delicate and exposed position ... But it remains his duty to give prompt and accurate information objectively about Government action and policy. It is not his job to try to persuade the press to boost the Government ... I do not have and have never had any intention to centralize control of Government information in

10 Downing Street, and I have no plans to extend the responsibilities of my Chief Press Secretary.

Ingham got his computer system (after securing the support of the Cabinet Secretary, Sir Robert Armstrong), but his ambition to bring the Whitehall information machine under his personal control was balked – at any rate, for the time being.

Mrs Thatcher's declaration – that it was not Ingham's 'job to try to persuade the press to boost the Government' – seems at first sight to be so palpably false, it is a wonder it can have been made with a straight face. Only if one studies her reply more closely can one, perhaps, detect behind it the slippery hand of the civil service drafter. Technically, it was correct to state that persuading the press to boost the Government was not his *job*: in so saying she was not denying that that was what he *did*. On such subtle distinctions are Whitehall careers built.

Why was it necessary to go through these linguistic contortions? What was wrong with seeking to manipulate the press? Why not admit what everyone on the inside track knew for a fact: that Ingham devoted himself, body and soul, twelve hours a day to boosting the Government; that he used the MIO not as a channel for ensuring the smooth transition of facts from rulers to ruled, but as an instrument for even more high-octane Government-boosting?

The answer was simple. If it was once admitted that Ingham's job was to procure for the Government the most favourable coverage possible, and hence to increase its popularity, he could no longer be regarded as objective. If he was not objective, he was not acting in accordance with his duties as a professional civil servant. And if his behaviour was deemed improper, what of the MIO, whose members were instructed by Ingham to 'encourage' their ministers to do this, that or the other? Ingham's alleged neutrality, in other words, was the rock upon which the entire edifice rested. Remove it, and the theory of a Government Information Service whose sole function was to dispense objective facts would have come crashing down. Hence the necessity for the fiction that he did not 'persuade the press to boost the Government'.

It is hard to think of any other public official whose duties were so hedged around with half-truths and evasions. He was in a sense like the head of MI5 or MI6 – organizations whose existence for years was never officially admitted. He was there, but he was not there; he managed the news, but he did not manage the news; he was neutral, but he was not neutral: he ran the Government Information Service, but then again . . .

Another illustration of Ingham's actual, rather than his professed, role came just three months after Mrs Thatcher's assurances to Owen. At the Prime Minister's insistence, the 1983 Conservative election manifesto had promised the abolition of the Greater London Council (GLC). It had seemed a good idea at the time. Unexpectedly, however, in October, an *Evening Standard* poll had found 54 per cent of Londoners opposed to abolition. Tory GLC councillors were aghast at the plan, as were a substantial number of Conservative MPs and peers. To add to the Government's problems, the GLC was running a sophisticated advertising campaign.

On 30 December, Ingham addressed himself to the problem in a seven-page memorandum. He called for 'a plan of campaign . . . comprehensive but flexible', which would 'treat, as a matter of urgency, dissident elements among the Government's own supporters to ensure they are neutralized if not positively harnessed to the Government's cause'. He also demanded 'remedial action with troublesome journals, whether national, provincial or specialist'; the placing of 'special articles' in sympathetic newspapers ('eg, *Sunday Express*, *News of the World*, regional press'); and ministerial appearances on 'phone-ins or discussion programmes, including the *JY Prog* [the *Jimmy Young Programme*]'. In addition, Ingham also proposed 'a comprehensive diary to which all Departments contribute relevant dates, events and Ministerial engagements which might be turned to good account'. It is difficult to square this memorandum, either with the Prime Minister's earlier assurances about her Press Secretary's role, or with Ingham's own statement to the newspaper editors in Cardiff in May that 'with respect, the Government does not manage the news'.

Ingham's 'plan of campaign' was soon in operation. In the first week of January 1984, the minister responsible for abolishing the GLC, Patrick Jenkin, began hawking round Fleet Street an article explaining the Government's case. The *Sunday Times* turned it down. The *Sunday Express* published it on 15 January. On 18 January, Ingham's other measures were approved by a Cabinet sub-committee. On 20 January, details of his proposals leaked. 'As a Tory dissident I must confess I rolled about in my chair, laughing until the tears fell down my cheeks, at the news that Mr Bernard Ingham has drawn up a seven-page memorandum on how to "neutralize" us all,' wrote George Tremlett, a GLC councillor, in the *Guardian* three days later. 'Ye Gods and little fishes, has it really come to this? How long, I ask, will it be before the gentlemen in white coats come to take Mr Ingham away?'

These leaks were becoming a serious embarrassment to Ingham. He abhorred such breaches of trust, wherever they occurred. Fancy notions about civil servants having a 'higher duty' to Parliament or the nation passed him by. In September 1983, he told the MIO that the leak of a minute from Michael Heseltine about Cruise missile deployment was 'taken very seriously indeed'. When the culprit, a clerk in the Foreign Office named Sarah Tisdall, was discovered and jailed for six months, he applauded the sentence. He saw Clive Ponting, the MoD official who revealed details of the sinking of the *General Belgrano*, as a particularly odious viper. On 10 September 1984, on the eve of Ponting's trial at the Old Bailey, he told the MIO of his wish that the case be heard by a particularly severe judge: he only wished Judge Jeffreys of the 'Bloody Assizes' of 1685 was available. It was, presumably, a joke.

The best means of stopping leaks in the Government Information Service, in his view, was to make sure the right kind of person was appointed in the first place. Never had a Prime Minister's Press Secretary taken such a close interest in the careers of Whitehall's information officers. 'Bernard wanted the very best people to work in Number 10,' recalled one of his most senior colleagues, 'and he had no compunction in digging them out of other departments. And if people went to Number 10 and were no good he was quite ruthless about it.' One by one, the brightest entrants to the Information Service were given six-week attachments to the Number 10 Press Office. By the summer of 1984, Ingham had worked his way through more than thirty. Those he felt he could trust he backed for promotion.

But this alone was not enough. His associates speak of his strong desire, amounting almost to a sense of personal mission, to 'sort out' public relations in Whitehall. First, he wanted to end the practice whereby some departments – notably Trade and Industry, the Treasury and the Foreign Office – appointed ordinary civil servants to run their information offices. They were not 'professionals'. They had not worked for him at Number 10. They were in-house 'natives'. In the great symphony of Government presentation, as Ingham envisaged it, they were the ones who could be expected to hit the wrong notes.

Secondly, he wanted to improve press officers' pay and conditions of service. According to Neville Taylor: 'Bernard has had – and I have got to use the phrase – a great chip on his shoulder that until he got to Number 10 he never felt he'd been taken as seriously as an information officer as he would have been as an administrator ... Throughout his career, he's had this feeling that it's unfair, that for the work we did we should have been at least one grade further up.'

And the third necessary reform, in his humble opinion, was that he should be placed formally in charge of the whole operation. Ever since its establishment in 1949, the Government Information Service had been technically subordinate to the Central Office of Information, a strictly non-political body, responsible for advertisements, exhibitions and public service films. Thus the Director-General of the COI (in 1984 it was Donald Grant, whom Ingham had defeated for the Press Secretaryship) was also Head of Profession for all full-time information officers. Theoretically, he was Ingham's superior. He was paid more. It was Grant who sat on the appointments boards and recommended the promotions. Although Ingham could – and frequently did – use his political muscle to defeat Grant on particular issues, he regarded the situation as ridiculous. What did the boss of the COI – stuck in a gloomy office block in Hercules Road in Lambeth – know about life at the sharp end, dealing with the media across the river in Whitehall day in, day out? He coveted the job. 'I believe it was the case,' recalled Neville Taylor, 'that he actually wanted to be Director-General of the COI and Press Secretary. I believe that to be true. I also believe it to be true that there was quite a debate within the Cabinet Office and Number 10 as to the way in which his power would be, could be, increased by combining elements of the two jobs.'

Ingham's tentative manoeuvring was brought temporarily to an end in the autumn of 1983, by the premature disclosure of his ambitions in the press. Asked on 31 October – by the indefatigable Tam Dalyell – about her intentions, the Prime Minister had been obliged to reply: 'No new responsibilities have been given to my Chief Press Secretary and I have no plans to change the status of the Director-General of the Central Office of Information.'[6] But Ingham had been around Whitehall too long to be defeated that easily. If he could not have the job himself, he would do the next best thing. He would have an ally appointed to it instead.

Accordingly, in September 1984, it was announced that, following Donald Grant's scheduled retirement, Neville Taylor would move from the Ministry of Defence to be the next head of the COI. Taylor, of course, was the man whom Frank Cooper had regarded as Ingham's nark at the MoD during the Falklands war. 'My appointment,' Taylor agreed later, 'may well have been partly due to the fact that he and I were known to get on.' As a further sop to Ingham, the salary of the Prime Minister's Press Secretary was increased – by nearly £3,000, to £32,350 – to match that of the COI chief. But the most significant fact was not released to the press. This was contained in a letter from Sir Robert Armstrong to Taylor setting out the terms of his employment: in future, the Director-General of the COI was required to consult the head of the Number 10 Press Office on all senior appointments.

To an outsider, it was a trivial change; to an insider, it was a significant accretion of power – which is why Ingham had fought for it. He was now well on the way to becoming what he had dismissed as malicious gossip twelve months earlier: 'a so-called "Information Overlord"'.

EIGHT

Licensed to Leak

'I'm the man who is licensed to leak . . .'
Bernard Ingham, speech to mark the fortieth anniversary of Calder
High School, January 1990

The fountainhead of Ingham's power was his relationship with the Prime Minister, and as he approached his fifth anniversary in Number 10 that continued to run pure and strong. Few people were granted a better and more complete view of what was going on in Government than Mrs Thatcher's Chief Press Secretary. The only information kept from him was the output of the Joint Intelligence Committee and the other organizations responsible for security. 'Knowledge is power,' as Neville Taylor put it, 'especially in the information business. Because if you know what's going on, then other people have to come to you.' Ingham used this power, in part, to keep his colleagues up to the mark: 'if you're aware that Bernard is seeing all submissions going in, then you make damn sure that in your own department you find out what's going on before it gets there . . . He is very much better at keeping people on their toes than anyone else I have ever seen' – another trait he shared with the Prime Minister.

The minister responsible for co-ordinating Government presentation was the Lord President of the Council and Leader of the House of Lords, Viscount Whitelaw. Late every Thursday morning, after the weekly Cabinet, he would wander across to Ingham's office. 'We would just have a general gossip,' recalled the amiable Whitelaw, 'about what was going on, what had happened at Cabinet, what the sort of mood was. He would see all the bare bones and I would try and give him some indication of the mood in order to help him with the tone of the briefing. I think that's the terribly difficult thing: the tone of the briefing. We also tried to foresee events, to see what we thought Government departments might do better. His political judgement was very good.'

Ingham did not attend the full Cabinet but he was often called in to the smaller – and actually more important – Cabinet committee meetings.

Nominally, his advice was confined to policy presentation; actually, he helped shape decisions. The nature of his job, he once said, entailed an 'input into policy-making, as well as a communicator's output'.[1] A good example occurred at the beginning of 1984, when trade union membership was banned at the Government Communications Headquarters (GCHQ). There was an outcry at what was seen as a denial of democratic rights. Armstrong, supported by the Foreign Secretary, Sir Geoffrey Howe, negotiated a compromise: the unions could stay at GCHQ in return for a promise that they would never strike. The Prime Minister was dubious. Ingham was consulted. 'It will look like a U-turn,' he declared, simply. 'It will *be* a U-turn.'[2] Armstrong's compromise was rejected.

A few months later, Alasdair Milne, the Director-General of the BBC, was given a similar insight into Ingham's fondness for issuing off-the-cuff policy directives. He was entertaining the Chief Press Secretary to lunch at Broadcasting House and the conversation turned to the Corporation's future. 'Just take advertising on Radios One and Two,' Ingham told him, 'and don't argue!'[3]

If he spoke his mind, it was because the Prime Minister encouraged him to do so. In September 1984, at the height of the miners' strike, the editor of the *Sunday Express*, Sir John Junor, visited Mrs Thatcher in her study. Junor was an old friend, but to his surprise, Ingham was invited to sit in on the conversation. 'It was evident that Ingham was now very much part of the inner Cabinet,' he recalled. 'He intervened from time to time in our talk and it was obvious from the way the Prime Minister listened to what he had to say that she respected his judgement.'[4]

Ingham seemed to live a charmed life, for Mrs Thatcher's devastating assaults on her ministers and on other senior civil servants were legendary. These extended even to those whom she liked and promoted. 'Did you ever practise at Chancery?' she once inquired of her junior Home Office minister, David Mellor. He answered that he had not. 'I thought so,' she retorted. 'Not clever enough.' Sir Keith Joseph, leaving his office with Norman Tebbit for a meeting with her about British Leyland, was asked by his private secretary if he would be needing anything. 'Yes,' he replied. 'Ambulances for two at three.' One Cabinet Minister she sacked reputedly burst into tears; another, Lord Soames, complained after his dismissal that he would not have treated his gamekeeper 'in the way that woman treated me'. The fund of stories is endless. But not once did Mrs Thatcher extend this rough treatment to Ingham, even though he made plenty of mistakes. He was different from the others. His loyalty, unlike that of some ministers, was never in question, nor had he ever been known to make an uncomplimentary remark, even in private. Whatever he did, however maladroit, he did only for her. For that reason, if he committed an error, she would always direct her criticism at the press, holding the journalists responsible for getting it wrong; Ingham she absolved from blame.

In July 1983, he overstepped the mark by accusing Labour's Shadow Chancellor, Peter Shore, of talking 'bunkum and balderdash' – hardly an objective dispensing of factual information about Government policy. The Prime Minister, however, thought his blunt speaking wonderful. 'Mr Ingham was fully within his instructions as my Chief Press Secretary in making these points,' she declared, 'and he found characteristically vivid and colourful phrases.'[5] Six months later she addressed the centenary dinner of the Parliamentary Lobby and went out of her way to praise Ingham: a public servant 'of whom,' she said, 'I cannot speak too highly'.[6]

At the beginning of 1985 he committed his most serious transgression to date: one which should have tested even Margaret Thatcher's high opinion of him to the limit. The issue – it was to prove a veritable running sore over the next five years – was exchange rate policy, and the differing views taken of it by the Prime Minister and her Chancellor, Nigel Lawson.

Sterling had been dropping at an accelerating rate throughout 1984, from $1.45 to just over $1.15 by the end of the year. Previously, such a fall would have sent a British Prime Minister into panic. But Mrs Thatcher was sanguine. She shared the strict monetarist view of her economic adviser, Sir Alan Walters, that the pound had to be allowed to find its own level. Government intervention – buying sterling on the foreign exchanges to prop up its value – was a relic of the bad old days of the corporate state. In Thatcherite philosophy, the market reigned supreme. This, as the New Year opened, was the message which Ingham faithfully pumped out from the Number 10 Press Office. 'Thatcher No to crisis move on the pound' was the headline in the *Sunday Times* on 6 January. The story beneath quoted Ingham ('the highest sources in Whitehall') as indicating that the Prime Minister was even prepared to contemplate the previously unthinkable: parity, with one US dollar equalling one pound.

But further down Whitehall, in the Treasury, Lawson was beginning to change his mind. He was about to embark on the long process of apostasy which would, eventually, set him at such odds with the true believers in Downing Street that he would feel obliged to resign. He and his officials watched anxiously as, in the two or three days following the *Sunday Times* article, sterling's value continued to dribble away. On the morning of Friday 11 January, in an effort to stop the slide, and with Thatcher's full knowledge, the Bank of England raised its money market dealing rates, sending base rates up by 1 per cent.

At 2.45 that afternoon, as usual, Ingham met the Lobby correspondents of the Sunday press. What followed was highly illustrative of the risks inherent in his freewheeling role. He had not asked the Prime Minister about what he should say regarding sterling. He was unaware of the significance of the Bank of England's move a few hours beforehand. Instead, he simply launched into his normal routine, laying down the line in his customary, emphatic manner. 'You can be absolutely certain that we are not going to throw money at the pound,' the *Sunday Telegraph* recorded 'authoritative Government sources' as insisting. 'We are not going to defend a particular parity.' Intervention by the Bank of England, the 'sources' added, would be simply 'wasting Britain's substance'. The *Mail on Sunday* reported similar phrases: 'We are not throwing good money after bad.' The *Sunday Times* carried the dramatic banner headline: 'Thatcher ready to let £1 equal $1'.

In this unanimous chorus there was only one dissenting voice. As Ingham was briefing the Sunday Lobby, William Keegan, economics editor of the *Observer*, who had worked at the Bank of England for a year in the 1970s, was finishing lunch with a senior Treasury official. The Treasury man had told him a quite different story: that they had been perturbed by the previous week's *Sunday Times* article; that 'letting the pound fall to one dollar was certainly not official policy; that the Treasury and the Bank had deliberately engineered the rise in interest rates on the Friday morning. And they would do the same again, or more, on the Monday if the market was still selling sterling.' The *Observer* preferred this version of events to Ingham's. That weekend, alone in Fleet Street, it reported that the Government was planning 'a determined defence of the exchange rate.

> Ministers are now prepared to see interest rates rise at least another 1 per cent ... Until late last week the Government had followed a hands-off policy towards sterling, accepting a steady decline in its

value. Briefings to this effect from Number 10 are being blamed ...
for encouraging dealers to start selling large volumes of sterling last
week.

The BBC took delivery of the early editions of the Sunday papers soon
after nine o'clock on Saturday night. Which account of the Government's position was to be believed? The Chancellor and his senior
officials could not be contacted. They were all away for the weekend at
Chevening, the Government's country house, planning the next
Budget. (In fact, at that moment, Mr Lawson was down on all fours,
barking: the Treasury men were playing charades; the Chancellor was a
dog.) The BBC's political correspondent rang the Number 10 Press
Office for guidance. The duty officer stuck to the substance of the
Ingham briefing. The *Observer*, he said, was wrong; the others were
broadly right.

Next morning, the Treasury men awoke to hear the BBC announcing that the Government was prepared to let the pound fall as far as the
speculators cared to push it. It was the worst possible news. The Prime
Minister was soon on the telephone. So was the Governor of the Bank
of England. The long-term discussion of Budget strategy had to be
jettisoned in favour of a short-term scramble to shore up the pound.
Government information officers were ordered out of their beds and
into Whitehall to call round financial and political journalists, urging
them to ignore that morning's newspapers. The Bank had to intervene
on the Hong Kong markets that night as the pound lost three cents.
The next morning, Minimum Lending Rate, abandoned in 1981, was
reintroduced and interest rates were hiked by 1.5 per cent to a 'crisis'
rate of 12 per cent. 'I am afraid,' said Lawson in the Commons on
Tuesday, in what was effectively an apology, 'that there was a feeling in
the markets that the Government had lost their willingness and ability
to control their affairs ...'[7]

At a conservative estimate, the episode had cost the country £100
million in foreign reserves. It also had far-reaching political consequences. According to William Keegan: 'The searing effect of the
January sterling crisis was a major influence on Lawson, who now
displayed considerable interest in, and enthusiasm for, the EMS.'[8] Full
entry into the European Monetary System, Lawson concluded, would
lessen the speculative pressure on sterling. He was to pursue this

policy, overtly and covertly, in the teeth of the Prime Minister's opposition, until his resignation in October 1989.

What, meanwhile, had happened to the author of this débâcle? The answer was: nothing. On the Monday, he was summoned to see Lawson and senior Treasury officials. But by then the Prime Minister had let it be known that no blame should attach to 'my Bernard'. Once again, she held the press, not her Press Secretary, to be at fault. The deflated Lawson could only express the hope that Ingham would guard his tongue in future.

Had the error been made by anyone else, especially a minister, she would surely have turned the flame-thrower of her wrath fully upon them. There might even have been a non-attributable briefing to indicate the degree of her fury. But Ingham was different. She went out of her way to ensure that everyone knew he was still in favour. At a party full of political journalists, held in the Commons a few days later, she insisted on parading him round, ludicrously introducing him to people he already knew: 'Have you met Bernard? Bernard's marvellous. Isn't he marvellous? He's great. He's the *greatest*.' Naturally, when word of this special attention spread around Whitehall, as she intended it would, it served only to heighten his reputation. What might have finished the career of another official became, for Ingham, a fresh demonstration of his power.

By this time Ingham was taking an increasingly conservative view of the media and society. He had even come to subscribe to that hoary right-wing theory that the decline of national standards had set in with *That Was The Week That Was* – apparently forgetful that at the time of the 1960s 'satire boom' he was himself describing the Prime Minister as 'Sir Alec Strangelove', a bomb-happy 'political fossil'. In March, two months after the sterling crisis, he addressed the International Press Institute in the spirit, he said, of a 'candid friend':

> I believe that the Watergate syndrome, combined with the broadcasters' 'confrontation' approach to interviews and the determination to take the mickey out of authority, starting with *That Was The Week That Was*, seems to require that any self-respecting reporter should knock seven bells out of symbols of authority, and especially Government. This goes beyond the normal and expected tension between Government and press. Its effect on our democracy is, in my view,

corrosive . . . I can assure you that, working in the Government service, I find the reverence for fact and truth and balance more akin to that which was inculcated into me as a 16-year-old junior reporter on a West Riding weekly than I do in my close observation of quite a lot of contemporary journalism.

He accused many journalists of being conspiracy theorists, of over-simplifying, 'of laziness, laxness, or arrogance, or a combination of these'.

Can you honestly say that British journalism, even acknowledging its right to take a particular political standpoint, strives to be fair? Of course you can't. And the reason you can't is that it doesn't strike me any more that there is a driving compulsion to be fair.

This particular point, unfortunately, was not one which he developed to its logical conclusion. For the overwhelming beneficiary of any political bias and unfairness in the British press was, of course, his own employer. In 1990, Ingham was challenged on this point by Mark Lawson in a profile in the *Independent Magazine*:

LAWSON: When the *Sun* runs a story, as it does, which may or may not have come out of your briefings: MARVELLOUS MAGGIE SAVES THE WORLD. By the terms you've set out, that's bad journalism but, in terms of the Government, it does a lot of good . . .
INGHAM: But what about the *Mirror* ignoring it totally . . . ?
LAWSON: Yes, but that *Sun* story. They'd never give the other side. Is that bad journalism?
INGHAM: Well, the short answer is, I don't know because I haven't got the facts . . .[9]

In truth, the self-appointed scourge of the media was always curiously selective about where he applied the lash. Most of the sins which Ingham detected in the British media – invention, distortion, misquotation, wilful refusal to check facts, persistent failure to apologize, bias in news coverage – found their ultimate refinement in the *Sun*. With a readership of over 12 million, one in four of the adult population, it was the journalistic phenomenon of the Thatcher age. Yet he never mentioned it in his strictures – presumably because it was not guilty of the only sin which really mattered: it did not believe the Government to be 'chronically up to no good'.

In November 1985, he returned to the attack, this time in a lecture to the Media Society. He confessed to a 'liking for journalists in ones or twos – as distinct from the wolf pack', but he diagnosed 'four debilitating afflictions' which had gripped the profession. These were 'the le Carré Syndrome', sufferers of which believed the Government was 'not to be trusted and conspiratorial'; the 'Conan Doyle complication' in which deduction was carried 'to such excesses that two and two became twenty-two'; 'columnar pox, a social contagion particularly affecting diarists'; and, finally, the 'Coleman or Carpenter phenomenon ... which produces in reporters an inability to report just facts; only their own commentary on those facts will do'.

As it happened, by the time he came to deliver this diagnosis, the Government was already in the foothills of a crisis which would give the le Carrés and the Conan Doyles, the pox-ridden columnists and the Colemans and Carpenters plenty more to write about.

Ingham's involvement in what became known as the Westland affair turned him into a household name. Before it, he could still plausibly insist to the Media Society: 'I am not a public figure'; after it, he was one, whether he liked it or not.

He made his first significant contribution on Wednesday 18 December 1985. On that day Mrs Thatcher had assembled her most trusted inner core of advisers, among them Whitelaw, Armstrong and the Chief Whip, John Wakeham, to discuss the developing crisis. The Defence Secretary, Michael Heseltine, was refusing to accept that Britain's sole helicopter manufacturer should be sold to the American company, Sikorsky, as the Prime Minister wished. He had assembled instead a rival bidder – a European consortium of French, German, Italian and British firms – whose claims he was pressing with near-messianic fervour.

Bismarck in his later years is said to have remarked of the Schleswig–Holstein Question of 1863 that only three men ever understood it: Lord Palmerston, and he was dead; a French professor, and he had gone mad; and he, Bismarck – and he had forgotten it. Much the same might be said of the minutiae of the Westland imbroglio. It was, in truth, a battle in which helicopters were merely the weapons. At heart, it was a contest of wills between a Prime Minister accustomed to getting her own way and an ambitious politician who had decided to face her down. Afterwards, when he was asked in private if he regretted his stand, Heseltine always shook his head. He knew, he said, the unforgiving fate which would have awaited him had he backed down: a couple of years' banishment as Northern Ireland Secretary, accompanied by a steady drip of non-attributable briefings from Number 10 about his 'lack of judgement', followed by a well-trailed return to the back-benches. He had seen the way 'they' operated. No, thank you: he preferred to go down fighting.

In the process, the Government was turned into a shambles. In public, Heseltine was repeatedly contradicting the Prime Minister's agent, the wretched Trade and Industry Secretary, Leon Brittan. In private, he was briefing friendly reporters, protesting at the cancellation of Cabinet committee meetings, accusing Armstrong of writing misleading Cabinet minutes, and – on the very afternoon that Thatcher and her advisers met – giving secret testimony about his 'European option' to the Commons Select Committee on Defence.

The Prime Minister's group discussed the problem for several hours. She wanted to send Heseltine a letter setting out strict rules about how much he could say on Westland, to which he would have to assent in writing. According to the fullest account of the affair (*Not With Honour*, by Magnus Linklater and David Leigh, published in 1986), three different drafts were prepared and discussed. Eventually, Ingham was called in and asked his opinion. For once, he counselled caution. Heseltine might use such an ultimatum as a pretext to resign. The Prime Minister already had a politically damaging reputation for high-handedness. Another dissident ex-minister on the back-benches, especially one of Heseltine's calibre, was the last thing she needed. He advised against sending any letter. Coming from anyone else, this might have sounded to the Prime Minister's ears like cowardice; from the man whose usual motto was 'screw the buggers' it carried special weight. No letter was sent. Heseltine would have to be contained by other methods. It was, with hindsight, a serious mistake.

Three days later, on Saturday 21 December, Ingham learned that both Brittan and Heseltine would be appearing on the lunchtime radio programme, *The World This Weekend* – exactly the sort of open clash the Government needed to avoid. He rang Heseltine at his home in Oxfordshire and asked him to decline the BBC's invitation. Heseltine said he would, but only if Ingham also prevented Brittan appearing. However, Brittan's contribution had been recorded already. When the Defence Secretary duly arrived at the BBC's studio in Oxford on Sunday morning, he was told that Downing Street had been putting pressure on the Corporation to drop Brittan's interview. The BBC refused. Even as Heseltine prepared to speak, another call came through from Number 10, presumably from Ingham. Heseltine declined to take it. Both interviews were broadcast.

Such incidents convinced the Prime Minister that tougher tactics were required. On Friday 3 January 1986, Heseltine inadvertently provided her with an opportunity when he wrote and allowed to be published a letter to his friends in the European consortium. Poring over it that afternoon, Mrs Thatcher and her advisers spotted what they believed was an error. She instructed Brittan to contact the Solicitor-General, Sir Patrick Mayhew, and seek his opinion. This Brittan did the following day. Heseltine's letter had been published in that morning's *Times* and Mayhew, having studied it, agreed that at first glance part of it looked questionable. Brittan reported this view back to Number 10. Charles Powell, one of Mrs Thatcher's private secretaries, then contacted Mayhew's office and formally asked, on behalf of the Prime Minister, for the Solicitor-General to put his opinion in writing to Heseltine.

Mayhew completed his letter soon after 11.00 a.m. on Monday 6 January. It was promptly dispatched to the Ministry of Defence, with copies to Number 10 and to the DTI. They arrived at noon. Heseltine, in his words, was 'relaxed' about it. He had reason to be. Mayhew, an old friend, had warned him on Saturday night that a letter would be coming, and in the event it was hardly a damning document. Heseltine's original remarks had implied that *all* the other companies and governments involved in building a European battlefield helicopter would be concerned at a Westland link with Sikorsky; Mayhew required further evidence regarding two firms. His letter therefore concluded:

> On the basis of the information contained in the documents to which I have referred, which I emphasize are all that I have seen, the sentence in your letter to Mr Horne does in my opinion contain material inaccuracies in the respects I have mentioned, and I therefore must advise that you should write again to Mr Horne correcting the inaccuracies.

Heseltine sent the necessary extra information round to Mayhew that afternoon, and the Solicitor-General raised no further objections to the disputed sentence.

But in Number 10 and the DTI, armed with the Solicitor-General's opinion, the 'Get Heseltine' operation swung into action. Powell made one copy of Mayhew's letter and took it down to Ingham in the Press Office – an action which suggests they had already decided it was to be used publicly in some way. He then returned upstairs to take a call from his opposite number at the DTI, Brittan's Private Secretary, John Mogg. Mogg had just spoken to Brittan, who was out at lunch. He had read him the letter over the telephone. The Trade and Industry Secretary was keen to have it leaked, but only, in his words, 'subject to the agreement of Number 10'. This was a prudent precaution to take. As Brittan, an eminent QC, knew very well, advice from the Government's Law Officers was never disclosed. Besides, Mayhew's letter was marked 'Confidential' – 'unauthorized disclosure,' according to the official definition of that term, 'would be prejudicial to the interests of the nation'. Mogg therefore asked Powell if Number 10 would release it. Powell refused. The DTI would have to do its own dirty work.

The focus of activity now shifted to the office downstairs. Ingham, the Solicitor-General's letter in front of him, spoke on the telephone to Colette Bowe, Chief Information Officer at the DTI.

As it happened, there was no great love lost between the two. Bowe, a 39-year-old graduate from Liverpool, was an administrator, not a professional press officer. She pointedly did not attend Ingham's MIOs on Monday afternoons, preferring to send her deputy. She had also enjoyed a good relationship with Heseltine, working on his Merseyside task force. All these factors cast a chill over her dealings with Ingham. 'Quite apart from anything else,' recalled one senior colleague, 'there was a clash of personalities.'

There are two versions of their conversation that afternoon. One – Ingham's – is that Bowe sought his advice and he, foolishly, did not discourage her from leaking the letter. According to Hugo Young, who spoke to him in the course of writing his biography of Mrs Thatcher, Ingham (who years later still retained 'photographic recall of every twist and turn' of the affair) found only one thing with which to reproach himself: 'In the heat of the moment, he had not stated with sufficient firmness to Ms Bowe that she should have nothing to do with such an unorthodox procedure.'[10] The other version is Bowe's: that she was extremely anxious, in the wake of the prosecution of Clive Ponting, not to leak a classified letter, and had to be ordered to do so. The only point on which both agree is that Ingham, like Powell, refused to put the information out personally via Number 10.

There is no tape recording of what was said. So whom do we believe? The circumstantial evidence clearly substantiates Ms Bowe's account, for she had to be pushed and prodded into making the leak. There is no doubt that when she put down the telephone on Ingham, she was a very unhappy woman. She was sufficiently appalled at what she was being asked to do to seek professional advice. Sir Robert Armstrong subsequently confirmed that she had 'misgivings'; that she 'shared her burden'[11] with Mogg in Brittan's private office; that she wanted to follow the procedure set down for civil servants who believe they are being asked to do something 'unlawful' – that is, consult her Principal Personnel Officer and her Permanent Secretary, Sir Brian Hayes, neither of whom was in the building. Unless she underwent some miraculous change of heart while talking to Ingham, it is reasonable to suppose that she would have expressed these doubts to the *primus inter pares* of the Government Information Service. And what did he do? According to 'friends' of Ms Bowe quoted in the press at the time, he told her: 'You'll — well do what you're — well told.' Even if he did not put it in quite such crude terms, he offered naught for her comfort. Bowe, at least, expressed some qualms; he did not. Had he done so, given her well-attested reservations, the Solicitor-General's letter would probably not have been leaked. In other words, it was in his power during that crucial telephone call to put a stop to the whole business – and he did not do it.

The conversation between Ingham and Bowe, according to Armstrong, 'was in part technical as to methods of disclosure and so on'.[12] In the event, the fortunate recipient of the scoop was none other than Ingham's trusty Lobby friend, Chris Moncrieff. 'I was in the PA room at the Commons Press Gallery,' Moncrieff remembered.

At 2.15 p.m. a message came through from the DTI that I was to ring them. I called ... The letter was paraphrased, with just two words given in quotes ... 'material inaccuracies'. I think it was understood that this was unattributable as usual, but it was also something special. I mean, you could tell the nature of what you were getting was rather more important than the stuff Bernard gives you upstairs. It was made clear the information didn't need any checking. So I went off and put it on the tapes straightaway.[13]

Moncrieff's story, that Heseltine had been rebuked by the Government's own law officers, was running on the PA's tapes by 2.53 p.m. It came in time to make the later editions of the London *Evening Standard*. It dominated the following morning's press. 'YOU LIAR!' screamed the *Sun* (a headline for which the paper later had to apologize to Heseltine and pay damages). *The Times*, in more measured language, summed up the general tenor of Fleet Street's coverage: 'Heseltine told by Law Chief: Stick to the facts'.

The Prime Minister subsequently defended the leak on the grounds that the board of Westland was holding a press conference at four o'clock that afternoon: the directors, she claimed, needed to know the legal position regarding Heseltine's letter. Of all the many excuses trotted out in the course of this inglorious affair, this was the most pitiful. A simple telephone call to the board would have sufficed to convey the information. The letter could have been sent round by dispatch rider. But that would not have served Number 10's purpose. The media had to be briefed as they were in order to cause the maximum amount of public damage to Heseltine's credibility. Indeed, it is a misnomer to speak of a 'leaked letter': it was not a letter but two words, taken out of context, which were leaked. It was a smear.

The other question on which much ink has been expended is: how much did Margaret Thatcher know? She was in Downing Street when Mayhew's letter arrived, but Powell assured Armstrong, and Armstrong believed him, that he did not disturb her with it. Instead, he took it down to Ingham. This claim caused much merry cynicism at the time, but in retrospect it has a ring of credibility. To an unusual degree the Prime Minister was willing to leave press matters in Ingham's hands. She had commissioned the Solicitor-General's letter in the first place. She obviously hoped it would damage Heseltine. How that damage was to be inflicted was a matter for her good and faithful servants. There was thus a double layer of insulation surrounding her that Monday night. She was protected by her officials, and her officials were protected by the fact that the leak had originated in the DTI. Nobody in Number 10, it seemed, had any cause to worry.

The following morning, Ingham prepared his usual press summary and, soon after 9 a.m. went upstairs to the Prime Minister's study for the daily meeting. Naturally, his digest was dominated by the leaked law officer's advice. 'In the course of a discussion of business with members of her staff,' Armstrong later reported, 'which was not recorded and at which a considerable number of other matters were discussed, the Prime Minister was told there had been contacts between her office and the DTI. But not in any detail.'[14] The disclosure of Mayhew's confidential advice was obviously fine as far as she was concerned.

Mayhew, however, had been incensed to discover that his letter was chattering out on the club tapes less than four hours after he had written it. He wrote to Heseltine that same night to express his 'dismay' that his letter had been leaked in such a 'highly selective way'.

> Quite apart from the breach of confidentiality that is involved, the rule is very clearly established that even the fact that the Law Officers have tendered advice in a particular case may not be disclosed, let alone the contents of their advice. It is plain that in this instance, this important rule was immediately and flagrantly violated.

It is possible that Ingham had not been fully aware of the consequences of his collusion that Monday afternoon. In 1981, for example, in his private speech to the IBA, he had made it clear that he did indeed consider himself 'licensed to leak':

> I must tell you that I – and I am sure my colleagues – have never regarded the Official Secrets Act as a constraint on my operations. Indeed, I regard myself as licensed to break that law as and when I judge necessary; and I suppose it is necessary to break it every other minute of every working day, though I confess the issue is so academic that I have not bothered to seek counsel's advice.

But the Law Officers – the Solicitor-General and the Attorney-General – were in a position, and a mood, to stamp on such cavalier disregard for the rules. Bernard Ingham, the man who had applauded Sarah Tisdall's jail sentence and who had said he longed for Judge Jeffreys to try Clive Ponting, was about to feel the noose tighten around his own neck.

Mayhew had complained immediately to the Attorney-General, Sir Michael Havers. On Tuesday morning, Havers wrote to Robert Armstrong demanding a full inquiry into the leak. No action was taken. On Wednesday, Havers (in Armstrong's words) 'had some conversation with' the Cabinet Secretary about the progress of the inquiry. Again, no action was taken. Thursday was lost in the maelstrom following Heseltine's dramatic exit from the Cabinet. On Friday the 10th, Havers saw Armstrong personally and made it clear that neither he nor Mayhew was prepared to let the matter drop. Armstrong made one last attempt to dissuade him, at which point a thoroughly exasperated Havers threatened to send the police into Number 10 and the DTI. Armstrong called in Nigel Wicks, Mrs Thatcher's Principal Private Secretary, to hear this ultimatum for himself. The stonewalling could go on no longer. On Monday, a full week after the disclosure, and following three separate approaches from the Attorney-General, Mrs Thatcher gave her reluctant assent to an inquiry. Armstrong would conduct it personally. Copies of his report would go to the Prime Minister, the Attorney-General and the Director of Public Prosecutions.

Armstrong talked privately of 'unrest at the DTI'. Colette Bowe was said to be in a stage of near-mutiny. Her account of events, it was whispered, had been deposited in a bank vault. Clearly, she was not willing to be the scapegoat. Indeed, Armstrong had to ask the Attorney-General to grant her immunity from prosecution in return for her co-operation with his inquiry – something which previously had been given only to two people, one of them the Soviet agent, Sir Anthony Blunt. 'I believed I should be addressing the person who had actually passed the information,' Armstrong said later. 'It was evident that a truthful answer could be an incriminating answer . . . '[15]

Armstrong, accompanied by a Cabinet Office colleague, interviewed Ms Bowe for forty-five minutes at the DTI. Sir Brian Hayes was present; the meeting took place in his office. She asked about the legal position. Armstrong gave her the Attorney-General's assurances. Yet even with immunity guaranteed, she stuck to her version of events: she had not wanted to do it; Ingham had told her to do it. Back in Downing Street, the Cabinet Secretary then interviewed Ingham, who arrived unac-companied. The conversation also lasted about three-quarters of an hour. Ingham, equally, maintained his innocence. Armstrong then tele-phoned Bowe to confront her with this discrepancy. She would not budge. Nor would Ingham. Across this yawning chasm, even the Cabinet Secretary, with all his legendary drafting skills, could apply only the flimsiest of sticking plasters. The conversation between Bowe and Ingham, he concluded limply, was based on a 'misunderstanding'.

In all, Armstrong's inquiry consisted of brief interrogations of five officials (Ingham, Powell, Bowe, Mogg and John Michell, the official in charge of the DTI's air division), and a couple of telephone calls. It could have been wrapped up in an afternoon. Instead, it took him nine days, adding to the impression that Downing Street was in no hurry to discover the truth. The Prime Minister was handed his report on Wednesday 22 January. It had not been her intention to make it public. But Tam Dalyell, that perennial thorn in Ingham's side, had been told by two deeply disillusioned civil servants that Colette Bowe was the official who had leaked the Solicitor-General's letter. That afternoon, he 'named' her in the House of Commons. A horde of reporters immediately descended upon her. 'If you have any questions about leaks,' she told them cryptically, 'you should refer them to 10 Downing Street.' Westminster was fizzing with rumours that the Prime Minister herself would be brought down, Nixon-style, by her knowledge of her subordinates' wrongdoing. Mrs Thatcher had no choice but to agree to make a statement on the leak the next day.

It was an immensely delicate situation. None of the officials involved would be liable to prosecution under the Official Secrets Act if the leak had been authorized by a minister. It had: by Brittan. But Brittan, his political life at stake, was insisting that he had explicitly requested the prior authority of Number 10. Naturally, the Prime Minister had to be protected from any suggestion that she had connived at the leak. On the other hand, she could hardly expect Ingham and Powell to destroy their careers by confessing they had acted without her approval.

Narrowly, the Prime Minister survived. She did so by denying prior knowledge of the leak but throwing her protective mantle, retrospectively, around the actions of her officials. Ingham and Powell, she said, had 'considered – and they were right – that I should agree with my Rt. Hon. friend the Secretary of State for Trade and Industry that the [Mayhew letter] should become public knowledge as soon as possible.' Her only regret was the method. 'Had I been consulted, I should have said that a different way must be found of making the facts known.'[16] Brittan's position was now rendered intolerable; he resigned the next day. On Monday 27 January, Conservative MPs closed ranks behind Mrs Thatcher, and she survived an emergency debate in the Commons. Her story – 'stranger than fiction,' she called it – although shaky in places, just about held together. For her, the worst was past.

For Ingham, however, the moment of maximum danger was only just approaching. With Brittan gone and the Prime Minister apparently safe, he was the next most obvious target. Only a few months earlier, he had accused journalists of falling for the 'Watergate syndrome'. Now, there were plenty who believed Westland was the British Watergate, and who wanted to cast Ingham in the role of H. R. Haldeman. The House of Commons Select Committee on Defence had set up its own inquiry into the affair. It decided to 'invite' the five key officials involved in the leak to testify. This threw the Government into a fresh panic, for it was technically within the Committee's power to summon witnesses and have them imprisoned if they refused to appear. Once again, the Prime Minister turned to Armstrong. On 4 February, flown back specially from a pre-summit meeting in Honolulu, he wrote to the Committee:

> All five of these officials gave a full account of their role in these matters to me in the course of my recent inquiry, and co-operated fully in my investigation. The PM and the Secretary of State, DTI, believe that your Committee will recognize and share their view that it would be neither fair nor reasonable to expect these officials to submit to a second round of detailed questioning, of the kind that would be involved in giving evidence to your Committee.
>
> With the PM's agreement, I am writing to you to say that, if the Committee believed it would be helpful, I should be ready to accept an invitation . . .

This offer was not as generous as it appeared. There was no means by which the Committee could make an independent appraisal of the truth. All the facts were to be filtered through Armstrong, and he had already reached his own conclusions based upon them. It was the shadow, not the substance of open government.

Realizing the danger, the Committee's deputy chairman, the Labour MP, John Gilbert, proposed that they should turn down Armstrong's offer. He was outvoted by the Conservative majority. The next day, Armstrong appeared, complete with bodyguard and red dispatch box, the key to which hung from a large chain attached to his belt. The Keeper of the State's Secrets gave a bravura performance, turning away the wrath of the Committee with soft words which, in his mouth, never quite added up to 'giving permission': Downing Street, he averred, had given 'cover' but not 'covering authority' for the leak, a distinction which he held to be of the utmost significance. Powell and Ingham 'accepted, or they acquiesced in, or they did not object to – whatever phrase of that kind you like to use – that the DTI were going to make the disclosure'.[17] Afterwards, the Committee's bemused members agreed among themselves a compromise. They would drop their demands to see four of the officials. But they still wanted to see the Prime Minister's Chief Press Secretary.

Ingham's own mood, according to his colleagues, veered at this time between despondency and rage. He refused to talk to anyone about what had happened. 'He was going around muttering and swearing,' recalled one. 'He could not believe that he had been let down so badly by Colette Bowe.' By an exquisite stroke of bad timing, on the day that Armstrong gave his evidence to the Defence Select Committee, Ingham was due to give an evening lecture to the Worshipful Company of Stationers and Newspaper Makers, an invitation he had accepted six months earlier. He arrived at Stationers' Hall, in Ave Maria Lane in the City, to find it packed with reporters and camera crews. His response was to duck back outside and walk around in the snow until it was time for his lecture to start. Eventually, his anxious host, Ray Tindle, spotted him by the door. 'I've got him!' shouted Tindle as he steered Ingham to the podium.

There is a famous scene in *Scoop*, in which Lord Copper, at the outset of a prepared speech, suddenly realizes it to be disastrously inappropriate: glancing through it, it seems to him like 'a new form of driving test, by which the applicant for a licence sat in a stationary car while a cinema film unfolded before his eyes a nightmare drive down a road full of obstacles'. Ingham might have been forgiven similar emotions as he studied his own text – 'The Reporter: An Endangered Species' – which had been composed in calmer times. Here he was, off again, for the third time in eleven months, accusing the British media (half of which appeared to be present) of

> a cavalier approach to facts especially if inconvenient . . . a readiness to make deductions which are as creative in their approach to logic as some accounting is to sound finance . . . an excess of malice . . . insinuation – the branding iron of contemporary journalism . . .

All that most reporters really wanted was to write a story 'based on a document marked "Secret" . . . The occupational hazard of the public figure today is not to be misreported; it is to be misrepresented by interpretation' – to which Sir Patrick Mayhew and Mr Michael Heseltine would no doubt have said a loud 'Hear, hear!'

'Our democracy,' he concluded, 'needs lively, determined and scrupulous reporters.'

As he stepped down from the lectern, several members of the 'endangered species' crowded round him. 'Feel better now?' asked one. 'I didn't come here to be followed around by TV cameras and journalists,' snapped Ingham. He spent the remainder of the evening, as viewers of *News at Ten* later witnessed, dodging out of sight every time a camera appeared.

The face of this supposedly anonymous civil servant was now in newspapers and on television screens across the world. If nothing else, his new-found fame suddenly meant he started hearing from people he had lost touch with decades ago:

> Like Dr Jim Wilde, the first head boy of Calder High School, in Victoria BC; School principal Sheila Lever, in Oamaru, New Zealand; peripatetic teacher Rita Cherry, last heard of in darkest Khartoum; Brian Sutcliffe, Rolls-Royce representative in Rio; Stella Moss (and Jim Gibson) in Mississauga, Ontario ... The most touching communication I have ever received came during the Westland affair. A woman identifying herself as Betty Broadbent, who said she had taught me *Julius Caesar*, rang my wife when I was away to say that she hoped she could claim to be a part of my success. Nancy said this was the nicest thing anyone had said about me for weeks ...

'The black clouds of infamy,' he observed four years later, 'have their silver linings.'[18]

The following day, the Commons Defence Committee renewed its attempts to summon Ingham. The Committee's Conservative Chairman, Sir Humphrey Atkins, spoke to the Government Chief Whip, John Wakeham. 'Ingham won't accept an invitation,' Wakeham told him. 'However you do have the power to make Ingham come, and we won't block you.' But, he added: 'When you bring Ingham he will simply refuse to speak.'

Had the Defence Committee decided to press ahead at this point, the career of the Prime Minister's Chief Press Secretary would probably have been at end. The House of Commons is very particular about its rights; Atkins could have appeared before it and urged a vote requiring Ingham to attend, on pain of imprisonment; the Government, according to Wakeham, would not have imposed a three-line whip to stop him; the Committee would probably have mustered a majority. Then Ingham would have appeared and, to every question, as he was entitled, refused an answer. But such a spectacle, broadcast into every home in the country, would have had a devastating effect on his reputation. 'In my present job,' Ingham was fond of saying, 'I rely on one quality: credibility.' Where would his credibility have been by the time the Committee had finished with him? If he had done nothing wrong, why did he not speak? More to the point, if the Prime Minister had done nothing wrong, why did she not encourage him to say so?

It was this latter consideration which saved him. The Conservative members of the Committee were under intense pressure from their colleagues to put an end to the Westland affair. Summoning Ingham would have guaranteed it fresh life. Atkins led the retreat. He returned from his conversation with Wakeham and made a passionate appeal. 'What are you after?' he pleaded. 'Are you just trying to have somebody destroyed?'[19] The Committee backed down, saving its face by recalling Armstrong, who had again offered to answer for the civil service.

It was over. In April, Tam Dalyell initiated a second Commons debate on Ingham: no mere Press Secretary, he insisted, but 'a man who is an adviser on central decisions of Government in Britain, and whose power has grown exponentially, along a geometric progression, with the years during which he has occupied the office'; he was, 'with the arguable exception of Sir Robert Armstrong . . . the most important man making decisions in British politics'. Richard Luce, the minister responsible for the Civil Service, accused Dalyell of giving vent to 'obsessions'. Ingham was doing 'an excellent job', serving the Government 'professionally and with integrity'. The issue of Westland was 'worn to a frazzle'.[20] Whenever Thatcher was questioned about it in the future, she simply referred to the statements she had made at the time and declared that she had nothing to add.

Ingham had been lucky to survive. Just how lucky was revealed three years later, at the beginning of 1989, when Leon Brittan broke his long silence on the affair. In a television interview he stated that the leak 'was approved by Mr Charles Powell, the relevant Private Secretary at Number 10, and it was approved by Mr Bernard Ingham, the Prime Minister's Press Secretary . . . there would have been no question of the leaking of that document without that express approval from Number 10.'

This was the equivalent of one of the conspirators returning to the scene of the crime and depositing the smoking gun. Had Brittan made such an allegation at the time, Armstrong's defence – that the whole affair was based on a misunderstanding between Downing Street and the DTI 'as to exactly what was sought and what was being given' – would have dropped to bits. As it was, the nearest Ingham came to an official reprimand was in the report of the Commons Defence Committee, published that summer. 'The disclosure of the Solicitor-General's letter without his permission was an improper act,' concluded the MPs. 'Yet we understand from Sir Robert Armstrong's evidence that no disciplinary action is to be taken against any of the officials concerned. We find this extraordinary.'[21]

That Ingham had done wrong, there is no question. To what extent precisely, we do not know, and probably never shall. The worst case is that he helped arrange a smear against a Government minister, then bullied a troubled colleague into breaking the Official Secrets Act with the intention of hiding behind her skirts in the event of trouble; the best is that he turned a blind eye to a notably shabby piece of political chicanery – even the Prime Minister later said she 'regretted' the way the leak was sprung.

It did Ingham damage because he had always been so pious about his own standards and those of the Government, contrasting them with the debased behaviour of the British press. If no other good came out of Westland, it did at least put a stop to Ingham's sermons on the media for the next four years. This was a special relief to those who believed that neither press nor politician was in much of a position to damn the other's morality. After Westland, political reporters could say to Ingham, rather as Michael Corleone says to the corrupt senator in *The Godfather*: 'We are both part of the same hypocrisy.'

The affair had one other significant side-effect, in that it strengthened the Prime Minister's relationship with her new Private Secretary, Charles Powell, a 44-year-old diplomat, theoretically on a short-term attachment to Number 10. Her response to the attacks on his integrity was almost maternal in its protectiveness. Powell – whose capacity for work surpassed even Ingham's – now firmly established himself as her undisputed favourite. He worked not twelve but sixteen hours a day. Strictly speaking, Powell was merely one of three civil servants in Mrs Thatcher's Private Office, working to her Principal Private Secretary, Nigel Wicks. But gradually, from assisting the Prime Minister exclusively on foreign affairs, he widened his brief to embrace matters of domestic policy. Mrs Thatcher also struck up an equally warm relationship with his Italian wife, Carla. They would gossip on the telephone. They would joke about Charles. Mrs Powell would give her advice on which clothes to buy ... These were services which Ingham could not hope to render. Gradually, almost imperceptibly, he began to be nudged out.

But all this was not to become apparent until several years after Westland. In 1986, his relationship with the Prime Minister was as strong as ever. One by one, the principal actors in the story of the leak left the stage – John Mogg was transferred out of the Secretary of State's office to other duties, Colette Bowe left the Government Information Service to work for the Independent Broadcasting Authority, Robert Armstrong retired, Leon Brittan departed for Brussels – until only the central trio was left: Bernard Ingham, Charles Powell and Margaret Thatcher. They stayed together at the heart of the Government, bound by loyalties no outsider could penetrate.

NINE

The New Machiavelli

'From this arises the following question: whether it is better to be loved than feared, or the reverse. The answer is that one would like to be both the one and the other; but because it is difficult to combine them, it is far better to be feared than loved ... Men worry less about doing an injury to one who makes himself loved than to one who makes himself feared.'

Niccolo Machiavelli, *The Prince*, 1541

'We need a new version of Machiavelli's *The Prince* to explain the way in which the Lobby has been used by Number 10 ...'

Sir John Nott 1987[1]

Only three people had the privilege of meeting the Lobby and briefing them about the whole range of Government activities: the Prime Minister's Press Secretary, who saw them twice a day; the Leader of the House of Lords, who saw them every Friday morning; and the Leader of the House of Commons, who saw them on Thursday afternoons.

Ingham regarded the encroachment of these two ministers on to his territory as a tiresome distraction. Their briefings were yet two more opportunities for cock-ups: two more occasions when the Government might be caught out speaking with more than one voice. He began sending along members of the Number 10 Press Office, who would sit at the back, taking notes. This served two purposes. It alerted Ingham to any deviations from the authorized version of Government policy, as emanating from Downing Street; and it deterred the ministers concerned from making disloyal remarks. Anything they said would be taken down and would, most assuredly, be used in evidence against them.

At the beginning of 1986, the Leader of the House of Lords was William Whitelaw: co-ordinator of Government presentation, Deputy Prime Minister, and one of Mrs Thatcher's most trusted lieutenants. He might occasionally sympathize with ministerial dissidents; he might have his doubts about the Government's economic policies; but in the end he would always back the Prime Minister – a characteristic which had earned him, from some of his colleagues, the nickname 'the Devious Squire'. For Ingham, he was no problem. But Whitelaw's opposite number in the Commons, John Biffen, was a different matter.

Biffen was Thatcher's third Leader of the House since 1979. All three had posed difficulties. All three were to meet sticky ends. And all three were to have reason to blame Ingham for their misfortunes. The first, Norman St John Stevas, was sacked in 1981, and Ingham helped encourage the belief that he was dismissed for leaking details of Cabinet discussions. In Stevas's place came Francis Pym, the arch-wet whom Ingham dismissed as a notorious pessimist. When Lord Carrington resigned at the outset of the Falklands crisis, Pym had to be given the Foreign Office to balance the Cabinet. (He was to last in that position a mere fourteen months before his career, too, was terminated.) Pym's replacement as Leader of the House was John Biffen.

Biffen was no wet. He was a Thatcherite at a time when, in his words, 'Thatcher was closing grammar schools' and Ingham was writing about the wickedness of capitalism. But he had a thoughtful, original mind which made him difficult to categorize. He was, for example, the only Cabinet minister to oppose the sending of the Falklands task force and, later in the conflict, to defend the BBC against charges of 'treachery' from the Tory right – neither of which, given Ingham's gung-ho attitude, can have endeared him to the Chief Press Secretary. From the start, their relations were marked by a strictly professional coolness. 'Ours was never a relaxed and easy partnership,' said Biffen.

The Leader of the House had not been long in his new position when his staff told him that Ingham wanted to see him. 'He came over to the Commons,' recalled Biffen, 'and it was quite clear that he felt he had got a problem: that he had already had to put up with Stevas and Pym and now he had got me. He made it very clear that it was his job to present Government policy, as seen through the Prime Minister's eyes, and that the rest of us were all partially sighted. I was courteous, but made it clear I was not prepared to put up with this. From that time onwards, I felt no warmth towards him.'

Ever since Herbert Morrison first developed the practice in 1945, the Leader of the House has given his briefings at 4.30 on Thursday afternoons, after he has announced to MPs the Government's business for the coming week. Different Leaders have handled these occasions in different ways. Biffen gave careful thought to his own approach and decided that, rather than concentrate on detail, he would talk about the broad philosophical background to Government decisions. Surprisingly, the Lobby rather enjoyed these sessions. One reason was that Biffen, unlike Ingham, actually liked journalists. He was taken aback by the Yorkshireman's detestation of the Fourth Estate: 'His language was lurid. He really did treat them like shit. They were all up to no good as far as he was concerned. There wasn't one he wouldn't have suspected of being a child molester or of selling his grandmother into white slavery.' Biffen thought that such 'obvious contempt' for journalists was unwise, and that Ingham's instinctively hostile reaction to certain individuals was 'not always well-founded'.

It was slightly unfortunate, then, that in February 1983 it fell to Biffen to defend Ingham in the House of Commons against Tam Dalyell's attack. In addition to the absence of 'warmth' between him and Ingham, Dalyell was an old friend (indeed, as a student, the Labour MP had been a Tory, and Biffen had backed him, successfully, for the chairmanship of the Cambridge University Conservative Association). It was not that Biffen did not defend Ingham; he did. But somehow, compared to Dalyell's invective (a 'thug', he called Ingham, a 'truculent, arrogant bully'), his reply seemed flat and passionless. The best he could manage was 'to endorse and support what the Prime Minister said about Mr Bernard Ingham'. He even praised Dalyell for a 'fascinating' if 'controversial' speech and commended him as 'an engaging and resolute campaigner'.

On the whole, Biffen gave the impression that he regarded the affair as a slightly dotty occasion, which should not come between men of good sense. His murderous little joke about a 'rough-spoken Yorkshire Rasputin' – a description which stuck long after Dalyell's taunts had been forgotten – can hardly have endeared him to Ingham. Nor can his curiously ambivalent conclusion, that the Press Secretary should not be attacked too much because he 'may well have a future career outside the Civil Service'.[2] What species of weasel's words were these?

Biffen had been obliged to stay up all night, waiting to defend Ingham's reputation. He might have expected a note of thanks, or at least a telephone call. There was nothing. 'He felt no gratitude for what I'd done,' recalled Biffen. 'He may have thought I was too laid back in my remarks because I was an old friend of Tam.'

Nevertheless, the two managed to rub along for the next three years. Then came Westland, followed by a series of political setbacks. Unemployment began to rise again. The Cabinet was forced, under pressure from the back-benches, to drop plans to sell Land Rover to an American firm. Mrs Thatcher insisted, despite the misgivings of several ministers (including Biffen) that US planes should be allowed to bomb Libya from British bases. Her popularity hit an all-time low. Finally, on 8 May 1986, the Government had two bad by-election results. On Sunday, 11 May, Biffen gave an interview to *Weekend World* in which he boldly addressed the Prime Minister's alleged shortcomings. 'To assume that because a party has one dominant figure it thereby benefits is not necessarily true at all,' he asserted. Was he implying that Mrs Thatcher had liabilities? 'Oh yes, yes of course, that goes without saying.' He proposed that the Conservatives should fight the next election with a 'balanced ticket', giving due prominence to the more emollient aspects of Toryism – after all, 'nobody seriously supposes that the Prime Minister would be Prime Minister throughout the entire period of the next Parliament'.

Unfortunately for Biffen, that was exactly what Mrs Thatcher did 'seriously suppose'. She had a formula for these occasions. When a minister or civil servant displeased her, she would sweetly inquire of her intimates: 'Shall we withdraw our love?' That was precisely what she did. Few politicians have had Prime Ministerial affection whipped out from under them quite as quickly as John Biffen. She never said a word to him herself. On Monday morning he was given a dressing-down by Whitelaw. Then, late that afternoon, Lobby journalists began coming up to him. Had he heard what Bernard was saying about him? He had not, but the next morning it was there for all the world to read. According to the *Guardian*:

> His criticism ... last night provoked a fiery counter-offensive in which he was described as a 'semi-detached member of the Government' whose views were of little consequence in its thinking ... If Mr Biffen's intention was to irritate his leader, he appears to have succeeded. The scornful tone of the responses in official quarters was unmistakable. His remarks 'did not have to be taken seriously' and he was not 'fully integrated' into the Government...[3]

In *The Times*:

> The sources said that . . . Mr Biffen was a 'semi-detached' member of
> the Cabinet . . .

In the *Financial Times*:

> Mr John Biffen . . . was yesterday being authoritatively described as 'a
> well-known semi-detached member of the Government'.

The phrase was everywhere. 'Axe threat as Biffen gets biffing' was the
headline in the *Sun*:

> In an unprecedented bid to discredit Mr Biffen, Downing Street
> sources made it clear Mrs Thatcher 'did not give two hoots' for his
> views.
>   Others close to the Premier called Mr Biffen a 'semi-detached
> member of the Government'.
>   They said Mrs Thatcher 'sometimes has to pinch herself to realise
> he is a member of the Government'.
>   Significantly, no attempt was made to deny that Mr Biffen could be
> the victim of her looming reshuffle.

'As far as the Premier is concerned,' reported the *Daily Mail*, 'he is in the
doghouse.' In the *Daily Mirror*: 'She let it be known that in her view he is
liable to think something different every week – and what he says doesn't
matter anyway.' The British press had wheeled on Biffen with the
mechanized precision of a Busby Berkeley chorus line.

As with the Mona Lott episode four years earlier, what was striking
was the contrast between the words used non-attributably by Ingham and
those uttered publicly by Mrs Thatcher. At Prime Minister's Questions
on the day the 'semi-detached' stories appeared, she told the Commons
that Biffen had 'made many robust policy points on Sunday with which I
wholly agree'. It was this which the errant minister found most extraordinary. She scarcely spoke to him again from that day onwards. Certainly, she never once confronted him directly about what had upset her.
Instead, she had him murdered out of the corner of somebody else's
mouth – quietly, in the dark, away from public gaze. He never held it
against Ingham (in his lighter moments, he even acknowledged that
'semi-detached' was 'quite a good phrase') because he was convinced
that 'Ingham had not exceeded his responsibilities: he did it because the

Prime Minister wanted to make it perfectly clear she had withdrawn support from me, but couldn't yet drop me.' And so Biffen was left to twist in the wind for another year, before eventually being cut down and deposited on the back-benches two days after the 1987 General Election.

The analogy with the gibbet is not altogether misplaced. Dangling there, without the support of Number 10, Biffen was an awful warning to his colleagues of the penalty for lese-majesty. Observing the method of his dispatch, it was not surprising that many of his colleagues began inspecting the press with the care of Kremlinologists. 'They've become neurotic about it,' according to Viscount Whitelaw, 'and they all think it's Bernard all the time . . . A lot of ministers feel – people who've left the Government or resigned – that before the time came for the reshuffle, Bernard had been working against them to prepare the ground for it.' Several ministers, perceiving themselves to be under threat, took their worries to Whitelaw and asked him to intercede with Ingham on their behalf. During their Thursday morning 'gossips', the Deputy Prime Minister thus found himself asking the Chief Press Officer: 'Oh, Bernard, are you sure you're right about that?' He had to be careful in his approach, for this, as he later acknowledged, was 'touchy ground even for me'.

The briefings in which ministers were mentioned tend to divide into two sorts. There were the premeditated, set-piece denigrations, of which Pym's and Biffen's were the most obvious examples. These were almost certainly performed on the Prime Minister's explicit instructions: in another of Biffen's memorable metaphors, Ingham, on these occasions, was 'the sewer rather than the sewage'.[4] Then there were the less dramatic pieces of guidance: the hints, the pauses, the raised eyebrows, the supportive remark which was conspicuous by its absence. The message was not always negative. Sometimes, he would even go out of his way to praise a minister. Kind words about John Major, for example, were commonplace when he was Chief Secretary to the Treasury. The basis for this 'mood music', by which the Lobby judged who was on his way up and who was on his way out, were the Prime Minister's own private remarks, which Ingham would slip into briefings as he saw fit.

Patrick Jenkin, dropped from the Department of the Environment in 1985, was one Cabinet Minister who complained privately to his staff about Ingham. Another was John Moore, who cautioned his aides to remember that 'Bernard's first loyalty is to the Prime Minister, not to us'.

A third was the Conservative Party Chairman, Norman Tebbit. During the 'semi-detached' briefing about John Biffen, Ingham had taken the opportunity to refer to Tebbit as 'fully integrated'. Nevertheless, stories about the poor relations between the Prime Minister and her Party Chairman continued to circulate, and Tebbit became convinced Number 10 was behind them. Two months later, towards the end of July, he went stalking into Downing Street with a folder full of 'dozens' of hostile press cuttings. In his own, carefully-chosen words, they:

> must have resulted from regular press briefings by someone whose position give him credibility with the Lobby ... I realised that if Margaret had been previously unaware of the stories she would not have briefed Bernard Ingham ... to refute them; and his lack of comment must have added credibility to them.[5]

What was the truth behind this curious episode? Certainly, Margaret Thatcher was suspicious of Tebbit. She felt he had wavered over Westland and was plotting a future which did not include her. They had had a row about the US bombing of Libya. She was dubious about his managerial skills as Party Chairman. In the usual way, Ingham appears simply to have picked up these vibrations and transmitted them to the Lobby. Stephen Sherbourne, the Prime Minister's political adviser, took possession of Tebbit's cuttings file and passed on word of the Chairman's unhappiness. According to Tebbit:

> Her response next day was swift and the briefing coming out of Number 10 was that the stream of stories was baseless and the Chairman and Prime Minister were at one.[6]

He left the Government the following year.

Stevas, Pym, Heseltine, Biffen, Jenkin, Moore, Tebbit and, later, Howe ... 'We need a new edition of Machiavelli's *The Prince*,' said Sir John Nott in 1987, 'to explain the way in which the Lobby has been used by Number 10 to raise the cult of personality so far as the Prime Minister is concerned, at the expense of colleagues who have happened to disagree at the time.' Edward Heath claimed the Government 'uses the Press Office in Number 10 in a way that can be described as corrupt', going 'far beyond the achievements, even the aspirations, of any previous government'.[7] In John Biffen's view, too, Margaret Thatcher's use of the Lobby has been an essential tool of her style of statecraft:

First of all, she wanted a good cadre of people around her, like John Hoskyns [first head of the Number 10 Policy Unit] and Alan Walters [her economic adviser], to enable her to challenge the big departments, the Foreign Office and the Treasury. But particularly she used the Number 10 Press Office with tremendous effect, to put across the line that Governments must be united and Governments are spoken for by the Prime Minister. She has centralized, presidential powers – much more presidential than anything you'll find in North America – powers which had always been there, but had simply lain dormant.

Thatcher, through Ingham, had turned the doctrine of collective responsibility inside out. In the past, the rule which Prime Ministers had insisted upon was that the Cabinet could argue strenuously in private, but that in public a united front must be presented. Mrs Thatcher used the Lobby system in precisely the opposite way: Cabinet discussions were kept to a minimum, whilst she reserved the right to make public her disagreements with her own ministers.

Thus, it was implied, Stevas was a leaker, Pym a moaner, Heseltine a liar, Biffen unreliable, Jenkin hopeless, Moore disappointing, Tebbit distrusted, Howe dispensable. And these judgements came not from the Prime Minister's personal, political agent, whispering to individual reporters; they were the official pronouncements of the Civil Service spokesman for the entire Government, in twice-daily contact with the Parliamentary Lobby. Short of marching in to Number 10, like Tebbit, there was nothing much the minister concerned could do, for, technically, the briefing never took place. Even if an aggrieved minister did confront her, she could deny any involvement. In 1981, when James Prior tackled her about these 'leaks' from Number 10, she protested her innocence.

'Oh no, Jim, I never leak.'

'Well, if you tell me that I must accept it, but in that case your officials and press people certainly leak for you.'

'Oh, that is quite wrong: they never know anything, so how could they leak?'

As Prior commented: 'Either she was incredibly naïve, which I have no reason to believe, or she thought I was, and I frankly doubt that. I believe she really didn't think in terms of "leaks" herself at all – if she said it, then it had to be right: how could there be any question of a leak?"[8]

The essence of the game was deniability. If Ingham's briefings had been on the record, none of these attacks on Cabinet ministers would have taken place. Even Margaret Thatcher could not have been seen openly to attack her colleagues in such a fashion: she was, after all, in the words of that increasingly threadbare maxim, only the first among equals.

The realization of what was happening prompted a degree of soul-searching among some journalists who, hitherto, had gone along with the need for a Lobby system. Were they not, in a sense, the tools by which Number 10 was extending its power? One of Ingham's favourite examples of media irresponsibility was the way in which the mere presence of television cameras could incite a riot, stimulating lawlessness 'simply by screening it night after night'.[9] Did the analogy not hold good at Westminster as well? Did the existence of the Lobby not create news which otherwise would not have happened? In that case, Lobby journalists were no better than Ingham's dangerously corrupting TV cameramen: they had ceased merely to record events and become central players. In the summer of 1986, these questions had become so insistent that Ingham found himself facing an unexpected crisis. The Lobby system, the very basis upon which his office was built, began to collapse, partly under the strain he was imposing on it.

One morning in July, at the end of one of Ingham's eleven o'clock briefings, Anthony Bevins, political correspondent of *The Times*, asked if he could have a private word with the Chief Press Secretary. Bevins was one of the most assiduous Lobby journalists, forever poring over Government documents and ministerial statements, alert for discrepancies; always first on his feet at a press conference with a hostile question. He and Ingham had had a difficult relationship. Bevins was due to leave *The Times* shortly to become political editor on the soon-to-be-launched *Independent*. Its editor, Andreas Whittam Smith, wanted to make a gesture which would signal that his paper's name really meant what it said. Could they, he asked Bevins, pull out of the Lobby? Bevins was enthusiastic and it was this decision which he was staying behind to impart to Ingham.

Ingham, Bevins recalled, was 'absolutely incensed'. He went bright red. He called the idea 'silly' and 'childish'. This only made Bevins more determined. He wrote to the editors of the *Observer* and the *Guardian*,

Donald Trelford and Peter Preston, telling them of the *Independent*'s plan and asking if they would care to join a boycott of the Lobby. Both gave non-committal replies. In truth, the *Independent*'s action posed more of a problem for the *Guardian*, which was reluctant to see a rival upstaging it for the affections of progressive opinion. On 18 September, two weeks before the *Independent* was due to launch, Preston wrote to Ingham to tell him that, after the summer Parliamentary recess, his journalists would no longer be playing by the old Lobby rules:

> I have this week instructed my political staff that, when Westminster business recommences, they shall attend – as normal – your daily briefings, but that instead of employing any of the customary and increasingly threadbare circumlocutions ('Downing Street argues that . . . made clear last night', and so forth) they shall refer openly to 'a Downing Street spokesman' or 'Mrs Thatcher's spokesman' and, as relevant, quote what that spokesman says – whether it is a description of Mr Pym as 'Mona Lott' or Mr John Biffen as 'a semi-detached member of the Government'. I take your point that it would be wrong to turn you, a civil servant, into a national star turn, more ubiquitous than any of the ministers you serve: that's why I want the attribution to 'a spokesman' (whoever it is from your staff on the day) rather than a named individual – the practice we follow for other Civil Service departmental spokesmen.

To an outsider, this might appear a relatively harmless step. To Ingham, it struck at the heart of his Lobby operation and of his attempts to speak for the entire Government. He took this action by his old paper as a personal betrayal. With some *Guardian* journalists – notably the paper's political editor, Ian Aitken, whom he had known for twenty years – he severed all relations. When he learned that he and Aitken had both been invited to a mutual friend's retirement dinner, he refused to attend unless the *Guardian* man was struck off the list. His response to Preston (who had also regarded Ingham as a 'mate' in the 1960s) was acid:

> I can reply quite briefly since your letter is not for me. The Parliamentary Lobby Journalists exist as an independent body with their own constitution and rules. Under this so-called Lobby system, I do not invite political correspondents to briefings; they invite me. Their chairman, or acting chairman, presides and the terms under which

briefings are given are covered by their rules.

Consequently, if you wish to change the system you will have to find a way of addressing the Lobby . . .

That was his public stance. In private, he made it clear that moves to make his comments attributable to Downing Street would take place 'over my dead body'.

The Lobby was thrown into confusion. Ingham was due to give his next off-the-record briefing on 20 October. As a stop-gap measure *Guardian* journalists were asked by their colleagues not to attend it. Two days later, a special meeting of Lobby reporters voted to hold a ballot on whether the rules governing non-attribution should be changed. If the ballot had gone against Ingham, the Lobby system, in its existing form, would have ended – and with it, quite possibly, given his outspoken opposition to change, his career as Chief Press Secretary. Instead, on 29 October, the reporters voted by a narrow margin – 67 to 55 – to keep the briefings on the same basis as before.

An inquiry was held, to which Ingham submitted evidence. Given his unremitting hostility to the Lobby over the past seven years, accompanied by his frequently expressed desire to 'screw the buggers', one might have expected him to have welcomed the chance to give up his twice-daily jousts with the media. ('I have got news for you,' he had said in his private speech to the IBA in 1981. 'I have no objection to going on the record.') But, of course, when it really came down to it, he needed them even more than they needed him. In a written submission, he described the Lobby system as something which 'within the constraints imposed by Parliament ... facilitates the flow of information and guidance'. It was common journalistic practice, he asserted, to speak to 'informants' non-attributably: 'The Government cannot accept that the Lobby should seek to treat differently collective briefings with the Chief Press Secretary.' He concluded:

> The Government considers that, properly operated according to the conventions, the Lobby system can serve a useful purpose in our democracy and for that practical reason would wish to see it continue.

When he met the inquiry's members to discuss his evidence, he characteristically went straight on to the attack, stressing his belief that the system had to be 'properly operated'. Many journalists, he claimed, no longer seemed to appreciate the rules under which he gave his briefings. In the words of the inquiry report:

> It is no longer good enough to say that everyone understands. They clearly do not. Mr Ingham told us he thought that any references to information from his briefings should be non-specific – in particular the increasingly used terms 'Downing Street spokesman' or 'Downing Street said' . . . were not acceptable. In his view 'Government sources' was more accurate since he argued that he was speaking on behalf of the whole Government.

This latter point was really the crux of the matter. If Ingham spoke for the Government and not merely for the Prime Minister, then her interpretation – whether it was of policy or of colleagues – was automatically presented as the official view. Ingham could thus undermine a Cabinet minister, with or without the Prime Minister's prior knowledge, and the press would pass it on to the public as if it were the considered opinion of the entire Government. This had been the advantage of the Lobby system to Prime Ministers ever since Neville Chamberlain's time. It was this which put his collective Lobby briefings in a totally different category from the ordinary, off-the-record exchanges which are the stuff of everyday life, never mind everyday journalism.

Nevertheless – and rather surprisingly given the narrowness of the original vote – the inquiry accepted the logic of Ingham's argument: if you were going to keep the system, you had to operate it properly. And so what had begun as an attempt to make the Lobby less secretive and suggestible turned into a drive to make it more so. The report, completed in December, recommended that journalists attending Ingham's briefings should always refer to him as 'Government' or 'Whitehall sources', and that they be required to 'give a written undertaking that they are prepared to obey the rules of those meetings'. Any breaches of this 'tighter self-discipline' would lead to offenders being excluded by their colleagues from Lobby briefings.

'The *Guardian* will sign no such pledge of secrecy,' declared a leader in Ingham's old newspaper on 8 December, 'and finds it hard to believe that other newspaper editors will put their names to this voluntary endorsement of closed government.' In the event, they were not required to do so. Put to a vote in February 1987, this proposal was rejected.

When at last the smoke cleared after these months of wrangling, it was apparent that the Lobby system had been weakened badly. Nearly half its members (according to the October 29 ballot) favoured reform. Proposals designed to reimpose the old, strict discipline had failed. Two newspapers, the *Guardian* and the *Independent* (they were later to be joined by a third, the *Scotsman*), were refusing to attend Ingham's briefings. They relied instead on the substantial number of disaffected journalists still working inside the system, who were always happy to fill them in on what had been said. In their subsequent reports, the self-exiled papers, the *Independent* in particular, would sometimes take great pleasure in identifying Ingham by name. Ingham responded by making their lives as difficult as possible. 'They will not dine at this restaurant à la carte,' he was fond of insisting. If the 'buggers' refused his non-attributable guidance, they would not be given anything else, either. Even routine inquiries to the Number 10 Press Office about the Prime Minister's engagements would go unanswered.

The Prime Minister's famous trip to Moscow in March 1987 showed how political journalists now divided in Ingham's eyes: between those in the Lobby who had stayed loyal, and those outside it who could look after themselves. Downing Street had set aside twenty-two seats for reporters on the official VC-10, every one of which went to a member of the Lobby. The Number 10 Press Office refused even to help with the visas of some of those who were not in this select group. Joe Haines, by then Assistant Editor of, and columnist on, the *Daily Mirror*, had his passport returned to him and was told to do it himself. Haines telephoned Ingham. 'He said he wasn't going to help,' he recalled, 'wouldn't even tell me which hotel they were staying at, which was important to know. When I said "Why not?" he said "Because I'm in this to look after my friends". I said "you mean the Lobby?" He said "Yes".'

A few weeks before the Moscow visit, on the evening of 17 February, James Naughtie, chief political correspondent of the *Guardian*, visited Ingham at Number 10 to try to patch up relations, at least on a personal level. It was a stormy occasion. The next morning, Preston wrote again to Ingham 'to say how much I regret the individual anger, with added vituperation, that you seem continually to display towards this paper, and towards members of its staff. We have sought only to bring about some modest measure of reform in a system which we feel would benefit from it.' In his reply on 23 February, Ingham refused to respond to these points. As to the Moscow trip:

I give Lobby briefings during flights. Such briefings concern the visit itself as well as touching on matters of wider Governmental interest. You have decided, for your own reasons, that the *Guardian*'s journalists should not participate in Number 10 Lobby briefings in this country. It would be quite impracticable, in the narrow confines of the VC-10, for any *Guardian* members of the press team to absent themselves while I gave my briefings. Since you find the principle of collective Lobby briefings by Number 10 so offensive, I am sure that you would not wish to subscribe to them simply for the duration of the flight.

Ingham also turned down a plea for a seat from Anthony Bevins, asking the reporter if he proposed to hide in the VC-10's lavatory every time there was a briefing.

The treatment meted out in Moscow to Joe Haines, James Naughtie and Colin Brown of the *Independent* showed the price of antagonizing Ingham. Whilst their Lobby colleagues were whisked from the airport to the city centre in an official coach, Brown became involved in a furtive black market deal with a taxi driver 'with bald tyres'. They were put up in rooms without direct-dial telephones which made filing copy almost impossible. Ingham's morning briefings on how the visit was going were always non-attributable so Naughtie and Brown could not attend. Finally, on 1 April, when the rest of their colleagues were flown down to Tbilisi in Georgia for the last leg of the visit, there was no way they could follow. They simply gave up the chase.

That night, at 9.00 p.m., as the RAF VC-10 left Soviet airspace, a steward made his way to the press compartment in the rear of the plane bearing a silver tray and four bottles of champagne: a gift from the Prime Minister to the Lobby. The stories which had been filed to London ('SuperMag!', 'Maggiemania!'), six weeks before she called a General Election, were a politician's dream. A 2,000-word summary of their contents had been relayed every morning from the Downing Street Press Office to the British Embassy. The drinks, it was clear, had been well-earned. When, soon after the champagne, the Prime Minister herself and her Press Secretary appeared, it was smiles all round. Ingham wore the biggest grin. He had brought off, he declared, 'the big one': one of the most successful exercises in public relations Downing Street had ever mounted. It can only have added to his pleasure that somewhere, outside in the freezing night, far below and miles behind, Joe Haines, Jim Naughtie and Colin Brown were probably still locked in a row with customs at Moscow Airport.

After the Conservatives' success in the General Election of June 1987, Ingham saw the Prime Minister and offered to resign. He had long since overtaken Harold Evans's record to became the longest-serving occupant of his office. He was fifty-five years old, nearly eight years into the job, and on to his sixth deputy. Enough time had elapsed since Westland for it not to appear that he was departing under a cloud. According to an old friend: 'He went to her and said, "Now you've won, it's a good time for a parting of the ways." But she wouldn't hear of it. He would have been happy to go.'

Like many leaders who have remained at the top for a long time, Mrs Thatcher had become peculiarly dependent upon her closest advisers. Senior civil servants, Cabinet Ministers, foreign statesmen, Leaders of the Opposition – all had changed since 1979. But Ingham, and especially Charles Powell, remained reassuringly familiar. In the words of one highly-placed official: 'She gets comfortable with the people around her and she doesn't want to change. Michel Jobert, who was President Pompidou's *chef de cabinet*, once wrote that when relations are good, there's no need to finish a sentence. So it is with Bernard.' Another intimate described Ingham as 'part of the furniture': 'This Prime Minister wants to change everything – except Number 10. It's the one thing she's very conservative about. She loves familiarity.' Maybe against his own better judgement, Ingham agreed to stay. The following year, at a Press Association lunch, Mrs Thatcher described him, with heavy emphasis, as '*indispensable*'. It appeared to be literally true.

His fame had now spread far and wide. His performances at foreign summits had made him such a star with the international press corps that they always sought out his briefings, rather as tourists to Britain might go in search of beefeaters or pearly kings. These occasions had a ritual element to them. Ingham would arrive, order all cameras and tape recorders to be switched off, then growl: 'Usual terms: British sources.' He would next proceed to belabour the other heads of government, much as his mistress was said to be doing in the conference chamber. At the European summit at Fontainebleau in 1984, he ridiculed the German chancellor, Helmut Kohl. At Milan the following year, when the leaders were having what he later called 'a real old-fashioned fall-out', he made a disastrous foray into the world of irony:

> I was asked what Mrs T thought about it all. I replied, with masterly understatement, 'Well, she's not best pleased'. A great smile of satisfaction suffused across the collective face of the media ... 'Aha,' said I, looking at the rows of smug, self-satisfied journalists in front of me, 'I know what you will be writing tomorrow. This time the Prime Minister won't just be furious; nor livid; nor even volcanic with rage. Oh no, she will be positively erupting. Krakatoan on the Richter scale.'[10]

Unfortunately for Ingham, *The Times* somehow missed the joke, and quoted 'Mr Bernard Ingham, her spokesman' as saying that the Prime Minister 'has but one emotion – fury ... It is total volcanic eruption. Krakatoa has nothing on it.'[11] In the ensuing row, Edward Heath went on the radio to call for Ingham's dismissal (an increasingly common occurrence), while Ingham himself demanded that *The Times* print a retraction. At the foot of an article the following day, the paper faithfully reported that Ingham 'considered that both he and she had been entirely misunderstood. She was no more than vexed.' ('This episode,' said Ingham later, 'reinforced my long-standing view that nothing less becomes a press which so extols its Arthurian pursuit of the truth than its utter determination never to apologise if it can be avoided, and then only in the most illegible type available.')[12]

To the normally sedate world of international diplomacy, Ingham imported the language and tactics which had made him notorious at home. At the Commonwealth Conference in Vancouver in 1987, when Britain was alone among member nations in resisting the call for sanctions against apartheid, he rattled off figures allegedly showing that the Canadian prime minister was a hypocrite: why, Canada was actually *increasing* its trade with South Africa. The Canadian government angrily pointed out that the statistics were out of date. Other leaders professed themselves amazed at this non-attributable attack on their hosts. Bob Hawke of Australia called it 'a process of misinformation ... an abominably untrue statement, totally unfair to the Prime Minister and the people of Canada.' Robert Mugabe declared himself 'completely disillusioned and dismayed by the most dishonest way of informing the public that has been presented here this week'. Ingham ('a senior spokesman') was typically unrepentant: people might 'take some exception to the force with which we put our argument,' he said, 'but we take pride in the accuracy of our briefings'.[13] The Canadian press subsequently dubbed him 'Bernie the Bear'.

After a few years, he came rather to look forward to these confrontations. 'I expect there'll be the usual trouble,' he said, rubbing his hands, a week before the European Council Meeting in Copenhagen in 1988. '"Blood Lake Beside Black Pudding Mountain" – that kind of thing.'

He presented to the world a curious mixture of aggression and good humour, touchiness and bad grace. In 1989, the Prime Minister flew to Paris for the annual Anglo–French summit, at the conclusion of which there was a press conference in the Elysée Palace. 'I became aware of someone in the row behind me who was muttering and fidgeting,' wrote Patrick Marnham, Paris correspondent of the *Independent*.

> An inspection by my neighbour, Edmund Fawcett of *The Economist*, revealed that this restless, rather distracting person was Mr Bernard Ingham, who seemed to be enjoying himself. Perhaps he was exhilarated by his flying visit to Paris. The last question asked at the press conference was about Camembert cheese. President Mitterand said that all Camembert was excellent and Mr Ingham, in an urgent stage whisper, replied, 'but it can poison you'. I turned to look at him again, he was grinning happily.[14]

Marnham concluded his subsequent report of the press conference with a reference to Ingham's 'unexpected little joke'. His story was published on Tuesday. On Wednesday, the *Independent* carried a letter from Ingham. 'Just for the record,' he wrote, 'I did not say camembert can poison you.' On Thursday, there was a letter from Edmund Fawcett, confirming that he had heard the same remark. On Saturday, Ingham wrote again. 'Let's stop inventing things,' he suggested. The following week, Marnham recounted this curious exchange in the *Spectator* and revealed that he had a third witness up his sleeve, 'a public official' who had been 'seated near Bernard'. Only at this point did Ingham cease his correspondence.

Of course, we were not there. We do not know. But odds of three to one suggest that Ingham did say something of the sort Marnham described. Maybe he had forgotten it. What is revealing is that he should have been so insistent he was right, so determined to have the last word, that he ended up drawing attention to something which would otherwise have passed unnoticed. He seemed to have got matters out of proportion.

Several observers put this marked and increasing sensitivity of Ingham down to the length of time he had been in Downing Street. 'If you have a close relationship with the Prime Minister,' said Joe Haines, describing his own experience at Number 10, 'you have an enormous influence, and that influence is corrupting. You don't brook argument. You've made up your mind. You're a busy man and you don't want people arguing with you. I think it's affected Bernard as it would affect most people who do that job.' There is an additional danger, peculiar to public relations, of staying in the same post too long. One head of PR for a large corporation expressed it as follows: after a couple of years, 25 per cent of the journalists he dealt with had written something so hostile he felt they had personally let him down; for Ingham, whom he knew well, he assessed that figure, after a decade, at 90 per cent. At that point, he argued, a suspicion that everyone was up to no good – a 'bunker mentality' – was the inevitable result.

'A lot of people say that I have a contempt for journalism,' Ingham told one reporter in 1987. 'I don't.'[15] But in truth, both in his private and public remarks, he expressed an almost constant contempt for the profession with which he had to deal on a daily basis. Reporters, to pick only a few of the insults he had flung at them over recent years, were smug, self-satisfied, arrogant, gossip-infected conspiracy theorists. Naturally, given his temperament, he could not keep this prejudice to himself. It kept spilling over into his work as Government spokesman.

On 6 May 1988 he met the Lobby correspondents of the Sunday press for one of his regular, Friday afternoon briefings. The row over the Thames Television documentary, *Death on the Rock* (about the SAS's killing of three unarmed IRA terrorists in Gibraltar) was at its height. Ingham had been furious about the programme, which had uncovered fresh evidence suggesting that the unarmed IRA gang had been, effectively, executed. Now he told the assembled journalists that the British media was just 'a form of institutionalized hysteria'. The following morning, the *Observer*'s political correspondent, Victor Smart, rang Ingham at home to check he had heard correctly. Ingham confirmed the words and added more: 'There is nothing wrong with the British media that a renewed respect for facts, objectivity and fairness, rather than the false gods of invention and malice, would not cure.' And that, he said, was on the record. Smart was slightly amazed. A few minutes later, he rang him back. Did he mean that those words could be attributed to him in his capacity as Chief Press Secretary. Yes, Ingham confirmed, they could.

This was a story in itself. But there was more. The press had also been told that Friday by Ingham (unattributably) that the Prime Minister felt that broadcasters should be reminded of their responsibilities; that they operated within society and were obliged to uphold its institutions, notably legal proceedings. Emanating from the Home Office that same weekend were reports that the Home Secretary would be seeking an early meeting with the BBC and the IBA. Taken together with Ingham's unprecedented action in going on the record at an off-the-record briefing, it suggested a concerted Government campaign against the media. The *Observer* reported it as such.

Ingham's remarks caused an immediate controversy. Labour MPs denounced him as a creature of the Conservative Party. 'I was trying to start a debate,' he was reported as saying in the *Guardian* the following morning. 'It is a free society and people are entitled to write what they want, but the Government for its part is entitled to express a view on the media.' Once again, it seemed, for Ingham, 'the Government' had become interchangeable with the personal pronoun. To his chagrin, he found that more attention was being paid to his brief comments than was being given to an entire interview with Mrs Thatcher published exclusively in that morning's *Sunday Times*. He had committed the unpardonable sin of distracting attention from his employer. He threatened to have nothing more to do with Smart. With the editor of the *Observer*, after an initial, hectoring phone call the moment its first edition came out, he began a detailed correspondence about the exact context of his remarks, placing copies of his letters in the House of Commons Press Gallery.

The Sunday Lobby, in fact, was to prove a particular bane in Ingham's life. His remarks to it in January 1985 had been followed by a three cents drop in the value of sterling. His accusation about the media's 'institutionalized hysteria' had caused him problems in May 1988. That November, his handling of it was once again to land him in trouble – perhaps his most serious error of all, apart from the leaking of the Solicitor-General's letter.

I should perhaps confess here that I was a member of this subsection of the Lobby myself throughout 1987 and 1988. It was a curious business. We would gather in the entrance hall of Number 10 every Friday afternoon, just before a quarter to three. A charming lady named Rose would come and collect us. We would leave the hall, turn right and right again, and be ushered into Bernard's office. (Everyone called him Bernard.) He would usually be settled in his mustard-coloured armchair, next to his desk, with his back to the window, waiting to receive us. The door to the safe in one corner of the room sometimes stood tantalizingly ajar. We would settle ourselves in chairs around the room. Rose would bring in tea – cups and saucers for the journalists, a mug for Bernard. We would begin.

It is important to appreciate that these were not 'briefings' in any formal sense. They were chats. 'What about so-and-so?' someone might begin. 'Is the Prime Minister worried?' 'Naooh,' Bernard would growl. 'Dammit, we've got more important things to bother about than that.' Across the blank notebooks, a dozen pens would begin to move. He might be gruffly monosyllabic. He might pound the arm of his chair. He might laugh – a noisy, gurgling chuckle, marginally more disconcerting even than his barks of disapproval. 'What about the Exchange Rate Mechanism?' a reporter might ask. 'Who cares about that?' 'Well, Geoffrey Howe made a speech –' 'I can assure you they are not discussing the Exchange Rate Mechanism in the Two Ferrets at Hebden Bridge.' His language was a strange, old-fashioned blend of the colloquial and the formal: 'You may come again, if I may say so.' His oaths were also slightly antique: 'By Jove! ... Dammit! ... Bunkum and balderdash!' Sometimes, if the spirit moved him, he would launch into a five- or six-minute monologue, laced with his own, homespun philosophy: 'One of the troubles with people today, if I may say so ...' Gradually, the pens would cease to move. He was off.

It was often impossible, in this torrent of Yorkshire grit, to work out which were Ingham's opinions and which were Mrs Thatcher's. This enabled him to plant stories which were neither true nor false, but inhabited some grey area in between. For example, when Bernard had a rant about the hypocrisy of highly-paid National Health Service consultants protesting about NHS cuts, several papers carried stories along the lines of 'Maggie to Move Against "Greedy" Doctors'. She never did; probably she never had any intention of doing so; but the headline served as a useful reminder to the British Medical Association that it should watch its step. (In the summer of 1989, he hinted that the Prime Minister was unhappy about the large salary increase awarded to Lord King by British Airways: King subsequently inquired anxiously of her if this was true; she placed her hands on his shoulders, looked him in the eye and told him not to be 'silly'.) Nobody complained about this bizarre style of news dissemination, for the very good reason that it often provided good copy. The point about Bernard was that he was so aggressively opinionated, there was always the chance he would say something usable. God, how our hearts would slip into our boots on those Friday afternoons when we walked in to find he was not there and his deputy, the lugubrious Mr Perks, was sitting in his chair.

The potential for error, for misinterpretation, for reading too much into too little or of missing something altogether, was obviously immense. One of the strangest aspects of Ingham's fulminations against the media was his repeated condemnation of speculation and the press's reliance on the words 'may' and 'could':

> The average newspaper, shorn of all stories carrying these invaluable technical aids – invaluable because they at once permit the wire of possibility to be stretched to its twanging limit without actually breaking the journalist's protection – would look like a moth-eaten rag ... these words 'may' and 'could' are also symptomatic of a journalism which manufactures news in a different way – by interpretation and comment. It is now often far more difficult for the reader of the average newspaper to determine what was actually said or done than it is to discover the reporter's interpretation of what was said or done.[16]

But this, as Donald Maitland concluded twenty years ago, is precisely what the Lobby system is all about. Nods and winks, kite-flying and speculation are the stock in trade of a system which is non-attributable. Ingham seemed to want to have it both ways. When the headline was wrong and did not suit his purposes ('Thatcher ready to let £1 equal $1'), he complained; when it was wrong but did suit him ('Maggie to Move Against "Greedy" Doctors') he said nothing.

Over the past few years, the Sunday Lobby has proved a particularly tricky device to handle. There is less political news around at the weekend. Consequently, the journalists who attend briefings, Ingham's or anyone else's, are always keen to find something – and if they find it, their papers are likely to give it greater prominence than it might have enjoyed had it emerged mid-week. For the person giving the briefing, this presents both a tremendous opportunity and a terrible danger. On Friday 4 November 1988, Nigel Lawson met the Sunday press in Number 11 Downing Street to offer non-attributable 'guidance' on his Autumn Statement. The result was an expensive disaster for the Treasury. Virtually every Sunday paper came away with the same impression and ran the same story: that the Government was considering means-testing benefits for the elderly. Mr Lawson gave an interview the following Monday, admitting the existence of the briefing and denouncing the reporters as liars. He was then challenged to produce the tape recording which his press officer had been seen making at the time. The Treasury, to its great embarrassment, reported that the tape was missing. Mr Lawson's explanation for the misunderstanding was that when he talked about 'targeting', he had actually meant extra benefits, not fewer. Without the tape, the only way he could convince Parliament he was telling the truth was to put his money where his mouth had been. The cost to the Exchequer was estimated at some £200 million.

Ingham could be forgiven for deriving a certain grim satisfaction from this particular incident. He had been abroad with the Prime Minister at the time of Lawson's briefing. No blame attached to him. Indeed, the incident proved his point: if the Treasury, like the Foreign Office, insisted on appointing ordinary civil servants to run their press relations, there was bound to be a cock-up. Now Lawson, the man who had reprimanded him over his sterling briefing in 1985, had had a briefing blow up in his face. When the battered Sunday political correspondents trooped into Downing Street the following week, Ingham merely shook his head and grinned: 'Don't come looking to me for sympathy.'

The Friday after that, 18 November, I was away on holiday and missed Ingham's briefing. On the Sunday morning I glanced at the *Observer*'s front page on a Paris news stand. The headline was 'Thatcher: No, Your Majesty', over a report stating that the Prime Minister would not let the Queen visit Russia. A good story. I looked at the *Sunday Times*: 'Queen can't go to Russia – Thatcher'. I rifled through the stack of British papers. 'Queen to be told: don't visit Russia' (the *Sunday Telegraph*); 'Queen told to call off Russia visit' (the *Mail on Sunday*); 'NIET Snub Russia, Maggie Will urge Queen' (the

Sunday Mirror). All were quoting 'Government sources'. All had the same tale to tell. There could be no doubt as to its origin. *Now* what was Bernard up to?

Relations between Buckingham Palace and 10 Downing Street are sensitive at the best of times, but they had been particularly delicate during Margaret Thatcher's premiership. As long ago as 1982 there had been authoritative reports that the two women did not get on and that the Queen 'dreaded' her weekly audiences with Mrs Thatcher.[17] In 1986, a Buckingham Palace press officer had given a briefing to the *Sunday Times* in which he spoke of the Queen's worries about the handling of the miners' strike and her 'misgivings' over the bombing of Libya. The monarch was said to be 'very much to the left on social issues' and concerned that the Thatcher Government was 'not caring enough'. There were clear disagreements between them over sanctions and the role of the Commonwealth. All in all: a minefield.

In response, the Prime Minister brought to her dealings with the Sovereign an almost oriental formality and discretion. Nobody curtsied lower or more deferentially. She made a point of turning up at the Palace for her weekly audience fifteen minutes early. With her inner circle, she might pass a comment or two on a minor royal, 'but when it comes to the Queen,' said an intimate, 'not a whisper'.

As it happened, by the middle of November, a new 'Queen versus Thatcher' story was already beginning to circulate in Westminster. On the 11th, the Queen had attended a dinner hosted by the Speaker of the House of Commons. Labour had just lost the Glasgow Govan by-election to the Scottish Nationalists. Her Majesty put this down to the voters' poverty. 'They have got nothing,' she is supposed to have remarked, adding, somewhat Antoinettishly, 'I know, because I have sailed *Britannia* there.'

The *Sunday Express* was preparing to run this story as an 'exclusive' when Ingham met the Sunday Lobby on the 18th. The Govan by-election was not mentioned. Instead, the journalists had a different question about the Queen, based on reports coming out of Moscow: given the new spirit of *glasnost* and *perestroika*, would she soon be paying a state visit to the Soviet Union?

Ingham did not say 'no', but he launched into a long monologue about the difficulties a visit would pose which left the reporters in no doubt about Downing Street's position. 'It came pouring out, with very little prompting from us,' one journalist recalled. 'All this stuff about the murder of the Tsar, cousin of the Royal Family, and so on. He was clearly getting over a view he wanted got over.' Ingham talked of the 'butchering' of the Romanovs, of how 'constitutionalists' might be offended by a visit, of the dangers of seeming to 'reward' the Soviet regime with a stamp of royal approval before it had made sufficient concessions on disarmament and human rights ... Ingham's answer filled six pages in one reporter's notebook. They all knew, even as they were taking it down, that this had the makings of another row. 'Here we go again,' whispered one Lobby veteran.

What followed, from Mrs Thatcher's point of view, could scarcely have been worse. Advice tendered by the Prime Minister to the Sovereign is highly confidential. Yet here it was, plastered all over the press. Worse, the stories appeared to confirm the damaging rumours that the Prime Minister saw herself as superior to the Queen, treating her as a glorified roving ambassador to be dispatched hither and thither as she saw fit.

The briefing burst that weekend over a bewildered Foreign Office and Buckingham Palace. An FO official claimed that, 'from a political point of view, there would be quite a lot of merit in a royal trip'.[18] One of the Queen's press officers believed 'the historic problem of the murder ... would not necessarily stand in the way of a visit'.[19]

Ingham was in trouble. On Monday, lest anyone was in any doubt, the non-Lobby papers named him as the source of the stories. On Tuesday, from his vantage point in the Commons Press Gallery, he watched the Prime Minister uncharacteristically thrown off balance by an intervention from the Labour MP Dennis Skinner who demanded to know why she was 'stopping the Queen from going to Russia'. Mrs Thatcher, obviously flustered, replied (in the royal plural) that 'we do not discuss this matter. The matter has not been addressed in any way at all.'[20] The Labour benches dissolved into disbelieving laughter. Neil Kinnock demanded to know how she could reconcile this assertion with Ingham's briefing. Three senior Labour Privy Councillors and twenty-seven MPs put down an Early Day Motion demanding a statement.

That night, in the words of the Court Circular, Mrs Thatcher 'had an audience of Her Majesty'. Most unusually, Buckingham Palace discreetly let it be known that the Prime Minister had apologized for the briefing. The *Daily Telegraph* carried an editorial entitled 'Damaging

Gaffe' about the regrettable breach of confidentiality: 'for an official to commit such a breach was an impertinence . . . A bad day's work.'[21]

We do not know what transpired between Mrs Thatcher and her Chief Press Secretary, but we can guess. To his colleagues, he appeared terribly low. There were rumours in Fleet Street that he was about to resign. He rang the organizer of the Sunday Lobby to complain that his identity as the source had been leaked. 'I feel very fed up,' he said. When the political correspondents arrived for their briefing that Friday, he could barely bring himself to say a word. 'I am not prepared to speculate to this Lobby in the future,' he declared. The reporters were back on the pavement within fifteen minutes.

However aggrieved Ingham might have felt, he had nobody to blame but himself. He had seen some official correspondence, or heard the Prime Minister talk, or both, and decided, probably on his own initiative, to pre-empt any invitation from the Soviet government. It was, to say the least, a ham-fisted way to send a message to the Russians. Ingham had always claimed he was no Machiavelli. Incidents of this sort certainly went a long way towards acquitting him of that charge.

But if his enemies within the Government and outside it thought this marked the beginning of the end for Ingham, they reckoned without the Prime Minister. It was like the sterling disaster of 1985; just as Mrs Thatcher went out of her way to demonstrate her loyalty to him then, so she did now. Ingham was about to confound his critics and bounce back with greater power than ever.

TEN

Minister of Information

'There may be many complaints levelled, justifiably or unjustifiably, against the Government Information Service; but one
there is not: party political partiality. Our independence, our
ability to transcend party . . . is one of the peculiar strengths of
our system.'

Bernard Ingham, address to the IBA, 1981

'A code of ethics is essential . . . to protect those members
who are expected to expound untruths on behalf of the
Government, produce dodgy material or leak documents in
the Government interest.'

Member of the Government Information Service, speech to the
conference of the Institute of Professional Civil Servants, 1988

In February 1988 the new Secretary to the Cabinet and Head of the
Home Civil Service, Sir Robin Butler, received a disturbing letter from
Ingham's old friend and colleague, the Director-General of the COI,
Neville Taylor.

For forty years, the COI had been responsible for all Government
advertising. But in 1987, thanks chiefly to pressure from Lord Young,
Whitehall departments (to use their euphemism) had been 'untied'. They
were now free to hire private companies to handle their publicity and
marketing. Taylor had watched with mounting unease as the Government's spending on advertising and promotion had proceeded to triple.
Much of this expenditure was devoted to persuading the public to buy
shares in the old nationalized industries. Most of the rest went into
campaigns. Some of these, like the health warnings about Aids, were
straightforward public information. Some, however, seemed slightly
more dubious, both politically and in terms of value for money.

For example, as Secretary of State for Trade and Industry, Lord
Young had called in the design consultancy Wolff Olins to give the DTI
a new logo. It was now, apparently, the 'Department for Enterprise'.

There was also Young's 'Enterprise Initiative' (cost: £7 million), ostensibly launched to remind companies about various aid schemes, but with the obvious additional message that this was a Government for free enterprise. Other, equally questionable 'initiatives' were being planned by other, equally ambitious ministers, who realized they, too, could spend millions promoting their achievements to the electorate. Suddenly, for advertising agencies, PR consultants and marketing firms, the once notoriously parsimonious Whitehall beckoned like a second Klondyke. By 1988 it was outspending even such industrial giants as Unilever.

Taylor put up with it for a year. Eventually, tired of being told to stop interfering, he took his concerns direct to the Cabinet Office. He threatened resignation. He demanded a full-scale inquiry into what he saw as both a waste and an abuse of taxpayers' money. Butler agreed. This review was about to begin when, in March, Taylor had a serious heart attack. Ingham – who had supported his stand, on the grounds that here were more bloody amateurs interfering in the professionals' business – sent him a large bunch of flowers in hospital with the message 'Love from Bernard'.

Gradually, it became apparent that Taylor, who was lucky to survive, would not be returning to his old post. As a consequence, the review subtly broadened in scope to consider the whole future of the COI. On 28 July, the Cabinet Office circulated a letter on the future of Government publicity which clearly had been drawn up in consultation with Ingham. This effectively reduced the COI to little more than a services agency. Henceforth, the Treasury would be the final arbiter on matters relating to value for money; the Cabinet Office ultimately would rule on the 'propriety' of individual campaigns. But for all practical purposes, in the words of the letter:

> The principal source of advice to Ministers and Heads of Department in this field is the Departmental Head of Information. Heads of Department should ensure that the Head of Information always has sufficient opportunity to advise on proposals for paid publicity . . .[1]

The Heads of Information, of course, reported through the MIO to Ingham.

All that was necessary now was to dispose of the last important outpost of the ailing Taylor's empire. That happened six months later. On 9 February 1989, eleven weeks after the controversy over the Queen's visit to Moscow, it was formally announced that Ingham was to be made Head of Profession for all Government Information Officers.

The evolution of bureaucracies is dry stuff. It excites the interest of historians rather than journalists. So perhaps it is not surprising that the news of Ingham's promotion produced not a ripple in Parliament. The press barely mentioned it. Yet it was much more significant than most of the episodes which had caused so many storms. What had happened was without precedent. Ingham now had four separate functions. He was the Prime Minister's personal media adviser. He was the non-attributable spokesman for the entire Government. He had responsibility for the 'recruitment, training and career development' of 1,200 information officers. He co-ordinated an advertising and publicity budget of some £168 million. In any other country he would have been given the proper title: Minister of Information. The appointment also represented a further, significant centralization of power in the hands of the Prime Minister: unlike the Director-General of the COI, Ingham, through the Head of the Home Civil Service, was responsible to her alone. In 1983, Mrs Thatcher had told David Owen: 'I do not have and have never had any intention or plan to centralize control of Government Information in 10 Downing Street, and I have no plans to extend the responsibilities of my Chief Press Secretary.' Now she had done both.

It had happened through a combination of Ingham's ambition and poor Neville Taylor's ailing heart. First, Ingham had utilized his chairmanship of the MIO, neglected by his predecessors, to 'co-ordinate' Government information. Then, when his attempt to widen his role was blocked, he had ensured that the COI's Director-Generalship was given to an ally. The status of his own post as Downing Street Press Secretary had been raised, along with his salary; his right to advise on appointments formalized. Finally, when the chance came for the COI to be broken up, he had made sure he was there to pick up the important pieces. Power had come to him, in part, simply because he had been around so long.

One does not have to be one of Ingham's despised conspiracy theorists to see the implications of this. Under the rules of the Civil Service, restated by Sir Robert Armstrong in 1985, officials owe their allegiance 'first and foremost' to the minister for whom they work. But information officers have a dual loyalty. Their careers are now to a large extent determined by the Prime Minister's Press Secretary. What do they do if their minister wishes to go one way and Number 10 another? And when they are called in to advise their ministers, whose advice is it that they are passing on: their own, or the line laid down by Ingham at the MIO? Ingham, in Neville Taylor's words, has an 'open line' into every department, down which he can both speak – and listen:

> The Press Secretary at Number 10 can find out what is planned to be said – action, proposals, policies and so on – every day and umpteen times during the day merely by picking up the phone and saying 'Neville, what's your Secretary of State up to?' Perhaps no formal paper has gone anywhere. The Prime Minister is unlikely to pick up the phone. The Private Secretary's a bit wary about it because it's a more formal channel. The better the contact between the Press Secretary and the Heads of Information, the better informed Number 10 is.

By 1989, at least one Cabinet Minister was telling his special adviser not to talk too openly in front of the Department's Chief Information Officer: the person concerned had once been Ingham's deputy at Number 10. Indeed, it has become difficult to find a departmental head of information who has not worked for Ingham at some stage. His contacts are equally good further down the chain of command. By the end of 1985, he could boast that fifty Whitehall press officers had served at Number 10 on a six-week or two-month attachment. By the end of 1990, that figure had risen to almost 100. His judgements of people, in Taylor's opinion, tended to be 'a bit quirky':

> Whereas most of us come to a view over a long period of time, balancing one thing against another, Bernard's views on most things are both extreme and simplistic. All his geese are swans. People are either 'no bloody good' or 'possibly alright' or 'brilliant'. Everybody fits into one of three categories. All the people who have ever worked for him, whom he selected, are marvellous – not one single failure among them. People who haven't worked for him, it's: 'Never heard of him. If they're any good, why didn't they come to Number 10?'

This raises longer-term questions. No Chief Press Secretary has ever stayed on at Number 10 beyond the term of the Prime Minister they served; rarely is there even a transition period. They leave Downing Street on the same day as their employers. For that reason, none of Ingham's predecessors had even sought, let alone been offered, the post of Head of the Government Information Service: first, they recognized they were not in a position to take a detached, long-term view of the profession; secondly, they were, by the nature of their work, seen as the partisan agents of a particular Prime Minister.

These reservations applied to Ingham with peculiar force. Few Press Secretaries had been as closely identified with their Prime Ministers as he had with Thatcher. An incoming Labour government might be forgiven for regarding an information service recruited by him as stuffed with like-minded people. In 1987, for example, one of Ingham's assistants, Christine Wall, had gone directly from Downing Street to work full-time for Conservative Central Office; another member of the Government Information Service, Alex Pagett, had moved across to work for the Scottish Tory Party.

In the past, this would not have mattered. But now, because of the virtual destruction of the COI, a new government would be in a position to act on any suspicions. A precedent had been established, of control from Number 10. In 1974, Joe Haines's first action on re-entering Downing Street had been to purge the Press Office of anyone whose loyalty he suspected. A future Joe Haines would inherit responsibility for the careers of more than 1,000 men and women across Whitehall. The purge could grow in proportion. Sir Robin Butler, custodian of the flame of Civil Service neutrality, was well aware of the danger, discussed it with ministers, and floated the idea that Ingham should give up the Chief Press Secretary's job to concentrate on being Head of Profession. The Prime Minister would not hear of it.

Ingham regarded such fears as so much twaddle. Two months after his appointment, in April 1989, he received a letter from the information officers' trade union, the Institute of Professional Civil Servants (IPCS). This enclosed a draft 'code of ethics', drawn up after their last conference had heard first-hand reports of life inside the GIS. Peter Cook, a press officer at the Department of Employment, claimed that he and his colleagues had been 'put under increasing pressure from ministers to work on projects which at best can be described as favourably disposed towards Government policies and at worst blatantly party political'. They had been required to write 'articles of a party political nature on behalf of their ministers for insertion in the press', and he gave examples of dubious campaigns, such as Action for Jobs 'which said little about the Department of Employment's services but much about the Conservative Party's views on unemployment and the unemployed'.

Peter Dupont, an official at the COI, had called for a code of ethics 'to protect those members who are expected to expound untruths on behalf of the Government, produce dodgy material or leak documents in the Government's interest'.

The IPCS's suggested guidelines were fairly innocuous: for example, that it was 'the responsibility of Information Officers in the Government Service to describe and explain Government policies; it is not their function to justify or defend them'; that 'Information Officers in Government Service should avoid identification with the political philosophy of any particular administration' and that 'Information Officers in Government Service shall not distort or suppress information for reasons of political expediency, advertising or sponsorship.' The wording was based on evidence from Lord Bancroft, former Head of the Home Civil Service, to the House of Commons Treasury Select Committee.

Ingham, however, seemed to take it as a personal affront. He sent a copy of the code with a covering note to Robin Butler. 'I propose to give the letter short shrift,' he wrote. 'It is outrageous that the IPCS gave the letter to the media – the Press Association, I understand – even before I had the opportunity to consider it. I think I should make it clear I do not intend to conduct business with them on this basis.' He wrote back to the union refusing even to discuss it. This remained his public stance on the issue. When, in his new role as Head of Profession, he held a recruitment seminar at a hotel in York, he discovered that the proceedings had been gatecrashed by a reporter and photographer from the *Mail on Sunday*, wearing buttonholes and posing as wedding guests. 'Bugger off!' he yelled at them. 'And if you want it on the record: Sod off!'[2]

How did he find the time? That was what his current and former colleagues found so puzzling. In the words of one retired senior civil servant: 'Here we are, in the middle of this supposedly wonderful managerial revolution in Whitehall, and what do we do? We put in charge of 1,200 people, overseeing the expenditure of millions of pounds, a part-time itinerant spokesman . . . '

Certainly, Ingham did not neglect the traditional aspects of his work. One minute he was busying himself with the appointment of the new Director of Public Affairs at the Metropolitan Police, the next he was telling the Lobby that the reports that Kenneth Baker was to be appointed Conservative Party Chairman were 'fevered speculation'. He was closely involved in setting the scene for Mrs Thatcher's 1989 Cabinet reshuffle. The Prime Minister was determined to shift Sir Geoffrey Howe from the Foreign Office and Ingham discreetly prepared the ground. When, in July, the BBC's *Nine o'Clock News* carried a report that Howe and Nigel Lawson would not be moved, he was on the telephone within five minutes, demanding to know of the Corporation's political editor, John Cole, whether he had a better reading of the Prime Minister's mind than her Chief Press Secretary.

Despite such indications, Howe failed to spot the scaffold which was being erected for him. On 24 July, the Prime Minister summoned him to Number 10 and offered him the Home Secretaryship. He refused and, after consulting with his friends, came up with a veritable shopping list of demands as the price of his departure from the Foreign Office: Leader of the House of Commons, Lord President of the Council, the chairmanship of various Cabinet committees, a house in the country, and – crucially – the title of Deputy Prime Minister. Only on these terms would he remain in the Government. He had too strong a following in the party to be sacked outright. Mrs Thatcher, reluctantly, gave him what he wanted. Her technique, as usual, when confronted by such disloyalty, was to pay lip service to the proprieties in public and unleash Ingham in private. The following day, Howe was blackjacked at the eleven o'clock Lobby briefing. The title of Deputy Prime Minister, previously awarded to Lord Whitelaw in recognition of his special role in the Government, had, Ingham asserted 'no significance'. It did not mean automatically that Howe would be sent for by the Queen in the event of Mrs Thatcher's political or bodily demise. It did not mean he would be in charge at home when the Prime Minister was abroad: given the effectiveness of modern communications, she would remain in control at all times.

Constitutionally and technically, this was no doubt correct. But it was also clearly intended as a signal that Mrs Thatcher had given Howe nothing of substance. Once again, the press reports the next day left nobody in any doubt that Ingham was the source of this 'guidance'. 'Government sources,' reported *The Times*, 'emphasized that the title of Deputy Prime Minister is a "courtesy".' The *Daily Telegraph* used the same phrase:

> While Sir Geoffrey was insisting that he would continue to have an important influence on Government policies at home and abroad,

those close to Mrs Thatcher were describing the role of Deputy Prime Minister as a 'courtesy title' with no constitutional status.

The *Daily Mail* was more blunt:

Whitehall sources firmly refused yesterday to confirm the claim that Sir Geoffrey had been offered the Home Office. Meanwhile, his new role has already been downgraded by Downing Street. It was suggested that the titles he has acquired are constitutional fiction – and in any case the Prime Minister does not think they matter.

This was a brutal way to treat the cabinet's most senior member, and Howe never really recovered from it: he resigned fifteen months later with his authority in tatters. David Howell described Ingham's briefing as 'nauseating and intolerable.'[3] That was the general feeling. When Howe made his first appearance as Leader of the House, he was greeted by more than a minute of cheering from the Tory benches – an unprecedented display of support, and a clear signal to Thatcher and Ingham.

The Prime Minister, characteristically, took no notice. When, on 25 October, Nigel Lawson told her of his dramatic decision to resign as Chancellor of the Exchequer, she did not even bother to let Howe, her supposed 'deputy', know what was happening. The only advisers she consulted were Charles Powell and Bernard Ingham. Many in her own party were now frankly critical of her obvious reliance on these two unelected officials. She was said to be isolated in Number 10. Her judgement was going. She treated her colleagues with contempt. 'One way to restore confidence in Cabinet government,' proclaimed Sir Barney Hayhoe, a former minister, 'would be to have Bernard Ingham and Charles Powell moved to quieter pastures before the end of this year. Such a signal would be welcomed by her ministerial colleagues as well as by back-bench members.'[4] Lord Hailsham, the former Lord Chancellor, went further. Ingham, he said, had been used 'unscrupulously on occasions' to undermine ministers. 'This is dishonourable conduct towards colleagues.' (Later, questioned about Hailsham's remark in the Commons, the Prime Minister declared herself 'very surprised that he made it. It is totally untrue.')[5]

In the wake of his departure from the Treasury, Mr Lawson, too, grumbled to his friends about Ingham's behaviour. That November, he bumped into a prominent left-wing columnist in the cloakroom of the Savoy and told him that if he wanted a good topic, he should write about 'the use of black propaganda by Number 10'. Whether he meant the Press Office or some other persons, he did not say.

What did Ingham care? His position went from strength to strength. In November 1989, he was promoted to Deputy Secretary, the third highest rank in the Civil Service. In February 1990, he unleashed another of his tirades against the media, the first since that memorable night in Stationers' Hall at the height of the Westland crisis. 'I sometimes compare press officers to riflemen on the Somme,' he told a Press Gallery luncheon, 'mowing down wave upon wave of distortion and taking out rank upon rank of supposition, deduction and gossip, while laying down a barrage of facts behind which something approximating to the truth might advance.' He trotted out his familiar compendium of journalists' diseases – the Le Carré syndrome, the Conan Doyle complication, the Coleman/Carpenter phenomenon – and something he called 'separatitis':

> its symptoms are an insistent, and some would say unreasoning assumption of rights to the exclusion of all responsibilities. An unshakeable belief in the media's entitlement to lead a privileged existence which sets its practitioners apart from, and above, the ordinary mortals on whom they depend for their livelihood, protection and security. A conviction that whatever they do is sanctified by the blessed state of freedom which they enjoy.

'Somehow, dammit, we rub along,' he concluded. 'But I think it would help at times if some of you weren't so blessed precious.'[6] Afterwards, he agreed to grant the BBC his first radio interview. The following morning, the nation awoke to hear, for the first time, the gravelly tones of the Prime Minister's Chief Press Secretary talking about 'the conspiracy theory which, I think, motivates journalism as a craft'. The interview included this memorable exchange:

INTERVIEWER: And the electronic media?
INGHAM: Oh, you've got to accept your share of the blame, too.
INTERVIEWER: What's the electronic media's share of the blame? Where are we guilty?

INGHAM: Well, you suffer from the diseases of journalists. Dammit, you're journalists aren't you?

INTERVIEWER: You don't feel, then, that the electronic news medium in Britain is trying to maintain an independent report of what is happening in Britain?

INGHAM: I think it *thinks* it's trying to maintain that.

INTERVIEWER: What of the view, though, the other side of this, that journalists might believe the Government *is* up to something, that it –

INGHAM: Well, you're now proving my point.

INTERVIEWER: Even by asking the question?

INGHAM: Yes.[7]

'Bernard's behaving like a second-term president,' said one of Mrs Thatcher's former advisers who heard the broadcast. Ingham had achieved all he wanted. He was going to say what he liked. He had nothing to lose.

Outspokenness in public was matched by an equally combative style in Whitehall, where he patrolled the walls of his newly-built empire, alert to any potential encroachment. He always kept one eye open for Tim Bell, the self-advertising advertising executive and Prime Ministerial favourite. Bell had advised the National Coal Board on public relations during the miners' strike of 1984, and Ingham had been infuriated by the abrupt dismissal of his friend, Geoff Kirk, who had been handling the industry's press relations since Ingham's days on the *Yorkshire Post*.[8] The following year, Lord Young had wanted to dispense with his information officer at the Employment Department. 'But she had been recommended by Bernard Ingham,' recalled Young, 'who had always been very helpful to me. I had no wish to upset him.'[9] Bell had come up with the solution: an employee of his named Howell James, who had handled PR for Capital Radio and TV-am, became Young's 'Special Adviser'. In 1987, Young had taken another Bell man, Peter Luff, to do the same job at the DTI. Now, in 1990, with the Government experiencing 'presentational difficulties', who should step forward to assist but the ever-present, ever-helpful Mr Bell.

He suggested to Kenneth Baker that certain key ministers should employ outside public relations advisers to improve their 'media profiles'. He volunteered himself to take on the challenging task of improving the image of the Home Secretary, David Waddington. Ingham read of the scheme in the *Independent on Sunday* on 29 April. He had wrecked it within thirty-six hours. On Monday afternoon he sent a memorandum to all Heads of Information in Whitehall, gleefully describing what he had done. It provided a telling glimpse of Ingham in action, and of his power to call even Cabinet ministers to heel:

As Head of the Government Information Service, I telephoned Mr Kenneth Baker, Chancellor of the Duchy of Lancaster, this morning about the reported appointment of Public Relations Minders to three Cabinet Ministers: Home Secretary – Tim Bell; Kenneth Clarke [Health Secretary] – John Banks; John MacGregor [Education Secretary] – Robin Wight.

I said I was doing so in response to serious concern which had been expressed to me by Heads of Information, especially as there seemed to be the possibility of further appointments.

I said we needed to deal with this issue immediately in order to prevent damage to the GIS. The announcement of the appointments, made without any consultation with the Heads of Information concerned, was seen as a grave reflection on the competence of the GIS – indeed as an insult to it.

The GIS had and, I was sure, would continue to do its level best for the government of the day.

But it was inevitably getting a lot of flak these days and this kind of episode would be damaging of its morale unless there was proper consultation and explanation.

It was absolutely essential that Ministers and Messers Bell, Banks and Wight handled the GIS with kid gloves, given the circumstances of their appointment.

Mr Baker regretted the publicity and said no announcement had been made. It had leaked out ... He was sorry if it was felt the appointments, and the manner in which the appointments had become public, reflected on the competence of the GIS. That had not been the intention and it did not reflect the view in which the GIS was held.

I said that we needed to dispel that impression immediately. I asked him to make it clear to all inquirers – and to the GIS – that these were party appointments and did not and were not intended to reflect upon the competence and abilities of the GIS. Mr Baker agreed to do this.

I strongly urge you to communicate these sentiments to your

Permanent Secretaries and to deploy them as necessary with your Ministers.[10]

No more was heard of Mr Baker's scheme. Ingham's memo was published in the following week's *Mail on Sunday*. No leak inquiry was established.

Despite Ingham's new executive powers, business proceeded with the Lobby as before. On 27 June he was reported to have 'erupted in fury' at the four o'clock meeting. He was being asked repeatedly if the Government proposed to apologize to Parliament for having misled it over the sale of Rover to British Aerospace, when he suddenly snapped that he was 'not going to put up with any more of this'. But wasn't it a legitimate matter of public interest? Ingham's reply was emphatic: 'I am not going to grovel before this Lobby!'[11]

Exactly one month later, on 27 July, he met the Sunday Lobby and delivered an unattributable karate chop to the unsuspecting neck of Sir Alan Walters, the man whose backstairs influence had precipitated the resignation of Nigel Lawson. Sir Alan had published a book, *Sterling in Danger*, attacking the Exchange Rate Mechanism of the European Monetary System. Rather embarrassingly, it had been revealed recently that he was still seeing Mrs Thatcher. Pressed in the Commons, she had described him as 'a family friend'. But the reporters were left in no doubt that he, too, had now fallen from grace. 'Downing Street hits out at Walters,' said the *Observer*, on 29 July, quoting 'one Downing Street insider' as remarking: 'Alan Walters plays no part here. He can canvass his own views . . . It is all out of the text books. It hasn't been tested.' In the *Sunday Correspondent*, 'a source close to the Prime Minister' called Walters's ideas 'half baked'. 'Walters frozen out by cool Thatcher,' reported the *Sunday Times*, quoting 'senior sources'. In the *Sunday Telegraph* it was 'Cabinet snubs Walters over Europe'; in the *Mail on Sunday*, 'No 10 snub for "friend" Walters' ('Downing Street sources pointedly said Mrs Thatcher had not seen [him] for well over two months . . .').

First Lawson, now Walters: if there was 'black propaganda' from Number 10, it had at least been distributed with an even hand.

That summer, Ingham celebrated his fifty-eighth birthday. It was clear that he would stay with Mrs Thatcher as long as she needed him. He was due to retire in two years' time, at the age of sixty. If she went before then, he admitted openly, he would go, too. Otherwise, his retirement date looked like being conveniently close to the next General Election. His name had been connected with a few jobs outside – editor of the *Yorkshire Post*, head of public relations at the Prudential, a chair in Government Communications at Newcastle University, funded by his old friends in British Nuclear Fuels – but they never amounted to much more than gossip. He talked of writing a book, and several publishers came to see him at Number 10. Lord Weidenfeld was said to be hawking the serialization rights around Fleet Street. But unfortunately, as he made clear to his disappointed visitors, he had kept no diary and had no intention of writing a kiss-and-tell autobiography. 'It will be an exposition of the job for my successors,' he explained, 'not a memoir.' Visions of a six-figure advance, which he could have commanded with ease, apparently held no attractions for him.

In fact, the belief in Westminster by the summer of 1990 was that he was no longer as close to Mrs Thatcher as he had been. It is the view of several witnesses, who are in a position to know, that there has been a decided shift in the balance of power in Number 10. One very highly-placed official, who saw the Prime Minister and her Press Secretary almost every day for some years, believes that gradually, since the mid-1980s, he has lost his unique place in her affections:

> She certainly trusted him, but she didn't always share with him what she was thinking. I wouldn't have said – although she had a great respect for him – I wouldn't have said he had a relationship with her like that she had with Charles Powell. Powell came to establish a close bond with her, and that changes the relative influence of the others . . . Subsequent Principal Private Secretaries have found [Powell] a difficult colleague to cope with. It's a very over-protective relationship.

Influence, as courtiers have found since at least the days of the Pharaohs, is proportionate to access. Ingham's access to Thatcher was great, but it was as nothing compared to that enjoyed by her Private Secretary. Although Powell got off to a slow start when he joined the Prime Minister's staff in 1984, it was no exaggeration, six years later, to say that he saw more of her than any other person, including her husband. He saw her throughout the day in Downing Street. He saw her at night at official receptions and banquets. He attended every talk she had with every visiting foreign leader. He accompanied her on every tour abroad. He and his wife saw the Thatchers socially. They even spent Christmas Day with them at Chequers.

The Inghams were simply not in this league. It was the *Guardian* all over again, with the Jenkins/Powell figure up in the officers' mess and Bernard slaving away below with the poor bloody infantry. A telling demonstration of their relative status was provided in June 1988, when Ronald Reagan paid his farewell visit as President to see Mrs Thatcher. The Powells joined the Reagans, the Thatchers, the Geoffrey Howes and the George Schultzes for the intimate candle-lit dinner; Ingham was left outside to hand out details of the menu to the press.

Powell also established his own links with journalists, separate from Ingham's. On one famous occasion he dined with Conrad Black, owner of the *Daily Telegraph*, and was rumoured to have discussed the political reliability of the paper's editor, Max Hastings. This was trespassing on to the Chief Press Secretary's closely-guarded turf and, not surprisingly, jealousies have stirred. What was once a most powerful axis – for a while, the nearest Britain had to a genuine Deputy Prime Minister – has now been replaced by a well-attested, unmistakable, mutual *froideur*. Such are the squabbles of good and faithful servants.

CONCLUSION

Crowned with Glory

'This business of communication is fraught with peril. It is a
wonder I survive. Perhaps I won't . . . '
Bernard Ingham, speech to Calder High School, January 1990

At the beginning of October 1989, the Hebden Lodge Hotel, a modest
establishment on the busy main road of Hebden Bridge, had a sudden
influx of guests from London. There were so many Heads of Information from Whitehall under one roof, the manager could have been
forgiven for thinking he had a convention on his hands. In one room
were Bernard and Nancy Ingham; in another, Neville Gaffyn, former
Head of Information at the Department of Education, and his wife, Jean
Caines, Chief Information Officer at the Environment Department; a
third room was occupied by Romola Christopherson, in charge of media
relations at the Department of Health. Eventually, some thirty Government press officers, many of them clutching mobile telephones, including Brian Mower and Jim Coe from the Home Office and the Ministry of
Agriculture, were to be seen swarming around the town. All were friends
of Ingham. All had worked for him at Number 10. All had come north to
celebrate his tenth anniversary as Chief Press Secretary.

It was a cross between a pilgrimage and a works outing. They ate half a
celebratory cake (Ingham had shared the other half with the Prime
Minister and her staff in Downing Street earlier in the week). They piled
into cars and drove down the narrow lanes to Derek Ingham's farm.
They clambered up to a local beauty spot high above the town. 'I hope,'
declared Ingham, 'I am not the first and last Chief Press Secretary to
conduct his entire world media operation by yuppie phone from the
cloud-enveloped balcony of Stoodley Pike.'[1] They saw Nutclough Mill
where Ingham's father used to work, now restored by a heritage preser-
vation group and kept as a living museum; the Ebenezer Chapel, where
Ingham started out as a journalist, now an antiques centre; and Garnet's

beloved Co-operative Society, now converted into a three-star hotel, specializing in parties from America. Gone were the smoking chimneys, the warehouses, the grimy slums. Hebden Bridge, with its pizzerias and its Tourist Information Centre, had changed over the past twenty years nearly as much as its most famous son.

The visit was a remarkable demonstration, both of Ingham's personal hold over the Government Information Service, and of his pride in his old home town. The political correspondents would have loved to have covered it, but they missed it – their attention was concentrated across the Pennines, in Blackpool, where the Conservatives were holding their annual party conference. Ingham, professional to the last, made sure the story went as an exclusive to the *Hebden Bridge Times*. 'Not all his colleagues could attend,' reported his old paper, 'and those overseas sent goodwill messages.' So did Margaret Thatcher.

It was to her that he owed his success. That is not to decry his own achievement. It was his ambition, his determination and his relentless hard work which had lifted him out of Hebden Bridge in the first place, taken him via Halifax and Leeds to London, through Fleet Street and Whitehall to Number 10. He had not buried his talents in the back garden; he had taken them out into the world.

But the unprecedented power and influence which he amassed during his years in Downing Street were entirely due to her. A decade earlier they had struck an unspoken bargain. He gave her most of his waking hours, and his unstinting loyalty. In return, she gave him a free hand with the media, her complete support and an occasional blind eye. The result has been unique in British political history. One day, no doubt, some historian will write an authoritative account of Margaret Thatcher's statecraft: of how she centralized power in Number 10, turning the Cabinet, in the words of one former minister, into a 'rubber stamp', by taking decisions in ad hoc committees with like-minded colleagues; of how she exploited the fact that she had to answer for the entire Government at Prime Minister's Questions to enable her to immerse herself in every department's affairs; of her adroit manipulation of the powers of patronage vested in her office, promoting and ennobling to keep her party loyal.

Her use of the Press Office and the Lobby system fell under the same category: chopping ministers off at the knees, whilst publicly appearing to give them her support; having her own passions and prejudices aired in the media as if they were Government policy, even if there was a majority in

Cabinet against them; sometimes distancing herself from her own administration when it suited her to do so. As Mrs Thatcher pushed the powers of her office to the limit, so, in her shadow and in her service, Mr Ingham did the same with his. 'Future Prime Ministers,' according to Sir John Nott, 'have a lot to learn from it all.'[2] Labour says it will do things differently if it returns to power. We shall see.

As a public servant, he exemplified her virtues – hard work, drive, directness, mastery of detail – and her vices – dogmatism, stridency, hunger for power, intolerance of dissent. Not surprisingly, therefore, when Mrs Thatcher began to lose the confidence of the Tory Party in the autumn of 1990, Ingham was picked out as one of the symbols of what had gone wrong. There was some justice in the charge. The crisis was precipitated by the resignation of one of his most resentful victims, Sir Geoffrey Howe, who had never quite recovered from Ingham's brutal dismissal of his title of Deputy Prime Minister as a mere 'courtesy'. Howe's action, in turn, cleared the way for another man who had experienced Ingham's way of doing business, Mr Michael Heseltine. And Heseltine's long-awaited leadership campaign was supported, over- tly and covertly, by several ex-ministers who nursed grievances of their own against the Chief Press Secretary. It was a Conservative nightmare. It was the revenge of the unburied dead.

Even some of Mrs Thatcher's staunchest supporters now urged her, as part of the price of restoring confidence in her premiership, to dispense with Ingham's services. 'Mrs Thatcher's exotic triumvirate of Charles Powell, Bernard Ingham and Sir Robin Butler could do with a change,' declared a leader in *The Times* on 20 November. The *Spectator* was even more emphatic. 'She cannot brook opposition,' the magazine asserted on 17 November; 'in particular she allows Mr Bernard Ingham to rubbish Cabinet colleagues in a way that can be described at best as divisive and at worst as grossly disloyal'. The magazine called upon her to 'appoint a Press Secretary capable of putting the civil back into service'.

But by then, it was too late. On 21 November 1990 Ingham issued what was to be almost his last press release on Margaret Thatcher's behalf. It consisted of seven words uttered by the Prime Minister as she left Number 10. 'I fight on,' it declared, 'I fight to win.' The following day she decided to resign, bowing at last to the reality of her position.

In the days which followed many explanations were advanced for her demise: her attitude to Europe, the Poll Tax, the Tories' disastrous showing in the polls. But, at the heart of all these, was her style of leadership – and Ingham's contribution to that style was crucial. His place in the pantheon of the Thatcher years is unique and assured; at her side for eleven years and a month, he outlasted every member of her original cabinet; every official; every aide. He was in almost at the beginning; he was there at the very end.

On 9 November 1989, exactly one month after conducting his colleagues around Hebden Bridge, Ingham attended a memorial service for the former political editor of the *Daily Mirror*, Victor Knight.

Assembled in the journalists' church of St Bride's on Fleet Street were many men whose paths had crossed his over the years: James Callaghan, who had come to speak for Douglas Houghton at the Sowerby by-election when Ingham was a sixteen-year-old junior reporter; Joe Haines, whom he had first met as an industrial correspondent; Edward Heath, upon whom he had poured such scorn in the *Leeds Weekly Citizen* and who had lately denounced the operations of the Number 10 Press Office as 'corrupt'; William Whitelaw, who had briefed Ingham after Cabinet meetings and who had seen those same operations at first hand; and Francis Pym, whom Ingham had dismissed as Mona Lott.

Heath, Whitelaw and Pym sat together – the Old Guard of a Tory Party whose day had passed. Haines watched them from the pew opposite, and was surprised, 'on this solemn occasion', to see Heath suddenly begin to laugh, the shoulders giving their familiar heave. He passed his order of service to Whitelaw, pointing to something. Whitelaw looked at it, then his face, too, broke into smiles. They let Pym in on the joke. It was extraordinary.

Ingham had been asked to give a reading from the Book of Proverbs, and it was only as the Hallelujah Chorus came to an end, and the Chief Press Secretary stepped into the pulpit, that Haines realized the source of their amusement. The text he was to read was printed on the service sheet. 'Get wisdom, get understanding,' began Ingham. 'Forget it not, neither decline from the words of my mouth.' And then he went on:

Forsake her not, and she shall preserve thee: love her and she shall keep thee.

Wisdom is the principal thing. Therefore get wisdom, and with all thy getting, get understanding.

Exalt her, and she shall promote thee: she shall bring thee to honour when thou dost embrace her.
She shall give to thine head a garland of grace; a crown of glory shall she deliver to thee.

Heath and Whitelaw were like schoolboys trying to suppress a fit of the giggles at morning assembly. Ingham, 'even redder in the face than usual', made his way back to his pew. Afterwards, Haines tried to find him, but he had already slipped away through the throng of journalists and politicians and was lost in the crowd on the busy London street.

APPENDIX

Prime Ministers' Press Secretaries

RAMSAY MACDONALD (1929–35)
STANLEY BALDWIN (1935–7)
NEVILLE CHAMBERLAIN (1937–40)

George Steward (1929–1940)
Official, Foreign Office News Department; appointed Press Relations Officer, 10 Downing Street, 1929; Chief Press Liaison Officer of Her Majesty's Government, 1937.

WINSTON CHURCHILL (1940–5)

No press adviser appointed.

CLEMENT ATTLEE (1945–51)

Francis Williams (1945–7)
Editor, *Daily Herald*, 1936–40; Controller of News and Censorship, Ministry of Information, 1941–5; appointed Adviser on Public Relations to the Prime Minister in 1945.

Philip Jordan (1947–51)
Journalist; civil servant; died in office.

Reginald Bacon (1951)
Journalist; Treasury civil servant.

WINSTON CHURCHILL (1951–5)

Thomas Fife Clarke (1952–5)
Lobby correspondent, Westminster press local newspapers; Principal Press Officer, Ministry of Health, 1939–49; Controller, Home Publicity, COI, 1949–52; appointed Adviser on Government Public Relations and Adviser on Public Relations to the Prime Minister, May 1952.

ANTHONY EDEN (1955–7)

William Clark (1955–6)
Diplomatic correspondent, *Observer*, resigned in November 1956 over his opposition to Eden's Suez policy.

HAROLD MACMILLAN (1957–63)

Harold Evans (1957–63)
Local newspaper reporter, 1930–9; Ministry of Information, 1942–5; Public Relations Officer, Colonial Office, 1945–57; appointed Public Relations Adviser to the Prime Minister, 1957.

ALEC DOUGLAS-HOME (1963–4)

John Groves (1964)
Lobby correspondent, Press Association and *The Times*, 1947–58; Head of Press Section, HM Treasury, 1958–62; Deputy Public Relations Adviser to the Prime Minister, 1962–4; Acting Adviser, 1964.

HAROLD WILSON (1964–70)

Trevor Lloyd-Hughes (1964–9)
Political correspondent, *Liverpool Daily Post*, 1951–64; appointed Press Secretary to the Prime Minister, 1964.

Joe Haines (1969–70)
Political correspondent, *Scottish Daily Mail*, 1960–4, the *Sun*, 1964–8; Deputy Press Secretary to the Prime Minister, Jan–June 1969; Chief Press Secretary, 1969. (Subsequently, Chief Press Secretary to the Leader of the Opposition, 1970–4.)

EDWARD HEATH (1970–4)

Donald Maitland (1970–3)
Diplomat. Head of News Department, Foreign Office, 1965–7; Principal Private Secretary to Foreign Secretary, 1967–9; Ambassador to Libya, 1969–70; appointed Chief Press Secretary, 10 Downing Street, 1970.

Robin Haydon (1973–4)
Diplomat. Head of Foreign Office News Department, 1967–71; High Commissioner, Malawi, 1971–3; Chief Press Secretary, 10 Downing Street, 1973.

HAROLD WILSON (1974–6)

Joe Haines (1974-6)

JAMES CALLAGHAN (1976–9)

Tom McCaffrey (1976–9)
Civil servant. Chief Information Officer, Home Office, 1966–71; Press Secretary, 10 Downing Street, 1971–2; Director of Information, Home Office, 1972–4; Head of News Department, Foreign Office, 1974–6; appointed Chief Press Secretary to the Prime Minister, 1976.

MARGARET THATCHER (1979–1990)

Henry James (1979)
Civil servant. Various posts in Government Information Service, including: Chief Information Officer, Ministry of Housing and Local Govt., 1969–70; Director of Information, Department of Environment, 1971–4; Director-General of the COI, 1974–8. Chief Press Secretary to the Prime Minister, May–Oct 1979.

Bernard Ingham (1979–1990)

Notes

PREFACE: 'Albion'

1 *Leeds Weekly Citizen*, 11 June 1965.
2 Ibid, 28 February 1964.
3 All references are drawn from the *Leeds Weekly Citizen*: to Heath, 11 February 1966; to Maudling, 24 July 1964 and 16 April 1965; to Hailsham, 25 December 1964; and to Powell, 20 January, 1967. ('I have given Powell the facts,' wrote Ingham on 27 January 1967. 'God alone can give him understanding. And it will be an all-forgiving deity that perseveres in that daunting task.')
4 Ibid: to house, 22 April 1966; to eleven-plus, 25 June 1965; to unions, 10 June 1966; to full employment, 13 March 1964; to socialism, 10 April 1964; to 'serfs' 5 June 1964; to 'fellow slaves', 25 September 1964; to the 'Golden Calf', 10 July 1964; to Mammon, 15 January 1965.
5 Ibid: to the Tory press, 21 August 1964; to a Labour press, 16 October 1964.
6 Ibid, 29 July 1966.

ONE: Dear Bernard

1 Quoted in Hugo Young, *One of Us* (Macmillan, 1989), p. 166.
2 Interview in the Halifax *Courier*, 20 July 1989.
3 Interview in *The Thatcher Decade: The Most Important Man*; BBC Radio 4, 18 April 1989.
4 Craig Brown, *A Year Inside* (Times Books, 1989), p. 124; Ingham speech to Calder High School, 13 January 1990.
5 The visitor, John Junor, recounts the episode in his autobiography, *Listening to the Midnight Tram* (Chapman, 1990), p. 309.
6 'She is not a relaxed person . . .': interview in the *Sunday Express*, 1 October 1989; 'an instinctive rapport . . .': interview in the *Sunday Telegraph*, 6 February 1983.
7 Speech to the Guild of Newspaper Editors, May 1983.
8 Interview in the *Sunday Express*, 1 October 1989.

TWO: Hebden Bridge

1 *Leeds Weekly Citizen*, 14 October 1966.
2 Ibid, 11 February 1966.
3 Ibid, 25 June 1965.
4 Speech to Calder High School, 13 January 1990.
5 *Hebden Bridge Times*, 5 December 1947.
6 Speech to Calder High School, 13 January 1990.
7 Speech at the opening of the Labour Party Christmas Fair; quoted in the *Hebden Bridge Times*, 13 December 1957. The fair was opened by 'Mr Peter Shore, BA, prospective Labour candidate for Halifax . . .'
8 *Hebden Bridge Times*, 27 April 1951.
9 Ibid, 20 May 1957.
10 Speech to the Worshipful Company of Stationers and Newspaper Makers, 5 February 1986.
11 Speech to the Guild of British Newspaper Editors, May 1983.
12 Speech to Calder High School, 13 January 1990.
13 Speech, 5 February 1986.

THREE: Reporter

1 *Hebden Bridge Times*, 9 November 1956.
2 Ibid, 21 February 1958.
3 Speech to Calder High School, 13 January 1990.
4 *Guardian*, 8 January 1963.
5 Ibid, 29 July 1963.
6 Ibid, 23 January 1964.
7 City of Leeds Labour Party papers deposited at the West Yorkshire Archive Service, Leeds; Box 41 'Nomination Papers'.
8 *Guardian*, 2 October 1963.
9 *Leeds Weekly Citizen*, 5 June 1964.
10 Ibid, 10 April and 7 August 1964.
11 Ibid, 9 October 1964.
12 Interview in the *Sunday Express*, 1 October 1989.
13 *Leeds Weekly Citizen*, 21 May 1965.
14 Speech to the Guild of British Newspaper Editors, May 1983.
15 *Leeds Weekly Citizen*, 21 December 1965.
16 Ibid, 4 February 1966.
17 Ibid, 28 January 1966 and 16 April 1965.
18 Ibid, 5 March 1966.
19 Ibid, 20 May 1966.
20 Ibid, 3 December 1965.

21 Ibid, 8 July 1966.
22 Ibid, 14 October 1966.
23 Ibid, 8 July 1966 and 3 March 1967.
24 Speech to the Worshipful Company of Stationers and Newspaper Makers, 5 February 1986.
25 Speech to the Guild of British Newspaper Editors, May 1983.

FOUR: Press Officer

1 Tony Benn, *Against the Tide: Diaries 1973–76* (Hutchinson, 1989), p. 452.
2 Interview in the *Sunday Telegraph*, 6 February 1983.
3 Ibid.
4 *Leeds Weekly Citizen*, 17 February 1967.
5 Clive Jenkins, *All Against the Collar* (London, 1990), p. 88.
6 Barbara Castle, *The Castle Diaries 1964–70* (Weidenfeld and Nicolson, 1984), p. 443.
7 Harold Evans, *Downing Street Diary* (Hodder and Stoughton, 1981), p. 26.
8 *Leeds Weekly Citizen*, 17 December 1965.
9 Ibid, 4 June 1965.
10 Ibid, 11 March 1966.
11 Speech to the Guild of British Newspaper Editors, May 1983.
12 Lord Carrington, *Reflect on Things Past* (Collins, 1988), p. 262.
13 Quoted in Robert Jenkins, *Tony Benn: A Political Biography* (Writers and Readers, 1980), p. 227.
14 Antony Part, *The Making of a Mandarin* (Andre Deutsch, 1990), p. 172.
15 Tony Benn, op. cit., pp. 412–3.
16 *Guardian*, 3 July 1975.
17 Tony Benn, op. cit., p. 414.
18 Ibid, p. 416.
19 Ibid, p. 452.
20 *The Thatcher Decade: The Most Important Man*, BBC Radio 4, 18 April 1989.
21 Tony Benn, op. cit., p. 460.
22 Ibid, p. 463.
23 Ibid, pp. 463–4.
24 Ibid, p. 560.
25 Tony Benn, *Conflicts of Interest: Diaries 1977–80* (Weidenfeld and Nicolson, 1990), pp. 23–4.
26 Ibid, p. 257.
27 Ibid, p. 289.
28 Speech, 5 February 1986.

FIVE: Prime Minister's Press Secretary

1 Interview with the author.
2 Speech to the Media Society, November 1985.
3 Ibid.
4 Quoted in Richard Cockett, *Twilight of Truth* (Weidenfeld and Nicolson, 1989), p. 5.
5 Ibid, p. 6.
6 Ibid, p. 15.
7 William Clark, *From Three Worlds* (Sidgwick and Jackson, 1986), p. 163.
8 Ibid, p. 196.
9 Ibid, p. 209.
10 James Margach, *The Abuse of Power* (W. H. Allen, 1978), p. 118.
11 Harold Evans, *Downing Street Diary*, p. 28.
12 Marcia Williams, *Inside Number 10* (Weidenfeld and Nicolson, 1972), pp. 53–4.
13 Written evidence to the Lobby's inquiry into its own future, 1986.
14 Quoted in Denis Healey, *The Time of My Life* (Michael Joseph, 1989), p. 298.
15 'The Lobby Correspondent's Role', *Listener*, 21 January 1965.
16 Marcia Falkender, *Downing Street in Perspective* (Weidenfeld and Nicolson, 1983), p. 98.
17 Written evidence to the Lobby inquiry, 1986.
18 James Callaghan, *Time and Chance* (Collins, 1987), p. 407.
19 Written evidence to the Lobby inquiry, 1986.

SIX: The Yorkshire Rasputin

1 Hansard, 7 February 1983.
2 Speech to an IBA seminar, 28 October 1981.
3 Ibid.
4 Ibid.
5 Andrew Thomson, *Margaret Thatcher: The Woman Within* (W. H. Allen, 1989), p. 226.
6 Speech to the Media Society, November 1985.
7 Jim Prior, *A Balance of Power* (Hamish Hamilton, 1986), p. 135.
8 Ibid, p. 163.
9 Hugo Young, op. cit., p. 229.
10 Prior, op. cit., p. 135.
11 Thomson, op. cit., p. 224.
12 Quoted in Thomson, p. 222.
13 Harold Evans, op. cit., p. 22.
14 Barbara Castle, op. cit., p. 631.

15 Hansard, 2 February 1982.
16 Quoted in *The Times*, 5 January 1988.
17 Norman St John Stevas, *The Two Cities* (Faber and Faber, 1984), p. 83.
18 *Leeds Weekly Citizen*, 10 March 1967.
19 Evidence to the House of Commons Defence Committee, 9 November 1982, para. 1718.
20 Quoted in Robert Harris, *Gotcha!* (Faber and Faber, 1983), p. 23.
21 Ibid, p. 116.
22 Quoted in Derrick Mercer and others, *The Fog of War* (William Heinemann, 1987), p. 50.
23 Ibid, p. 161.
24 Evidence to the Commons Defence Committee, op. cit., para. 1724.
25 Harris, op. cit., p. 116.
26 *The Thatcher Decade: The Most Important Man*, BBC Radio 4, 18 April 1989.
27 Mercer, op. cit., p. 53.
28 Harris, op, cit., p. 118.
29 Ibid, p. 118.
30 Quoted in Hansard, 28 April 1986.
31 Quoted in Michael Cockerell and others, *Sources Close to the Prime Minister* (Macmillan, 1984), p. 74.
32 Interview in the *Sunday Telegraph*, 6 February 1983.
33 Quoted in Cockerell, op. cit., p. 181.
34 Roy Hattersley, *Press Gang* (Robson Books, 1983), p. 28.
35 Hansard, 7 February 1983.

SEVEN: Conducting the Orchestra

1 Tony Benn, *Conflicts of Interest: Diaries 1977–80*, pp. 368–9.
2 IBA seminar, 28 October 1981.
3 *Guardian*, 7 July 1980.
4 Quoted in Cockerell, op. cit., p. 49.
5 *The Times*, 7 September 1983.
6 Hansard, 31 October 1983.

EIGHT: Licensed to Leak

1 IBA seminar, 28 October 1981.
2 Hugo Young, op. cit., p. 356.
3 Alasdair Milne, *DG: The Memoirs of a British Broadcaster* (Hodder and Stoughton, 1988), p. 164.
4 John Junor, op. cit., p. 309.
5 Quoted in *The Times*, 6 August 1983.

6 Quoted in Cockerell, op. cit., p. 232.
7 Hansard, 15 January 1985.
8 William Keegan, *Mr Lawson's Gamble* (Hodder and Stoughton, 1989), p. 156.
9 *Independent Magazine*, 24 February 1990.
10 Hugo Young, op. cit., p. 443.
11 Fourth Report from the House of Commons Defence Committee, Session 1985–6, paragraph 174.
12 Defence Committee, op. cit., Armstrong's evidence, paragraph 1289.
13 Magnus Linklater and David Leigh, *Not With Honour* (Sphere, 1986), pp. 137–8.
14 Defence Committee, op. cit., paragraph 184.
15 Ibid, paragraph 193.
16 Hansard, 22 January 1986.
17 Defence Committee, op. cit., Armstrong's evidence, paragraph 1297.
18 Speech to Calder High School, 13 January 1990.
19 Linklater and Leigh, op. cit., p. 202.
20 Hansard, 28 April 1986.
21 Defence Committee, op. cit., paragraph 213.

NINE: The New Machiavelli

1 Interview with the author for *Panorama: Thatcher's 3000 Days*, transmitted on 5 January 1988.
2 Hansard, 7 February 1983.
3 *Guardian*, 13 May 1986.
4 Interview with BBC television's *On the Record* programme; the BBC declined to transmit the remark.
5 Norman Tebbit, *Upwardly Mobile* (Weidenfeld and Nicolson, 1988), p. 250.
6 Ibid.
7 Hansard, 2 February 1989.
8 Prior, op. cit., p. 134.
9 Speech to IBA seminar, 28 October 1981.
10 Speech to Calder High School, 13 January 1990.
11 *The Times*, 1 July 1985.
12 Speech to the Media Society, November 1985.
13 Quoted in the *Sunday Telegraph*, 18 October 1987.
14 *Spectator*, 11 March 1989.
15 Interview in the *Sunday Telegraph*, 31 May 1987.
16 Speech to the Worshipful Company of Stationers and Newspaper Makers, 5 February 1986.

17 Anthony Sampson, *The Changing Anatomy of Britain* (Hodder and Stoughton, 1982), p. 6.
18 Quoted in the *Observer*, 20 November 1988.
19 Quoted in the *Sunday Telegraph*, 20 November 1988.
20 Hansard, 22 November 1988.
21 *Daily Telegraph*, 24 November 1988.

TEN: Minister of Information

1 Quoted in National Audit Office report, Publicity Services for Government Departments (HMSO, 1 December 1989), p. 54.
2 Profile of Ingham in the *Sunday Times*, 7 May 1989.
3 Quoted in the *Daily Mail*, 27 July 1989.
4 Quoted in the *Independent*, 28 October 1989.
5 Hansard, Prime Minister's Questions, 31 October 1989.
6 Speech published in the *Sunday Times*, 11 February 1990.
7 BBC Radio 4 *Today* programme, 8 February 1990.
8 Sunday Times Insight Team, *Strike* (Andre Deutsch, 1985) p. 198.
9 Lord Young, *The Enterprise Years* (Headline, 1990), p. 143.
10 *Mail on Sunday*, 6 May 1990.
11 *Private Eye*, 6 July 1990.

CONCLUSION: Crowned With Glory

1 Speech to Calder High School, 13 January 1990.
2 *Panorama*, op. cit., 5 January 1988.

Index